Mysteries
in Broad Daylight

A Journey into the Deeper Meaning
of Everyday Life

Mark Dillof, Ph.D.

Mystical Kentuckian Press
Louisville, Kentucky
2012

Copyright © 2012 Mystical Kentuckian Press
2533 Broadmeade Road, Louisville, KY 40205
(502) 458-7171   mdillof@me.com   www.deeperquestions.com
All rights reserved. No part of this book may be reproduced in any form or by any means, electronic or mechanical, including photocopying, recording or information storage and retrieval systems, without permission in writing or e-mail from the publisher.

First Edition

EPUB Edition: ISBN: 978-0-9855953-0-2
Kindle Edition: ISBN: 978-0-9855953-2-6
Paperback Edition: ISBN: 978-0-9855953-1-9

Book cover design by Alex Piascik
http://apmotiondesign.com/

Book formatting by Janet Dooley
janet@r5i.com

Dedicated to my parents, for encouraging me in my unusual vocation
and to
my clients, students, friends and family, throughout the years, in Binghamton, cyberspace and elsewhere, who've joined me in many a thought-provoking dialogue.

"May the Great Mystery make sunrise in your heart."

--Sioux Indian aphorism

Table of Contents

Chapter One: Introduction 1
Part I: Pursued By a Question: A Mystery Trilogy 11
Chapter Two: Irrepressible Questions: A Dialogue in Five Acts 13
    Act I: The Last Temptation of Dorothy 14
    Act II: A Farewell to Happy Talk 25
    Act III: Dancing with Schopenhauer 35
    Act IV: Fat Enough to Fill the Void 49
    Act V: The Last Train Leaving the Burrow 58
Chapter Three: First Philosophical Intermission 71
    Some Questions for Readers to Explore 77
Chapter Four: Unsettling Questions: A Dialogue in Four Acts 79
    Act I: Act I: A Contradiction that Tastes Like Amaretto 80
    Act II: Smoking, Drinking & Gambling to Infinity 97
    Act III: I Woke Up to Find My Tattoos Had Gone 118
    Act IV: Two Detectives Inquire. Into a Metaphysical Conspiracy 130
Chapter Five: Second Philosophical Intermission 145
    More Questions for Readers to Explore 152
Chapter Six: Dangerous Questions: A Dialogue in Five Acts 157
    Act I: A Yogi Becomes Consumed By Road Rage 158
    Act II: To Hell with the Infinite! 175
    Act III: Wading Through the Water 192
    Act IV: What Gets You Through the Day? 208
    Act V: Are You Ready? 223
Chapter Seven: Reflections on the Third Dialogue 235
    Mind-blowing Questions for Readers to Explore 245
Part II: Essays Found at the Bottom of a Cocktail Glass 249
The Conservation of Suffering Principle 251
Living in the Moment for a Moment 267
Nuts are for Anarchists, Organic Foods for Fascists 273
Pepsi Flavored Coke 279
The Psychological Appeal of Angry Whoppers 281
Tattoos and the Quest for Identity 285

The Deeper Meaning of Zombies 289
The Deeper Meaning of Dr. Epstein's Gas 293
The Deeper Meaning of Green Kryptonite 301
A Multiple Choice Exam Called Your Life 307
Friendship's Darker Dynamic 311
Socialism's Incestuous Relation to the Mother 315
The Deeper Meaning of Adultery 321
The Secret of Uncanny Valley 325
The Mystery of Bobby Fisher's Madness 333
The Law of Attraction as Flight from Reality 337
What Makes for a Free Spirit? 341
The Anxiety Underlying Global Warming Hysteria 345
The Transformative Power of Doing the Opposite 349
The Psychological Fascination with Batman 355
The Deeper Meaning of the Faux Brownstone 359
The Deeper Meaning of Michigan J. Frog 363
Shoelace Tying as Revelation of Divine Wisdom 367
Is a Tightrope Walker a Balanced Person? 373
The Secret of Judaism's Two Triangles and the Mystery of
Antisemitism 375
Is Nature Evil? 387
The Metaphysics of Fitted Bed Sheets 391
Do You Love Your Fate? 397
The Secret Symbolism of Magic Tricks 401
The Mystery of Mountain Climbing 405
When the Door to the Bus Opens, Get On 407
The Case of the Blown Newspaper 413
The Case of the Bottlenecked Bicyclist 417
How Not to Bring Yourself with You, When You Move 421
The Mystery of Being Home and Yet Not Being There 425
Part III: Concluding Thoughts & Suggestions to the Reader 427
Are You For Real? 428
Theoretical Background 433
A Philosophical Puzzle 435
Suggestions for Expediting the Process of Self-Transformation 437
About Mark Dillof 446

Chapter I
Introduction

With apologies to Freud, a cigar is rarely just a cigar. For that matter, neither is a glass of scotch, a workplace conflict or a new hairstyle simply what it appears to be. Delving deeper, we discern that everything resonates with symbolic significance and offers clues to life's profoundest enigmas! Yes, odd though it may sound, a lost golf ball can be a doorway into the mystery of who we really are and the meaning of life. And, a toasted corn muffin--if we are able to fathom its secret import--can lead us to the highest wisdom and enlightenment.

In the chapters that follow, we'll decipher our interests, desires, conflicts and anxieties. As we lift the veil of mundane familiarity, the world will emerge as a mystery in broad daylight. We'll then attempt to unravel it.

Be Forewarned

Socrates states that, "Philosophy begins in wonder." Asking deep questions, the type that we shall be pursuing here, intensifies wonder tenfold. That's the pleasant news. But the reader should be cautioned: The encounter with life's enigmas isn't simply wondrous. On the contrary, any real detective investigation--and the exploration of life's depths is the greatest of detective adventures--also contains elements of danger.

Where, then, lies the danger? Seeing the light can be unsettling, disorienting and often downright terrifying. It would have to be that way, for the dawning of the light reveals the unreality of what we normally take to be real, as well as the untruth of that which we take to be true. Thus the light, which is ontologically acidic, causes the very foundations of our existence to disintegrate.

Why, then, undertake this perilous journey? It's because the knowledge that we can gain has the power to end our mental and emotional perplexities. Ultimately, nothing is more healing than insight into who we really are and what life is all about. It isn't, though, the only reason to set forth on this journey. We might also do so out of a lust for life, one lived in the light of truth, rather than in illusion. What is, therefore, needed is courage, self-control, a yearning for a truer mode of existence, and a faith that what one may discover is well worth the hardships one may suffer. That's what enables a person to endure the vertiginous anxiety that is a concomitant of powerful insights.

Turning to Face that Which Has been Pursuing Us

Alas, it may already be too late for the reader. Whether or not we have been pursuing life's deepest enigmas, these enigmas may have started pursuing us! Indeed, one day, amidst our quotidian activities, the scales could fall from our eyes and the world transform into what it essentially is, a gigantic question mark, amazing beyond all measure. In most cases, the mystery emerges for just a fleeting moment, like the moon peeking out of the clouds, only to be obscured again, for the remainder of the evening.

The encounter with the mystery, though it lasts but a twinkling, throws the very foundations of our existence into doubt. That doubt then attracts a swarm of sphinxlike questions, such as, "Who really are you?" and "What is this strange affair, called life, really about?" The questions can ambush us at unexpected moments--during a sales meeting or perhaps in a restaurant, while waiting for the sandwiches to arrive. The questions can even haunt our dreams.

We might be tempted to flee the cosmic riddle by subscribing to a dogmatic worldview--whether it be a religious belief, a scientific theory or a metaphysical position--with its false promise of certitude and clarity, completeness and closure. We might also attempt to shield ourselves from its power, by means of endless distractions and busyness. It can happen, though, that we get tired of running or that our curiosity gets the best of us. And so, we brace ourselves and turn to face what has long been pursuing us, the riddle of existence.

If we do turn to face the riddle, we are rewarded by insights that liberate us mentally and emotionally. Furthermore, our courage begins to compound daily, granting us the fortitude to pursue even more perplexing riddles. We become, then, philosophers, detectives searching for clues to life's deepest enigmas. We may still desire happiness and may earnestly strive to lead a sanctified life--for it's been said that only the good can know life's deepest secrets--but our guiding star is the great mystery.

A detective needs clues, but where are they to be found? Life must be lived, if it is to be understood, but living is insufficient. After all, we can gain a lifetime of powerful experiences but still not grasp life's deeper meaning. Therefore, the diligent also seek wisdom from the profoundest thinkers, be they living or dead, and then wrestle with the questions themselves. Sensing the limits of discursive thought, we might also engage in spiritual practices, from prayer to meditation. These doorways into the mystery--experiential, intellectual and intuitive--certainly have their merits. There exists, though, another source of clues, of which few people are aware...

The Secret Path that Lies Hidden in Broad Daylight

Our interests, desires, activities, conflicts and anxieties contain a hidden depth. As we have suggested, not only do they tell us who we are, they also reveal what life is all about. I.E., they contain both psychological truths and ontological truths (insights into the nature of ultimate reality). Of particular value, is the negative dimension of human existence--not life's devastating tragedies, but rather the daily kicks and pricks, the petty annoyances and aggravations that we suffer. Illuminating the negative not only relieves much of its sting, but is the fastest route to wisdom.

Most readers will find the ideas introduced here to be new, if not revolutionary. They have, though, their theoretical antecedents--certain brilliant, but now obscure schools of existential thought, that appeared in the 1930s and 1940s. We'll briefly touch upon them at the conclusion of this work. Suffice it to say that we shall delve--just as those existentialists had done--to a level deeper than psychological analysis, where lie the philosophical assumptions that weave the very warp and woof of the human experience. For many years, these insights have been hibernating, in the cave of forgotten ideas, where lie notions as ancient as those of Parmenides and Heraclitus. May they now awaken and sally forth with us, into a dark world much in need of illumination.

The main body of this work consists of the trilogy of dialogues, followed by a related series of essays. Together, they are intended to be lessons in the art of deciphering the mysteries of everyday life. There is no art of more practical value, for to illuminate one's world is to enjoy a greater felicity.

A Rather Intense Group of People

I'll explain how the dialogues came about. For over ten years, I met on Monday evenings with the same six or seven people. This wasn't group therapy, for none of my clients suffered from a psychological malady. They were simply discontent with their lives and yearned for a more fulfilling mode of existence. So they arrived, each week, to my philosophical counseling center--the living room of my apartment, in Binghamton New York--and sought whatever insights we were able to provide each other.

We would often begin our discussion with one of the members of the group presenting a particular problem or merely with something that he or she found perplexing. It could be anything, from a disagreement at the workplace to a sudden compulsion to gamble, from a marital conflict to a wish to have a certain design tattooed on one's arm. It then became a doorway into the profoundest of questions. The trilogy of dialogues derives from our conversations together.

Discerning the hidden depths of everyday life--as our group did together during those years--is a sublime experience. It's also rare, for few people are aware of the meanings with which the workaday world is imbued and fewer can decipher the symbolic appeal of a sunny side up egg sitting on their plate or the meaning of their fear of public speaking or the myriad other mysteries in broad daylight that surround them.

The Search for Subjective Truth

The conversations that comprise the trilogy have a very different subject matter, than do Plato's dialogues. The protagonist of Plato's dialogues is, of course, Socrates. We find him leading his students on a search for objective truth, which is to be found in the realm of eternal Forms, or Ideas, be it the Idea of courage, justice, love, or goodness. Objective truth is independent of opinion and perspective. That two plus three equals five, that George Washington was president of the United States or that Philadelphia is a couple of hours, by train, from Manhattan is universally true. The dialogues contained here, by contrast, aren't a search for objective truth. Rather, they're an investigation into each person's subjective truth, their outlook on life, or way of seeing.

One's subjective truth, worldview, or outlook on life, is a difficult thing to uncover. Here is the Zen-like problem of the eye not being able to see itself. If we wore a certain type of eyeglasses, we might remove them and examine them to see how they are distorting our vision. We might then discover that we were viewing the world through rose-colored glasses or perhaps through gray-colored glasses. Since we cannot do that, the perception of one's way of seeing the world can only come from a certain type of powerful insight. Sometimes, when in the midst of a familiar interest or activity, we may have a paradoxical moment of self-seeing, in which the eye does see itself.

It's valuable to uncover our outlook, for our problems ultimately derive from the world our mind creates, which we must then inhabit. If, for example, we are paranoid, the world that we create will be one that confirms our suspicious view of other people and the universe; we shall inhabit a dark and dreadful place indeed. As Milton stated, "The mind is its own place, and in itself can make a heaven of Hell, a hell of Heaven."

Self-knowledge is liberating because it frees us from the

constrictions that constitute our way of seeing things. Consequently, it frees us from the foolishness--and, invariably, from the adversity and misfortune--that stems from the narrowness of our perspective. That is why self-knowledge is the only real pathway out of Hell.

Philosophy in a Cocktail Glass

These dialogues are concerned with the quest to achieve happiness and fulfillment. Were my clients successful in their quest, they would neither be dissatisfied with their lives nor would they be on a journey with me to discover the root cause of their problems. Consequently, we devoted the sessions to uncovering how they sought to be in the world, their ontological assumptions. To uncover their mode of being, we explored their interests, desires, conflicts, actions, anxieties, and all else about them--for clues to their fundamental answer to the question of how to be real.

Whether or not we realize it, we are always concerned with the big questions. If we examined our interests, desires, pursuits, and activities, we would discover that they are actually answers to various ultimate questions. Strange though it may seem, even activities as mundane as buttering a bran muffin or driving a golf ball into a hole are attempts to solve the riddle of existence! No doubt, neither a donut nor a ballgame is a satisfying answer to an ultimate question. As we shall see, the essential reason why suffering exists is that our proposed answers to the ultimate questions prove inadequate.

There are a number of ultimate questions, but there are certain ones whose existential import is immediately apparent. They are those concerning our day-to-day efforts to achieve selfhood, or reality as a person. As our daily struggles indicate, the quest to achieve reality as a self is certainly problematical. How different is the life of animals. A cat doesn't stay up at night wondering about its life's purpose. A dog doesn't envy another dog's fortune and fame. And, at least as far as we know, a chicken doesn't debate with other chickens about the nature of God. Only man's very being is contingent upon satisfactorily answering life's ultimate questions.

How, though, is it even possible for something like a fried egg or a baseball game or a promotion to senior vice-president able to appear as an answer to an ultimate question? Some years back, Erich Fromm wrote a book called *The Forgotten Language.* (1957). Fromm was referring to the language of symbols, myths, dreams and fairy tales. Here, though, is the curious thing that Fromm didn't consider, at least as far as I know: our everyday interests and activities are written in this same symbolic language.

Take, for example, popular consumer products. Their real appeal is symbolic, but not like the depth psychologists had believed. I.E., while they may involve sexual fulfillment (Freud) or power (Adler) or the quest for psychic wholeness (Jung), they ultimately derive from a more fundamental longing, which is ontological. More specifically, these products are answers to the perplexing question, what is real?

For example, we drink Coke because it promises to connect our transient earthly existence to the everlasting or eternal, because it's the "real thing," as they used to call it, in their ads. We use Dawn dish detergent because its name suggests the early morning, the time when the world seems fresh and clean, indeed, the time before the fall, religiously speaking. Washing dishes is therefore associated with self-renewal, and with connection to a truer, more real mode of existence. We wear jeans because their uniform quality--they are all made from blue denim--promises to overcome our sense of separateness, isolation and alienation from other people. Furthermore, the fact that jeans are made of natural fibers is an expression of our desire for authenticity, for a "real" life. Similarly, we might wish to drive a car called "Infiniti," because one criterion for true reality, that we seem to all have, is infinitude. We long to be beyond limits.

Throughout the day, many things can deeply affect us, without our consciously realizing it. We can decipher them for clues to who we are and what we're ultimately seeking. What lies ahead is a detective adventure. It involves interpreting symbols and gathering clues, that we might solve the deeper enigmas of human existence.

I might add that I'm certainly not the first to suggest that there exists a hidden ontological depth to the everyday. Jean-Paul Sartre had such a moment of wonderment, back in the 1930s. As Simone de Beauvoir tells it, Sartre was sitting at a table in a Parisian bar, drinking a peach brandy, when another philosopher, Raymond Aaron, approached him and declared: "If you're a real philosopher, you can find philosophy in that cocktail glass." Sartre was electrified by Aaron's challenge! Could it be, he wondered, that all of our desires, interests and activities are infused with profound meanings? Sartre's eureka moment led him to investigate the deeper meaning of everyday life.[1]

My eureka moment came in college, when a professor--an existential analyst nonpareil--suggested that my fondness for potato chips had a profounder significance than I could ever have imagined. That epiphany opened my eyes to the wondrous depths of everyday life. This book is, in essence, a self-study course, replete with hundreds of examples of this mode of analysis, along with a plethora of thought-provoking questions. It's been designed so that you may experience not one, but numerous such epiphanies.

A Road Map and a Preamble

You will note that each of the three dialogues is separated by a philosophical intermission, in which we explore some of the key ideas that emerge from the various conversations. Then, the last dialogue is followed by some further reflections. Part II includes various essays--each another doorway into the depths--accompanied by some powerful questions. I had the members of the Monday evening group read the essays, as homework. You'll find them useful as case studies. They'll help you to learn the art of illuminating the symbolic and mythic dimensions of your everyday life. Following the essays is Part III, the conclusion, which includes practical suggestions regarding your own journey, to self-awareness and self-realization.

The first of the three dialogues commences on the group's third anniversary. One of my clients, Dorothy, voiced a certain frustration and discontent that everyone there had been experiencing, to various degrees. They wanted to be reassured that they were making headway--after struggling, week, after week for three years--with all of the slippery questions that emerged. They were also unsettled by my focus on the negative dimension of human existence, which needs to

---

[1] The phrase "mysteries in broad daylight" is from Jean-Paul Sartre's *Being and Nothingness* (1943) Sartre states that he read it in a book by the French phenomenologist Gaston Bachelard.

be explored if it is to be illuminated. I sought to encourage them to continue their efforts, for the potential benefits justify the hardships of the journey. Ironically, it was in this session that we reached a critical mass, for that discussion, and all subsequent ones, took on a greater intensity and drive.

Apologia

One last bit of business, before we open the curtains and view the plays, at least in our mind's eye. Imagine writing a series of dialogues, in which one is not merely a central character, but a modern-day Socrates, certainly as bald, only not nearly as wise. As Carly Simon stated to me, in a dream, "You're so vain; you probably think these dialogues are about you." So, out of fear of the forces of Nemesis punishing me for my hubris, I decided to delete this manuscript from my Mac.

But, at the last moment, just when I was about to hit "delete," my muse, the daemon Sharon, stayed my hand. She insisted that I publish the manuscript, but that I dedicate a certain percentage of the royalties to the Oracle at Delphi, an idea that my accountant feels has merit. With my apologia now out of the way and with Nemesis and the Furies off to do another gig, let the mystery unfold...

Part I
Pursued by a Question
A Mystery Trilogy

Chapter II
Irrepressible Questions

A Dialogue in Five Acts

Dramatis Personæ:

Frank--A recently retired owner of a record company, in his late fifties.

Samantha--A shiatsu masseur, in her mid-fifties.

Tim--Owner of a landscaping business, in his early forties.

Ricky--A graduate student in music, plays in a rock band, in his mid twenties.

Dorothy --A teacher of high school English, in her mid thirties.

Mark--Philosopher, leader of this group, in my early to mid-fifties, at the time.

Scene:

[The scene is the same, for all five acts. Evening: A room with a couch and comfortable chairs. In one corner, there is a bookcase overfilled with books, along with a few sculptures. On the wall, there are paintings and photos. The room also contains small tables, assorted lamps, and plants. There is an electric piano, in one corner of the room. The various characters are sitting around the room, except for Ricky, who doesn't make an entrance until Act III.]

Act I: The Last Temptation of Dorothy

Tim

What's on the menu for tonight Doc?

Mark

Tonight, Tim, we continue on our journey into the heart of dissatisfaction, disappointment, disillusionment, heartbreak, misery, inner-torment, anguish, dread and despair... Did I leave anything out Frank?

Frank

No, I think you've covered all the bases.

Tim

Yes! Another evening in the Inferno!

Mark

Well, Tim, I appreciate your boundless enthusiasm. But our purpose is actually to leave the hell of an unexamined life.

Tim [Writing in his notebook]:

Hmm, to leave hell. That's even better!

Dorothy

Did you know that this evening marks three years since we've been meeting?

Mark

Have we all been meeting that long, Dorothy? Gee, it's true that time flies when you're having fun. Hmm, this calls for celebration.

Frank

Shall I uncork the champagne?

Dorothy

> Having fun? For the past three years, we've done nothing but talk about suffering, in its myriad, miserable forms!

Frank

> It took you three years to realize that?

Dorothy

> Maybe I'm a slow learner, but I'm not leaving this wretched group until I get what I came for!

Mark

> Hmm, I get a subtle feeling that something is vexing you.

Dorothy

> Meeting my old college friend, Myra, for lunch today got me thinking.

Mark

> Ah, Myra the shallow. You brought her here once. Yes, she's the Einstein who quotes Oprah and Dr. Phil. What words of wisdom did Myra have for you this time?

Dorothy

> Nothing in particular. But she's totally absorbed in her career, marriage, house, children, clothing, and shopping. And it's not just Myra. All my friends are that way. My sisters are too. They're never perplexed, like I am, by the big questions. While I'm searching for answers, life passes me by. And yet I can't stop searching.

Samantha

> Well, can't you still do the things your friends do? You're only 35. You're attractive and can easily get remarried. And the questions you have about life will still be waiting for you, when you return from your honeymoon.

Mark

Samantha has a valid point. What, then, is stopping you?

Dorothy

I can no longer absorb myself in life, in the way that people like Myra can.

Mark

Oh really. Why can't you?

Dorothy

I keep popping out of everything I do to examine it. Yeah, I'm like a bar of Ivory Soap. Plunge me into an activity and I'll soon float right to the surface. Why do I do that?

Mark

Maybe you're coming up for air.

Dorothy

I need air?

Mark

Yes, consciousness. I suppose that's what the air symbolizes to you. That's why you float up to the surface.

Samantha

I'm not sure I'm following you.

Mark

Perhaps Dorothy would be kind enough to offer you an example.

Dorothy

OK, last Saturday night I'm with my boyfriend, Phillip, and right in the middle of things I'm wondering, What does Phillip see in me? What do I see in him? What is the ground of romantic attraction? In what ways does Phillip differ from my ex? Was Plato right about love? Was Kierkegaard... So there, sitting on the couch, was, Phillip, myself and one hundred questions.

Samantha

Well, that's good! Phillip is probably looking for someone intellectual. After all, he knew you were an English teacher when he met you. Didn't you tell me that his first wife was a fluffy, bleach-blond bimbo? What a wonderful change for him to be dating an egghead, who obviously isn't concerned about her appearance.

Dorothy

What type of left-handed insult is that?!

Samantha

Well, I only meant that you have inner beauty.

Dorothy

Anyway, it's not so good, Samantha, because at one point Phillip turns to me and says: "Dorothy, I see that you keep your eyes wide open when you kiss. Please feel free to bring over your laptop, so you can jot down your thoughts while we make love."

Samantha

Sarcastic fellow, isn't he? I would have slapped him!

Dorothy

Maybe so, but he does have a point. That's why I sometimes envy my friends. They seem to drift through life with their eyes closed and their mind securely shut, but not I. No, I can't help but pop out to examine whatever I'm doing.

Mark

That sounds excellent!

Dorothy

Ha! If only my health insurance covered lobotomies. Then I could be happy like Myra. But they don't, so I'm cursed! I'm cursed! We're all cursed by consciousness!

Mark

Ah, the last temptation of Dorothy.

Tim

What's the last temptation, Doc?

Mark

Some higher power sends your soul an "Opportunity Knocks" card, you know, like they have in the game of Monopoly. You turn the card over and it reads: "You are invited to leave this shadowy world of shared illusions and journey to the light, to awakening! But you better act now, because this offer will not be repeated!"

Tim

Wow, that's quite an Opportunity Knocks card! I wouldn't think that anyone would turn down an offer like that.

Mark

They might get cold feet at the last moment.

Tim

Cold feet? Yeah, I can see it. Fear of the unknown. The longing to just live an ordinary life. Maybe that's the temptation.

Dorothy

Yes, it's a vision of the simple life that tempts me.

Mark

The simple life? Who do you know who leads a simple life? Your friends aren't horses, cows, pigs or chickens. Your sisters aren't houseplants. If they're human beings, they cannot help but pop out of their waking dreams to look at their lives, to reflect--just as you do--if only for brief terrifying moments.

Dorothy

They have moments of self-awareness? You'd never guess from talking to them.

Mark

Yes, and when they do, they immediately grab a bottle of liquor or some pills or the remote to turn on the TV.

Tim

I got one Doc. They reach for their cell phone or they check their e-mail. Or they remember some item they forgot to buy.

Samantha

Or they daydream about chocolate macaroons or their plans for the weekend.

Frank

Or they get into an argument or arrange to have someone whacked.

Mark

Ah, all very nice. Excellent examples of how we seek to annul our emerging self-awareness, through distractions, busyness, drugs-- any means possible.

Dorothy

How do you know that my friends do these things?

Mark

I really don't know, but I'd bet they do, because they're some of the types of vices that I've struggled with and still struggle with. And I know I'm not much worse than the average person... Am I? Well, am I? Hmm, I see that no one's saying anything.

Frank

Maybe you're just slightly worse.

Samantha

Look Mark, we know that you're not the Dalai Llama. But you're not a complete knucklehead either. And besides, you do serve some good coffee and occasionally pastries. So we've settled for you as our teacher. I hope you don't mind me being forthright.

Mark

No, not at all. If I know anyone suffering from delusions of grandeur, I'll send them to you to be cured.

Dorothy

I'd like to get back to what we were talking about. A few of my friends are really quite thoughtful. They read poetry, listen to classical music and discussions on NPR, read the arts and leisure section of the New York Times and practice yoga. They...

Mark

They're still desperate characters.

Dorothy

How can you make such a categorical judgment? You haven't even met them! I mean, they're all quite different. They vary from teachers to business professionals, from artists to housewives. Some are men, although most are women. They all have different personalities. Some are...

Mark

I meet nothing but desperate characters. How about you Frank? You've been around even longer than I have. What type of people do you meet?

Frank

Desperate, demented, dangerous and doomed.

Mark

So, Dorothy, unless the people you know are very different from the great majority of human beings inhabiting Planet Earth, they're desperate.

Tim

What makes people desperate, Doc?

Mark

It's neither having answers to life's ultimate questions nor being on a journey in search of answers. When neither is present, a person flees self-awareness like a...

Tim

Vampire before the emerging rays of the morning sun?

Mark

Great analogy, Tim! Yes, that's what it means to be desperate. And yet, Dorothy tells us that she envies those who live amidst the shadows.

Dorothy

Actually, I have mixed emotions. I'm often glad that I got onboard this night train into the depths. Sometimes I get impatient because I'm hoping to get somewhere with this, to finally have my life make sense.

Mark

That's perfectly understandable. You know, three years isn't really all that long. And you've made great strides. It's good that you're eager,

but maybe you didn't quite realize what was involved. Gee, maybe I failed to make it clear.

Dorothy

No, you made it clear. I knew it wasn't going to be all sweetness and light.

Mark

That's just as well, because the emerging light doesn't bring sweetness.

Dorothy

What?! Now we're finally getting somewhere here. You said that the light of awareness is liberating. And don't try to deny it! And besides, isn't that the premise of Plato's Allegory of the Cave?

Mark

Yes, the light is liberating. And yes, it's the premise of Plato's allegory.

Tim

Is that the one about the prisoners who live in a cave and the guards decide to free one of them?

Mark

Right Tim. Plato is saying that to live an unexamined life, is like living in a dark cave, shielded from the light of truth.

Dorothy

Isn't the prisoner happy to be freed? Isn't he just ecstatic about leaving the cave and walking into the beautiful sunlight?

Mark

As Plato tells it, the guards have to drag the prisoner out of the cave, while he's kicking and screaming. He doesn't want to leave!

Dorothy

OK, but when we finally do face the light of truth, isn't it sweet?

Mark

On those occasions, when you've faced the light and gained a powerful insight into yourself--and I mean the type of insight that stopped you in your tracks or threw you off your horse, so to speak--did it feel sweet?

Dorothy

I've always been thankful for such powerful, life-transforming insights.

Mark

Well, it's good that you're thankful, but do such insights feel sweet?

Dorothy

No, they don't feel sweet! Sometimes I feel that my world is spinning out of control and I'm losing my sanity. But, it's probably just me.

Tim

I doubt it's just you, Dorothy. Four years in the Navy and I never got seasick, but if I imbibe the smallest draught of self-knowledge--which doesn't happen very often --and it's like I'm lost at sea, in a canoe, in a perfect storm.

Mark

I had a philosophy professor who said that feeling sick to one's stomach is a sure sign that one had a real insight about oneself.

Tim

Why is that Doc? What's up with self-knowledge?

Mark

It reveals the horror, the hopeless web of irresolvable contradictions that comprise each of us. The light reveals the nothingness at our very core, the groundlessness of our very being, the unreality of our...

Samantha

I'm just wondering, Mark, wouldn't it make sense to balance things out with talk of happier, more cheerful matters? I'm wondering if maybe that's where Dorothy was headed.

Dorothy

Samantha, I wasn't necessarily objecting to Mark's focus on the dark side.

Mark

Not necessarily objecting. Write that down Tim... So what's the problem, Samantha?

Samantha

I'm not exactly sure. I need a moment to think about this.

Mark

OK, lets take a short break.

[Exeunt omnes]

Act II: A Farewell to Happy Talk

Samantha

There's something strange about what we've been doing here these past three years. Sometimes, I worry that it's abnormal.

Frank

You've got that right, sister. I think it's sick!

Samantha

I didn't mean sick. That's too harsh a word, Frank!

Mark

Hmm, maybe it is sick. Who was it that called consciousness a disease?

Frank

Dean Martin?

Mark

Consciousness does require sobriety, so Dean Martin's a good guess. But actually it was Fyodor Dostoevsky. In truth, a character in one of his novels says it.

Tim

How could an intellectual be down on thinking? I mean that's like Tiger Woods being down on golf.

Mark

He was arguing that nothing good comes from thinking, that it only leads to greater perplexity, causing us to end up hamstrung by self-doubts, unable to act. That's why the sneaker company advises people not to think, but to just do it. But we continue to think, so I guess we're sick.

Frank

See, I was right.

Samantha

Well, I don't feel sick, but my husband tells me that I get other people sick.

Mark

How so?

Samantha

Whenever we have friends over the house for dinner, I share with them some of the amusing pleasantries that I heard here... I really don't know why it gets them sick.

Mark

Like what?

Samantha

Oh, I tell them that their existence is entirely without foundation and that they better not look down or they're going to plunge into the void.

Dorothy

Hmm, Samantha, aren't you sort of like Typhoid Mary?

Samantha

Typhoid Mary? Oh, please. That's ridiculous!

Mark

Dorothy has a point. If you had been affected by the insights that you share with others, you would have fallen into a life-transforming despair.

Tim

Whoa! How could despair be life transforming?

Mark

Despair is the perception of the total impossibility of achieving happiness in the manner in which we've been seeking it. Make sense?

Tim

OK, despair is the end of the road.

Mark

Well, it's the end of the particular road that we've been on.

Frank

Yeah, it's curtains, baby, curtains!

Mark

Yes, but then the curtain opens up again to new mode of existence. After all, you're not about to try something really different unless you're convinced that what you've been doing is impossible. So despair is a catalyst.

Samantha

Then how have I been able to keep from falling into despair?

Mark

Apparently by distancing yourself from what you know. You tend to float above it all, like a cloud. You then look down upon the world and say, "How very interesting!" But, somehow or other, you've mastered the art of serving up existential insights to your dinner guests. Anyway, Samantha, I think that your distance between head and heart is bound to collapse.

Samantha

What happens when it does?

Mark

Then you'll have a visit from the dread spirit, the spirit of anxiety, which reveals our hideouts from the truth of life. At least that's how Kierkegaard...

Samantha

A rendezvous with the dread spirit? This is terrible!

Dorothy

Are you frightened?

Samantha

No, I'm not frightened. It's just that I'm having the family over for the weekend and I don't know how I'm going to fit another meeting into my hectic schedule.

Mark

Oh, I wouldn't worry. The dread spirit usually arrives at around 3:00 in the morning, when you don't have much else scheduled, other than dreaming.

Samantha

I got another question, owing to this being our third anniversary, as Dorothy reminds me. It dawned on me recently that this isn't your typical spiritual path.

Dorothy

Mark doesn't like calling this a spiritual path. [To Mark]: Didn't you say that it invites an air-headed, holier than thou attitude?

Mark

I suppose that I did say that it...

Samantha

I just want to be able to tell people what this group is about, if they ask me.

Mark

If you don't bring it up all the time, people won't ask you. By the way, who's been asking you? Have you been talking to the police again?

Samantha

No, it was just that one time.

Dorothy

The police?

Samantha

Don't you remember? Or maybe you were away on vacation that week. Mark's neighbors reported him to the police for supposedly having a satanic voodoo cult, involving vampirism and human sacrifice.

Dorothy

Is that what his neighbors think goes on in these meetings? Before you know it Binghamton will turn into Salem Massachusetts and you and I, Samantha, will have to grab our broomsticks and fly into the wild blue horizon, real fast.

Samantha

Maybe not. Mark explained to the detectives that he was offering philosophical counseling. After listening, for about ten minutes, they got bored and left.

Frank

But they'll be back.

Samantha

Mark, I had suggested that what we were doing was abnormal. And then Frank called it sick. I guess what I meant is that it's just a lot different from the path I'd been following. For one thing, it sure is a lot more negative.

Mark

You never mentioned this before.

Samantha

I used to have a guru who had his students focus on positive images--flowers and other things of beauty. He would tell each of us that we were precious jewels. The men were incarnations of various gods and the women of goddesses. It was very inspiring and uplifting!

Dorothy

Why aren't you still his disciple?

Samantha

Because, when I returned home, from those joyful weekends at the ashram, I still had my miserable life to deal with--the conflicts with my husband, the problems with my son and daughter, my job, my father who was ill and my anxieties.

Dorothy

But, you said the guru gave you affirmations to say to yourself each morning.

Samantha

He did, but I'd look in the mirror and I'd ask: "Who's a precious jewel? Who's a goddess? Whose the one?" And the mirror would answer me: "Not you Samantha!" So, I realized, one day, that I couldn't flee the darkness any longer. I realized that it was about time that I faced the music.

Mark

Ah, so you're here to face the music.

Samantha

I just sometimes wonder if there's a danger of going too far in that direction. It's one thing to face life's negatives, but I'm worried that dwelling on them, as we have these past three years, may be slowly turning us into vampires or maybe flesh-eating zombies. I don't mean literally, of course.

Frank

Not literally? Oh, that's a relief!

Samantha

Isn't there a danger of becoming morbid? For example, I had on a colorful dress earlier today, but changed into something more subdued when I remembered that I would be here tonight discussing Kierkegaard.

Mark

Kierkegaard was last week. Do you mean Schopenhauer?

Samantha

Yeah Schopenhauer, the wolfman of London, Joseph Stalin, whatever. That's why I made the comment about happy things.

Dorothy

Maybe Samantha has a point. Mark, you need to be more upbeat. Why not begin these discussions with a comedy monologue, and then try to incorporate some singing and dancing? If you did that, you'd have hundreds of students, clients, disciples or whatever the heck you call the lunatics, like myself, who attend your weekly sessions.

Tim

Doc, perhaps your new ad could read, "Learn to face the music and dance!"

Frank

Of course, the Doc might have to pay royalties to the Irving Berlin estate.

Samantha

Yeah, all this stuff about the dread spirit is bringing me down. Mark, we need some happy talk!

Frank

Doc, Samantha has inspired me to break into song. Hmm, what should it be this time? What...should...it... be? Maybe *South Pacific*.

Tim

Great musical, except for "Happy Talk." I hate that song.

Frank

Sorry, Tim. It's too late. Once I get inspired, I can't stop.

Tim

[Putting fingers in his ears]

Oh no! Open wide the gates of hell!

Frank [singing]

"Happy talk, keep talking happy talk.

Talk about things you'd like to do,"

[Samantha and Dorothy join Frank for the last two lines]

"You gotta have a dream, if you don't have a dream,

How ya gonna have a dream come true?"[2]

Samantha

Why do I suspect that Frank has been mocking me over the years?

Dorothy

That's because he has. He mocks everyone, including himself.

Tim

Don't be too hard on Frank. He can't help but sing.

Samantha

What's that supposed to mean?

---

[2] From "South Pacific" - music by Richard Rodgers, Lyrics by Oscar Hammerstein II Copyright © 1997

Tim

> The Doc discovered that Frank has a rare form of Tourette's Syndrome. It has only one symptom: In the middle of a conversation, he'll bursts into song. If he doesn't sing, there's a danger that he could explode.

Samantha

> Well, I never heard of such a condition, but it would certainly explain why he's serenaded us these past three years.

Mark

> In any case, that song--like so many other songs--is about dreams coming true. Motivational speakers and life coaches also encourage people to work hard so that they can live their dreams. But we're here to awaken from our dreams.

Samantha

> Why would we want to awaken from them?

Mark

> Because dreams have a curious way of turning into nightmares.

Dorothy

> That sounds like my former marriage--a romantic dream turning into a nightmare. Anyway, if I understand correctly, we dwell on the dark side of life because...

Mark

> I think that that's really Samantha's question too.

Samantha

> Yes it is.

Mark

> OK, the good can take of itself. It needs no examination. After all, do you wake up in the morning and say, "I feel great! I'm full of

joy! I'd better go see a doctor!" And doesn't Jung say, "There is no coming to consciousness without pain"? Well, that's' why we don't have happy, shmappy talk here.

Tim

Yeah, we're badass existentialists!

Mark

More importantly, the dark side of life is that it is the quickest route into life's profoundest mysteries. And who knows what wonders we may discover.

Dorothy

Let me retrace Ariadne's thread. I began by seeing you individually for marriage counseling. Then you invited me to join this group. And so down the rabbit hole I went, without knowing what I was getting into. And so, three years latter…

Mark

You hoped that you could patch things up with your husband, but the more the two of you examined your marriage the more it kept on unraveling.

Frank

[Singing]

"You can laugh when your dreams fall apart at the seams, when you're young at heart…."

Mark

Well, Dorothy, when your dreams started unraveling from insight, when they started falling apart at the seams, life's enigmas began to peek through the torn seams of your dreams… Samantha, I don't know if I fully answered your question.

Samantha

You did. I just need to take it all in.

[Short Intermission]

Act III: Dancing with Schopenhauer

Frank

> Hey, look who's here. It's Ricky! He must have snuck in during our coffee break.

Ricky

> Sorry I'm late, folks. I had to meet with my graduate school advisor.

Mark

> What was his advice?

Ricky

> That I concentrate on composing and conducting. Why limit myself to the piano when I can control the entire orchestra! [Gives insane laugh & collapses onto a chair.]

Mark

> Well, we're honored that you'll be joining us maestro. You look like you had a rough night and your breath smells like you've been drinking.

Ricky

> Yeah, my rock band's gig didn't get out till midnight. Then I had a class early this morning. And then I attended a student faculty party at a local pub. By the way, I read your essay. It's a hydrogen bomb!

Samantha

> I was wondering, do you think we could read some of it aloud?

Mark

> If you're willing to. My throat is getting a bit horse from laughing all day.

Dorothy

You dare to laugh!

Frank

Uh oh! Run for shelter. There's a twister headed our way!

Dorothy

You told us, right before the coffee break, that we were bidding farewell to happiness. You said, and I quote from my notes: "no more happy shmappy talk."

Mark

Laughter isn't about happiness. On the contrary, it derives from pain, failure, disillusionment and despair. When viewed from enough of a distance, we laugh.

Frank

You mean when the other fellow suffers pain, failure, disillusionment and despair. Yeah, then it's funny. Then we laugh.

Mark

Well, sometimes we laugh at ourselves. But OK, Frank, I'll admit it's not nearly as much fun as laughing at someone else.

Dorothy

But laughter makes us happy. We feel good. Endorphins are released and go surging through our bloodstream.

Mark

You do have a good point, Dorothy. OK, I retract what I said earlier. Happiness can stay.

Samantha

Really? That's great!

Frank

Uh, oh. Too much talk of joy and laughter. I feel a song coming on.

Tim

Someone call the mental hospital! Call Homeland Security! Call Carnegie Hall!

Samantha

Go for it Frank. Like Saint Paul said, better to sing than to explode!

Dorothy

I think he said better to marry than...

Frank

[Standing and Singing]

"Happy days are here again

The skies above are clear again

So let's sing a song of cheer again

Happy days are here again!"[3]

Mark

OK, take it Samantha.

Samantha

[Singing]

"Happy days are here again..."

Mark

No, I mean please read the essay!

---

[3] *Copyright 1929. Milton Ager (music) and Jack Yellen (lyrics) and published by EMI Robbins Catalog, Inc./Advanced Music Co.*

Samantha

"There must be something intrinsic to life's pleasures, joys, and satisfactions that makes them evanescent, thus bringing us back to the state of dissatisfaction...What is it about happiness that makes it evanescent?"

Frank

Yeah, that's what I'd like to know. How do they get the bubbles in the soda pop?

Mark

Bubbles in the soda pop? Frank, I think you're thinking of effervescent. I wrote evanescent, meaning short-lived.

Samantha

"Examine the relation between the good things in your life and the bad things. You will discover, not that the bad destroys the good, but that, on the contrary, the good entirely depends upon the bad! The pleasure of friendship depends upon the experience of loneliness. Those who most truly appreciate wealth are those who have known poverty... Those who have been to death's door can most appreciate life. Schopenhauer says that the "Good" is nothing more than a synonym for, "the removal of the bad."

Ricky

No, that's bull! That's complete bull! It's ridiculous to say that the good is nothing more than the removal of the bad. There are some things that are good in themselves.

Mark

Like what?

Ricky

Hmm, like a bacon cheeseburger!

Mark

The pleasure depends on a prior state of hunger.

Ricky

Hmm, what about the pleasure of being drunk or stoned?

Mark

It's nothing but relief from life's difficulties, problems and responsibilities, by returning to unconsciousness. And besides, there's always a price to pay.

Dorothy

Wait, I have one. What about a new romantic interest?

Mark

That's dependent on a prior state of loneliness.

Ricky

What about a beautiful sunny day. Ha! Now I got you. What's Schopenhauer say about that one?

Mark

As you know, from living in Binghamton, the appreciation of a sunny day is dependent upon the fact that it's cloudy all the time.

Ricky

What about the pleasure of good music?

Mark

It provides us with the sense of beauty, harmony and direction that we long for, but which is usually lacking in life. So it merely relieves the lack that exists in our soul.

Samantha

I'd like to read more, if it's all right with everyone. Maybe, then, the essay will make matters worse... I mean make more sense.

Mark

Yes, please read on.

Samantha

"As the bad departs, with the satisfied desire or the solved problem, so does the concomitant good!

Frank

Hey, what's going on here! Are you saying that the good and the bad are some sort of Siamese twins? And when the bad brother leaves town, the good brother leaves with him?

Mark

Exactly!

Samantha

I'll read more. *When the hunger vanishes, the pleasure of eating fades. The pleasure of a warm house vanishes as we forget what it was like to be shivering outside. Forgetting our loneliness, we begin to take our friend for granted. Our newfound joy in being alive diminishes as our near-death encounter begins to fade from memory."*

Tim

Doc, just to make sure that I'm following you, let me know if this sounds right: Let's say, I'm on a really turbulent flight. Man, am I glad when the plane finally lands safely. I'm ready to kiss the ground. But within five minutes I'm walking through the airport terminal, having completely forgotten about my near death experience. And when my memory of the turbulent flight fades into oblivion, so does my joy at being alive. And, then, before long, I'm experiencing some new anxiety or worry. I'm worried whether or not the person who's supposed to be picking me up at the airport terminal will be on there on time, for a change.

Mark

Yes Tim! It all stems from the correlative nature of good and bad. As we forget the bad, we forget the good. And as a matter of fact, according to Schopenhauer, the good is nothing in itself. The good is nothing more than the removal of the bad. Make sense to you Ricky?

Ricky

It's making more and more sense, but I don't like what I'm hearing!

Mark

What don't you like?

Ricky

Hmm. I really don't know what I don't like, but I know that I don't like it!

Mark

Could it be, if Schopenhauer is correct, that there is no such thing as pure, unadulterated happiness? Could it be, in other words, that lack, hunger and suffering pervade everything?

Ricky

Yeah, that's it! I had hoped that I could, one day, leave sadness behind. It would be after I graduated, met the perfect girl, became famous for my musical compositions, and bought a condo in Paradise. But, since attending these sessions, I've been feeling a shadow pursue me wherever I go. And reading this stinkin essay only brought it to a head. Man, it's been haunting me!

Mark

The shadow has always been pursuing you. You just never noticed it. It's the spirit of dread, which follows each of us.

Samantha

You'll have to wait in line, Ricky, Mark says that I already have an appointment with the dread spirit for 3:00 in the morning.

Mark

I was just using the term metaphorically to describe...

Ricky

The spirit of dread? Hmm, so that's whose been on my tail, and that's the guy I'm trying to lose. [Bounding up from his chair]: Actually, what in the name of Bach, Beethoven, Mozart and Elvis am I talking about? Music without any minor chords is insanely boring!

Tim

It tends to be boring, unless you're into dancing the Polka.

Ricky

> [Walks over to the electric piano in the apartment and starts playing a jazzed up version of Bach's Toccata and Fugue in G. Minor]

I have a confession to make.

Samantha

Let's hear it.

Ricky

> [Continuing to play Bach's Toccata, but more softly]

I no longer know what the hell I want out of life! I never really chose to be a musician. It's just that I was born with some musical talents and so I passively let life carry me along. Maybe, I really shouldn't be a musician. Maybe I should be doing something else. Like fixing computers!

>[Bangs on the keyboard]

Or maybe being a rodeo clown!

>[Bangs again on the keyboard]

Or being a podiatrist!

>[Bangs again on the keyboard]

I no longer know who I am!

Frank

Maybe, you never did. You're just coming to realize it, kid.

Ricky

I can't take this uncertainty, this state of limbo, any longer! I shall leave Plato's Cave. How do I get out of this matrix? I'll smash down the door!

>[Ricky walks over to the door and pounds on it violently.]

Mark

Ricky, that's just the door to my apartment and this isn't Plato's Cave! And why not use the doorknob?

Ricky

I must find out what it's all about!

>[Grabs a long lamp]

I shall grab life by the collar! I'll slam life against the wall and interrogate it until it reveals to me its secrets!

Frank

    Don't forget to read the lamp its Miranda rights.

Samantha

    [Rising to her feet, running towards Ricky and grabbing part of the lamp]

Ricky! Put down the lamp!

Ricky

    Why should I?!

Samantha

    Because the lamp cost Mark over $200! I know because I checked the price on EBay.

Frank [Addressing Samantha]

    Yenta.

Ricky

    [Letting go of lamp]

Sorry, I got carried away.

    [Samantha returns to her seats.]

Mark

    I really need to increase my apartment renters insurance.

Samantha

    Have faith Ricky. With that kind of determination, you are sure to find answers to life's persistent questions.

Mark

    Yes, but if you are to find what you are looking for, you must learn to endure, to forebear the anxiety of uncertainty, for there's a long road ahead. You'll need patience.

Ricky

Hmm, maybe you're right. In that case, I must learn patience, immediately! [Bangs again on the keyboard]

Mark

You might want to be patient about learning patience.

Ricky

Patient about learning patience? Ha! Ha! Ho! Ho! Hee Hee! OK, that makes perfect sense!

Mark

I'm glad it does. Very good. Please have a seat Ricky. All right, then, let us continue our reading about the conservation of...

[Ricky returns to his seat.]

Ricky

Dr. Mark, I realize that I have a tough journey ahead of me.

Mark

Yes, you do, Ricky. We all do.

Ricky

Now that you have heard my confession, I'd greatly appreciate your blessing, as I set out, with everyone here--with my spiritual brothers and sisters--on this dangerous odyssey in search of divine wisdom.

Mark

Confession? Blessing? Hey, what's going on here Ricky? I'm a philosopher, not a Catholic priest.

Samantha

Then how about an incantation? I realize that philosophers can't offer blessings, but are they allowed to offer incantations?

Mark

You've been attending too many new age seminars, Samantha. Incantations are the province of shamans, sorcerers and witch doctors.

Samantha

Maybe you can offer Ricky a Hebrew prayer. Perhaps something from the mystical Kabala.

Mark

The only Hebrew prayer I know by heart is the one that Jews recite before eating bread. And Ricky doesn't appear to be a loaf of challah, rye or pumpernickel.

Dorothy

Isn't there anything you can say on Ricky's behalf?

Mark

Oh, here goes: Philosopher Pythagoras--patron saint of mathematicians and melodious philosophers, and protector of well-meaning fools, scoundrels and rock musicians--I evoke your spirit! Open Ricky's ears to the music of the heavenly spheres! Allow the hidden harmony of the universe to rewire his disordered soul, from F flat diminished to G sharp major. May he never again lose the divine beat.

Dorothy

[tearfully]

That was very inspiring!

Ricky

Thank you, Dr. Mark. I'm dedicating to you my new etude for forty-eight electric guitars and a drummer. I'll never forget this moment!

Mark

Neither shall I. It was traumatic. I may need therapy.

Ricky

And I'd also like to thank Frank, without whose kindness, I'd never be here. I've already named my guitar after you Frank.

Frank

Don't forget to also thank your director, producer, and wardrobe consultant, while you're at it.

Samantha

What does Frank have to do with this?

Ricky

Frank is a good friend of my dad. They've been neighbors, since I was a kid. Frank told my dad about Dr. Mark's philosophy group. Frank recommended that my dad attend because my dad was feeling really down after Rusty, our dog, died.

Samantha

I don't remember your father ever attending.

Ricky

No, my dad hasn't made it down here yet. He said that he wasn't ready to open a can of worms. But my dad asked Frank if I could attend. And then Frank asked Dr. Mark. And that's why I'm here.

Samantha

I just love it when everything connects.

Mark

Then you should love philosophy, because it tries to connect everything in the entire universe.

Tim

Whoa! Ricky, Frank and the entire the universe in one cosmic convergence! Holy quantum physics! Holy Heisenberg! This is far out!

Act IV: Fat Enough to Fill the Void

Mark

Schopenhauer claims that there exists in each of us a void, which must be filled.

Ricky

Oh, yeah, Dr. Mark. Filled with what?

Frank

Filled with Ricotta cheese, sugar and flour, kind of like a cannoli?

Mark

No, according to Schopenhauer the void must be filled with suffering!

Samantha

Hey, what happened to happy talk?

Frank

OK, let's say that my mother-in-law comes to visit. My inner void runneth over with suffering. The old bat finally leaves, so now my inner void is empty.

Mark

But it can't stay empty for long! You will immediately get the inner void filled to the brim with a new problem, for nature abhors a vacuum.

Frank

It would have to be a pretty big problem to make up for my mother-in-law.

Mark

Well, actually, Schopenhauer says that a major problem can be replaced by two smaller ones, or by four even smaller ones or by eight...

Frank

What happens if I can't find a problem?

Mark

Has that ever happened to you?

Frank

No, not really. And rare moments of inner-peace never last for very long.

Samantha

Why, does something come to disturb it, like some jackass mowing his lawn 8:00AM, on a Saturday morning, when everyone's trying to sleep?

Frank

Yeah, sometimes it's a jackass, but mostly it's me. I get restless. It's like I'm searching for problems, difficulties, headaches, and hemorrhoids. It's like I can't be peaceful for two minutes without missing the stress. Am I out of my mind or what?

Mark

No, you're not out of your mind Frank. It's just that your soul is always hungering and your mind always searching for the true object of human desire. Unless you find out what it is, you'll always be restless, always seeking after the next thing...

Samantha

Or the next person?

Mark

Yes, the next person...

Samantha

Kind of like the actress Zsa Zsa Gabor?

Dorothy

Huh? I don't get it.

Samantha

She got married about twenty times.

Mark

Nice example, Samantha. Zsa Zsa never examined the inner dynamics of relationships. She never realized that what she was seeking was impossible. Instead, she blamed the failure on not having found Mr. Right.

Ricky

Are you saying that I shouldn't seek happiness?

Mark

No, I'm not saying that! What I'm saying is that as you pursue each new thing, try to uncover what it is that you're really looking for. Then you won't run madly through life's maze, like a junkie in need of a fix. You see; clarity destroys hope and brings peace.

Ricky

But isn't hope a good thing?

Mark

On the one hand, the hope for a better future can save us from despair and we can't accomplish big things without hope. But hope can also drive us insane with anticipation. Utopian revolutionaries, fools and madmen are full of hope. When their hopes fail to materialize, they bitterly curse life or find someone to blame. If they grasped the conservation of suffering, they wouldn't be deluded by hope, for they'd know that the changes they seek will only bring new problems, equal to the old ones.

Dorothy [standing up]

I've had it with this conversation! There has to be a way of overcoming the conservation of suffering! I demand a solution!

Frank

Speak, great philosopher king, deliver us boneheads from our blightedness.

Dorothy

Do you mean benightedness?

Frank

Yeah, that too.

Mark

OK, OK. The reason why there's a conservation of suffering is because we don't know what we're really seeking, consequently we hanker after the wrong things only to be disappointed. We end up replacing one form of suffering for another. What, then, are we really seeking?

Frank

I've been asking myself that a lot lately.

Mark

And how do you feel when you ask that question?

Frank

It's like I'm in a strange place, somewhere I've never been too before, maybe...

Tim

The Twilight Zone!

Frank

Well actually, I was going to say Staten Island, but OK the Twilight Zone.

Mark

Asking deep questions can have that un-grounding effect and it's not a bad thing.

Tim

What happens, if we get answers, if we catch a glimpse of the truth?

Mark

It's more like we catch a glimpse of the untruth of what we had believed to be true, and the unreality of that which we had believed to be real.

Tim

Wow, what happens then?

Mark

That perception ends our hopes, dreams and delusions. It ends time and it ends space. Indeed, it ends our world. It's the end of Tim. It's the real apocalypse.

Frank

Drop us a line, Tim, if you each the end of the world.

Dorothy

I have a thought. We've been trying to figure out what it is that we are really, really seeking, the obscure object of human desire. Well, whatever it is, that we're ultimately seeking must not just be a negative good.

Samantha

A negative good?

Dorothy

Yeah, like having lunch. It's nothing more than a relief from hunger.

Mark

Schopenhauer doesn't say if...

Dorothy

OK, Mark, but can there really be such a good, that doesn't depend on a prior bad, on a prior sense of lack?

Mark

Well, if you found it, you would transcend the conservation of suffering.

Dorothy

OK, but does it exist? Is there this one good that isn't just a lack of the bad?

Mark

Hmm, does it <u>exist</u>? Does <u>it</u> exist? <u>Does</u> it exist?...

Frank

Whoa, better lift the needle! Sounds like the record got stuck in the grove.

Mark

OK. OK. The obscure object of desire is... Hey, what time is it?

Frank

The watch that I awarded myself, when I retired from working for myself, says that it's time for another coffee break.

Ricky

But we just had a coffee break five minutes ago!

Frank

Sorry kid, union rules. We get a ten-minute coffee break every five minutes.

Ricky

That's not fair! That's not fair! I shall go on a strike to protest this corrupt union!

Mark

I thought that you were determined to learn patience. Anyway, I'll give you a clue, but it's going to sound mystical. Is that OK?

Ricky

I love mystical!

Mark

OK, then, here's something I learned from Sharon.

Samantha

Sharon? Who the heck is she? Is she your ex-wife or something? Has she ever attended these meetings? I don't remember you saying anything about a Sharon.

Mark

Sharon is a seer. Socrates had Diotama, who educated him regarding mystical matters. I have Sharon.

Tim

Wow! Does she really exist, I mean in the flesh? Can we meet her?

Mark

Well, Tim, for me Sharon is a sort of tutelary sprit, sort of a muse...

Tim

You mean a kind of daemon?

Mark

Yeah, yeah, she's a daemon...

Tim

Can anyone get one of these daemons?

Mark

You probably already have one, but haven't yet made contact with her.

Tim [Writing and looking at notebook]

Remember to make contact with my daemon.

Mark

Anyway, according to Sharon... the Self, God, the universe, the It--whatever you want to call it--is seeking to see itself. Its long journey in search of itself is known as Ricky.

Ricky

Hey, that's my name! I never realized that I'd been named after the Self, God, and the universe! Hooray for me!

Mark

No, you're misunderstanding me. It's also Frank, Dorothy and everybody. Each person is a different road that the Self takes in search of itself. Well, if it finally does see itself, then all longing ends, all suffering ceases.

Dorothy

So, if I'm following you, the Self is trying to grasp itself.

Frank

Ouch! [Makes motion with his arms] Trying to grasp oneself. Sounds painful.

Mark

Yes, it is painful, and that's why, according to Sharon, life is painful.

Dorothy

So the Self's obscure object of desire is none other than itself! How fiendishly clever all this is! How wondrous! How...

Ricky

I'm totally confused.

Mark

You wanted the mystical, so I gave you the mystical. But don't worry. It might make sense to you one day. The thing to do is to start by analyzing your everyday...

Ricky

I hope you don't mind me leaving early tonight, but I got homework to do.

[Intermission: coffee break]

Act V: The Last Train Leaving the Burrow

Mark

Frank told me he had something that he wished to explore with us this evening.

Frank

Yeah, for over ten years, I'd been thinking about selling my business. No more cutthroat competitors, unappreciative customers, thieving employees, a board of directors comprised of idiots, and having to deal with federal regulators out to trip me up at every turn.

Tim

Gee, Frank, I can't imagine why you'd want to leave Paradise.

Frank

The other reason for retiring is that there were things that I wanted to do--such as reading the gigantic list of books that the Doc has recommended that I read, traveling with my wife, spending more time with my family, gardening, fly-fishing, hunting, listening to opera and getting up late. But not necessarily in that order.

Samantha

Have you been able to make those changes?

Frank

Yeah, last year I retired and I've, more or less, been doing what I set out to do.

Tim

Ah, so now your cup now runneth over with joy!

Frank

Not quite. Retirement has been a disappointment.

Mark

Hmm, this is perplexing. What might have gone wrong?

Frank

I now realize that when I said goodbye to problems, anxieties and headaches, I was also saying hello to ho-humness.

Mark

Oh no! Schopenhauer had warned that this could happen!

Samantha

I'm not sure that I understand what you mean by ho-humness.

Frank

It's blaséhood, baby. It's life gone flat, like when you forget to put the cap back on the soda bottle and the next morning it's lost its fizz.

Tim

No gusto?

Frank

Yeah, my life is gustoless.

Samantha

Oh. OK, I haven't retired yet, but I had a similar feeling of letdown, a couple of years ago, when the last of my kids finally left for college. My husband and I thought 'Free at last!' but that feeling of freedom didn't last very long. New problems immediately filled the void.

Tim

Let me know if this is the same: I thought I'd be overjoyed when I completed my last final exam and got my college degree. But that joy didn't last long, for the next day I was thinking about work and paying back my student loan.

Frank

Are we all on the same page?

Mark

Sounds like it. In all these examples, when we finally get what we wished for there's a sense of letdown. Actually, the changes created new problems, for Samantha and Tim. But in your case, Frank, the big change, namely your retirement, meant a lack of problems and, therefore, a lack of challenges, resulting in boredom. Did I get it right?

Frank

More or less. It's not that I don't have any problems--believe me, I do--but they're nothing like the battles I fought every day when I owned my company.

Tim

What's worse Doc, being deluged by problems, upsets and anxieties or experiencing ho-humness?

Mark

Ah, let's see… who wins the misery contest? Schopenhauer contends that boredom is worse than anxiety.

Frank

Hey, then I'm the winner! No wait; I'm the loser.

Mark

Then I offer you both my congratulations and my sympathies.

Frank

Yeah, it's ironic. I finally achieve the security that I've been seeking all my life and now it's almost like I want this cruise ship that I call my life to be attacked by pirates.

Mark

Actually, your situation reminds me of a short story by Franz Kafka, called "The Burrow." It's about an animal, a mole-like creature, who builds this elaborate burrow. It's full of escape hatches, in case a predator attacks him.

Frank

Hmm, let's see how tightly the shoe fits. I own a home here in Binghamton, one in Myrtle Beach and an investment property in the Boston suburbs that I rent out to students. I've got savings, stocks, bonds, annuities, collectables, gold bullion, a pension, and a Swiss bank account. I also have political connections, country club memberships--all sorts of memberships. Is it all an elaborate burrow?

Mark

I suppose that Kafka would say that it is.

Frank

Then just call me mole-man. Anyway, how does the story end? Does a wolf eat the mole? Do his kids sell the burrow and send the old mole to an old-age home? Or does he just rot away in his burrow?

Mark

Kafka's story ends differently than you'd suspect. The mole finally abandons his burrow!

Frank

Huh? Why does he do that? It makes no sense, considering all the trouble he must have gone through building it. I mean, just dealing with contractors. And what about his need for security?

Mark

Maybe the mole felt that his burrow had become his prison.

Frank

Look, I can't be singing "Halleluiah I'm a bum." I have Mrs. Mole and the molettes to support, mostly these days by managing my investments.

Mark

Obviously, we need to secure our existence. I'm not claiming otherwise. I'm just suggesting using our perplexity as a doorway into deeper questions.

Frank

Like what sort of deeper questions?

Mark

Doesn't it seem curious that we desire both security and adventure? But if we get the one, we seem to lose out on the other. Are we, then, creatures of contradiction?

Samantha

Well, can't we seek some sort of balance? Can't we balance our need for security with our need for adventure?

Mark

You love that word "balance," don't you?

Samantha

I guess I do. I also like the word "harmony." Maybe my work as a Shiatsu masseur affects how I see the world. It's all about balance.

Mark

In point of fact, modern life is very much an effort at balance. As to whether such balances are successful, is another story.

Samantha

I'm not sure I'm following you.

Mark

> I know you like to drive to Ithaca. Ever walk along Cascadilla Creek Gorge, which connects downtown Ithaca to Cornell? There's been a project to put up guardrails along some of the slippery areas. That would make it safer, but it might also ruin the sublime beauty of the gorge. So here we have a rather unsatisfactory balance of adventure and...

Samantha

> I've actually hiked that gorge hundreds of times and I know what you mean.

Mark

> A real adventure has elements of hardship and danger. It's often anything but fun, so they try to balance the longing for adventure with the need for security, kind of like adventure theme parks and video games and other virtual adventures. That sort of balance is no balance at all.

Tim

> I've been on some real adventures, some dangerous, like climbing Mount Washington, during the winter--which was foolish--parachuting out of planes and going on a safari in Africa, during one of my vacations. And, of course, being stationed in Iraq. I'm surprised I've made it to the ripe old age of forty-two.

Mark

> I admire your intrepid spirit. But, let me ask you, how do you feel when you return home from each adventure?

Tim

> Like Lawrence of Arabia. When he returned to England, after his daring military adventures in the Middle East, he suffered from what Frank called ho-humness. And so Lawrence took up high-speed motorcycle riding.

Mark

OK, then the motorcycle racing was a sort of compensation, a way of dealing with the adrenalin deficit he experienced when he was back in England. I remember that Colonel Lawrence died in a motorcycle accident. And I know that you, too, like to ride your Harley. Did I get that right?

Tim

You sure did, Doc. It seems that the more thrilling the adventure the worse it is to return to business as usual. It makes my regular life seem as flat as a pancake.

Mark

It doesn't sound, then, that your adventure vacations make for a well-balanced existence.

Tim

They actually throw my life out of balance.

Mark

And yet you continue with them.

Tim

If I had an answer that worked, I wouldn't be here asking questions.

Mark

Good point, Tim.

Dorothy

Would weekdays and weekends be an example of the balance we're discussing?

Mark

They really are. I once had a friend, during my graduate school years, who was really extreme that way. He got a job with an investment company, selling insurance, mutual funds, and annuities--that sort of thing. From Monday morning until Friday afternoon he was Mr. Serious, selling insurance by day and attending classes, in the evening, towards his MBA. I still picture him in his suit and tie, carrying his brief case. But, come the weekend, he would go on a drinking binge. Yeah, from happy hour, on Friday afternoon, to throwing up on Sunday morning-- That was his life for a few years.

Samantha

That was his idea of balance?

Frank

It sounds like he was trying to balance being sober with being plastered.

Mark

That's true Frank, although I'd say that he was really trying to balance sober-mindedness with a desire for self-abandon, or maybe self-control with a desire to relinquish self-control. Or maybe, you could say that he was trying to balance a desire for order with a desire for chaos.

Dorothy

Why the heck would anyone want chaos?

Mark

Because order seems limiting.

Frank

Yeah, just like a burrow. Hey, it's all beginning to make sense!

Mark

Or you could say that my friend was trying to balance a purposeful channeling of his life energies with a Dionysian longing for freedom from constraint.

Tim

How'd it work out for your friend?

Mark

His effort at balance made him inwardly unbalanced. He ended up checking into an alcoholic rehab center. And I think that he got slapped with a paternity suit from a women he picked up in a bar. He sent me a postcard from some monastery in upstate New York. That was the last I heard from him.

Samantha

Kind of extreme, wasn't he?

Mark

Yes, most people are more moderate. Their notion of freedom from order, direction and limit isn't so bacchanalian or Dionysian. It's simply a weekend hike through the woods, with their dog, or sitting in an easy chair watching sports.

Tim

Can you review where we've been with this discussion?

Mark

OK, let's see, Tim. We discussed Kafka's *Burrow*. Ironically, both Frank and the mole gained security but ended up board. Samantha recommended balancing security and adventure. Then we discussed vacations and finally my drunken friend. Got it Tim?

Tim [writing]

I got it all down, thank you.

Dorothy

Are security and adventure life's basic opposites?

Mark

They may be expressions of more fundamental requirements for selfhood.

Dorothy

Like what?

Mark

Well, I'm thinking, as we're talking, that our desire for physical security might really be an expression of an underlying anxiety about our identity, after all isn't the desire for security, to a large extent, the desire to stay as we are?

Frank

Identity? Hey, I'm Frank. I know who I am.

Mark

Yes, I realize that you're Frank. But hasn't your view of the world changed over the years, and along with it your sense of identity?

Frank

Yeah, maybe. When I was in my twenties, everything was up for grabs. I was kinda like Ricky. Eventually, I began to feel comfortable in my own skin. OK, maybe identity does relate to security. But now, years latter, I'm not so sure who I am. And attending these sessions has only made it worse!

Mark

Right now you're open, Frank, and that's an excellent thing.

Frank

Oh yeah, open to what?

Mark

To the big questions. We need inner chaos, from time to time. Renaissance isn't possible without it. Of course, we can't stay open forever. Closure inevitably sets in, sometimes even for years, until the next crisis.

Tim

Doc, if periods of openness are so wonderful, then why does closure set in?

Mark

Good question.

Dorothy

I think it's because there's only so much inner-turmoil we can endure.

Samantha

You got that right!

Mark

Good point Dorothy. So we seek to consolidate our identity, to have our life exhibit constancy and continuity, which are requirements for selfhood.

Dorothy

Those periods of openness --they're like a metaphysical panic attack! And yet I find myself inviting them all the same. I must be a glutton for punishment!

Mark

No, it's just that you long for freedom.

Dorothy

Freedom from what?

Mark

Freedom from oneself, for it's really our identity that walls us in. That's our real burrow. By the way, I'm wondering if an adventure is really a longing to be free of our own self-imposed limitations. Maybe, it's an effort to incorporate what we left out of who we are.

Frank

Are you saying that the gods left something out when they created each of us? Are you suggesting that we're incomplete? Of all the nerve!

Samantha

You said that our identity was like a circle, and that there is always an outside of the circle, which is why we feel incomplete.

Mark

Of course, those were just my tentative thoughts on the matter. I need to ruminate, a bit more, over these questions.

Samantha

What do you mean tentative? We're following you and now you say that you're not even sure of the path. Tentative shmentative!

Frank

Let's tar and feather this tentative philosopher and tentatively drive him out of town!

Mark

Remember, I'm not a guru. I'm really akin to a sha... a sha... what's the word?

Frank

A schlemiel?

Mark

No, Frank, I meant Sherpa, a Tibetan mountain guide. I have an idea how we can all get up the mountain--because I've climbed other before--but I'm doing a lot of improvising here. That's why this is a real adventure. How much more exciting!

Tim

According to my notes, Doc, you suggested that the need for identity and the need for completeness are contradictory. Are you saying, then, that we can't reconcile them?

Mark

We can't reconcile these needs in the ways in which people usually try to reconcile them. Perhaps, though, it's possible to transcend the very terms of the conflict.

Dorothy

OK, so let's say that what we desire is contradictory. Is that why we can't ever get what we want? Is that why there's a conservation of suffering?

Mark

That's it!

Dorothy

Does that mean that we're doomed to be forever dissatisfied?

Mark

Or is it possible to transcend life's contradictions and get what we really desire?

Tim

Wow, Doc, this is a heavy stakes game.

Chapter Three
Philosophical Intermission

The dialogue "Irrepressible Questions" consists of five acts. Let's now explore, in a bit more depth, some of the ideas that emerged.

The title of the first act, "The Last Temptation of Dorothy," is an ironic allusion to Kazantzakis' novel "The Last Temptation of Christ." Christ's last temptation was to live an ordinary life. Apropos is Abraham Maslow's notion of the "Jonah Complex." Jonah was given a mission from God, which he initially refused. The Jonah Complex consists of a flight from a deeper, truer mode of existence. That temptation is everyone's. It's certainly Dorothy's temptation.

Dorothy envies Myra and her other friends, who seem to have absorbed themselves in their marriages, families and careers. A reflective person, like Dorothy, will often long for "the simple life," but Dorothy's image of the simple life is romanticized and delusory. In truth, most people are in flight from life's depths, and utilize various modes of distraction for that purpose--from liquor to TV. They are in despair, without realizing it.

Kierkegaard contends that unconscious despair is worse than conscious despair, for if you realize that you are in despair you then ready yourself for the type of sea change that would bring self-renewal. In any case, if we look beneath the surface, we see that Dorothy's friends are desperate characters, as are the majority of people. Their lives are certainly not worth envying.

Dorothy, though, is beset with serious questions about life. Thus she finds herself unable to become absorbed for long, before becoming reflected out, examining everything. Her attitude towards all of this is ambivalent. For one thing, Dorothy fears that too much thinking has caused her to lose her immediacy, as well as the energy that derives from naïve, unexamined enthusiasms. That's certainly a concern, but she could always reengage with life, after having raised questions about it all. (A dream that Dorothy has, in a subsequent dialogue, offers some insight into her problem.) And while envying her friends for what Dorothy perceives to be a simpler life, she also has a lust for a truer mode of existence.

Dorothy harbors the assumption, as do many people, that the light of self-knowledge will make one feel joyous. Quite the contrary, in Plato's *Allegory of the Cave*, the prisoner, who is released from his chains, had to be dragged to the light. Indeed, any moment in which we see who we are is anything but sweetness and light. Rather, it will usually feel sickening.

What is it about self-knowledge that is terrifying, devastating, and sickening? The emerging light of consciousness reveals our unreality! How is this possible? Whether or not we realize it, when we look at our life, we also judge its reality or unreality. We do so by means of a number of different criteria. For example, we ask: "Do I possess a consistent identity? Am I one, a unity, something whole?" Self-reflection reveals that we are not. Rather, we are riddled, through and through, with contradictions of all sorts that belie our claim to consistency and wholeness. These internal contradictions are reflected in the fact that we often desire opposite things. For example, we might desire adventure, but we also desire security. Or, for example, we wish to give our life order, but also rebel against order.

Throughout the dialogues, we seek to uncover these various antinomies. Contradiction, impossibility and despair are not, though, the end of the story. The good news is that a human being isn't simply a network of contradictions. In time, we may come to realize that we are the *awareness* of these contradictions; that awareness is our true self. This free awareness is akin to what the Advaita mystics call the Self, or Brahma. What a relief it is to let go of the incessant effort to try to get it together!

Act II: *A Farewell to Happy Talk*

Act II is entitled "A Farewell to Happy Talk," because we explore a common concern of those who pursue this path to self-knowledge and self-realization. Samantha is worried that we've been having too much discussion of the negative dimension of human existence. Why, indeed, explore the many varieties of human unhappiness? It's because insight can provide a cure. Anyone who travels this road will eventually discern that our fundamental effort to achieve reality as a person, or selfhood, is riddled with unresolvable contradictions, or antinomies, and therefore impossible to achieve. And that's the good news!

Samantha, in particular, felt overwhelmed by all of the talk of the darker side of life. She had once tried a path that involved a more "positive" approach to self-realization, but found it wanting. She found that there is no escaping the negative dimension of life. Sooner or later, one must face the music, i.e., one must seek to understand and illuminate the negative, which we experience as suffering.

In truth, suffering--when illuminated--is the fastest route to self-knowledge, deliverance, and self-realization. It reveals to us our inadequate answer to life's ultimate questions and what is lacking in our answer. If further examined, it reveals the question that life is asking us. As humans, though, we are constantly fleeing the negative. Thus the negative pursues us, like one might be pursued by one's shadow, and we are continually in flight from it. The thing to do is to turn around and face it that which has long been pursuing us. When we do, everything changes. For one thing, the anxiety that we had experienced transforms from our enemy to our teacher. That is why Kierkegaard used the phrase, "the school of dread."

There's a danger, though, that dwelling on the dark side could leave us feeling emotionally heavy and depressed. That's why discussions of life's negativities should be balanced with wonderment. Carlos Castaneda's teacher, Don Juan Matus, spoke of balancing the terrors of existence with wonderment about it all. Like, wonder, amazement and awe, humor is valuable, in that regard. The reader will observe that a certain degree of high-spiritedness pervades these discussions of life's negativities.

Act III: *Dancing with Schopenhauer*

Act III introduced the reader to the Conservation of Suffering Principle. The basic idea is that suffering, like energy or matter, can neither be created nor destroyed. Only the particular form that suffering takes changes. For example, becoming free of the source of our anxiety can leave us feeling bored. Furthermore, as Arthur Schopenhauer observes, everything that we think of as good is really only a lack of the bad. That is a shocking insight! It means that when--due to a particular need or desire being satisfied--the bad departs, so does the good along with it.

My analysis of why happiness is transient upsets Ricky's optimistic vision of a happy life. It often happens that one question leads to even larger questions. Thus when Ricky considers the implications of the conservation of suffering, he begins to realize that his life lacks purpose. Nor does he really know who he is and what he should do with his life.

Prior to the dawning of these questions, Ricky was living unconsciously. He was merely the product of various determinants, such as his upbringing, his natural abilities, and his inborn preferences. Now he has begun to be reflected out of his immediacy, such that he can examine it and freely chose what. He may, indeed, wish to remain a musician, but now it will be a free choice. This is actually a very positive development, for Ricky cannot be an authentic individual--and, therefore, fully human--until he has begun to ask the many fundamental questions that have emerged for him.

Of course, with freedom comes anxiety, but the lack of ground opens Ricky up to something new, a religious mode of existence, which involves the faith that our choices--benighted though we may be in making them--will eventually lead us to where we need to go in life. Indeed, as it turned out, Frank knows Ricky's father, who recommends that Ricky join the group. Ricky gets a lot out of these discussions. Was it luck or was it the hidden hand of providence? Ricky suspects the latter, which is why he requests that I offer him a blessing for the road that lies ahead.

Act IV: *Fat Enough to Fill the Void*

Here we continue with our investigation of the ontological origins of human suffering. We explore whether there exists, in each of us, something akin to an inner void. It must be filled with suffering, for nature abhors a vacuum. Thus, even if we free ourselves from a major problem in our life, the inner void must be filled with a new problem. On the other hand, the void could also be filled with a number of minor problems, but filled it must be!

If, on the other hand, we do not seem to have a problem to dwell on--as Frank discovers--we begin to feel restless, which is another form of suffering. We are beset by a hunger, an inchoate sense of lack that longs to take on a shape or a form. We might, for example, blame our discontent on not being successful or perhaps on another person. So much depends on what we determine to be the true source of our suffering!

The discussion then proceeded to the question of hope, which I argued is not always a good thing, for it can drive a person crazy with anxiety. We imagine, for example, that if we can only fulfill a particular goal--pass an exam, get into a college, marry our sweetheart, land a desirable job or purchase a house--that we are on the road to eternal happiness. Grasping the conservation of suffering destroys hope, for we perceive that despite the apparent improvement in our lot in life, that the quantity of our happiness is essentially the same after the desired changes in our situation have transpired. What inevitably happens when we obtain our desideratum is that we then hunt for a new object of desire. But realizing this frees us from a great deal of anxiety and brings peace of mind.

This leads us to some ultimate questions: Why is there a conservation of suffering? Simply stated, the reason is that we never seem to get what we really want. Indeed, we have no idea what we really want. What is this obscure object of desire? Dorothy concludes, rightly, that whatever it is, it must be a good without an accompanying bad. Eastern religion says that the ultimate longing is the desire of the Self (Brahman, God, the universe, the It) to see itself. But how can that which is infinite see itself? It cannot, for only that which is finite is graspable, or intelligible. Consequently, it seeks to reflect itself in that which is finite. Consequently, it mistakenly identifies with the finite self, or ego, of each person.

Playing the role of the finite ego, it then seeks each object of desire as that which would end its lack and thus reflect its infinitude. Alas, that which is infinite, i.e., the Self, cannot see itself reflected in the finite. Hence it fails to see itself, but miraculously, in the process, it does come to see itself as that which it has been seeking all along.

Act V: *The Last Train Leaving the Burrow*

Here we explored the contradiction between security and adventure. Like Kafka's mole-like creature--who builds a burrow only to feel trapped by the very security that he had sought to achieve--Frank too feels trapped and bored by his secure retirement.

Samantha suggests some sort of balance between security and adventure. There's certainly much to be said for balance. Indeed, some of the wisest thinkers have realized that life is often a balancing act between extremes. Aristotle's "Golden Mean" suggests that, as does Buddha's notion of "the Middle Way." But ultimately we are beset by contradictions and these irresolvable contradictions, or antinomies, haunt our existence, and we must come to terms with them.

The contradiction between the conflicting needs for security and adventure is seen to be an expression of related contradictions, including that between sober-mindedness (self-control) and self abandon. For Friedrich Nietzsche, the real conflict was between the Apollonian and the Dionysian. These various conflicts are really formulations of a more fundamental contradiction. On the one hand, to be real, to attain selfhood, requires that we have an identity. This self-identity requirement finds expression as a need for consistency, unity, and focus. But we also have a very different longing, one for completeness.

Identity is, by analogy, like a circle. No matter how large one draws the circle, there will always be something left out of it, for that's the nature of circles. Consequently, we shall feel incomplete. But, if one attempts to stuff everything into the circle of one's identity--such that one becomes like a bouillabaisse--one's life will lack unity.

The question arises, again, whether these contradictions that are based on the requirements for selfhood--self-identity and completeness--can be transcended in some way. As I had suggested earlier, the very awareness of the contradiction is its transcendence. The coming dialogues will have more to say about this.

Some Questions for Readers to Explore

A number of intriguing questions have emerged from these dialogues. Here are ten to get you cogitating. Don't even think of skipping over these questions or Schopenhauer's ghost will haunt you, and at the most inopportune moments!

1. Are you fleeing the big questions? If so, what are your modes of escape? Is it through distraction? Is it through TV? Food? The drama of a relationship? The drama of politics? Being a workaholic can also be a form of flight from the ultimate questions. Perhaps there are a variety of means, by which you seek escape.

2. Are you able to totally absorb yourself in whatever activity you engage in? Or do you find yourself popping out, at times, to look upon them, examine them, and ask questions about them, as does Dorothy?

3. Have you detected instances of the conservation of suffering in your own life? Can you, for example, describe a time when you hoped for something very much, but were either disillusioned upon getting it or getting it led to a host of new problems? Alas, it's been said, "Be careful what you wish for, for you just may get it." (To better answer this question, you might wish to read the essay on the conservation of suffering, in Part II.)

4. Have you ever had an important moment of insight that shook the foundations of your world? What precipitated it?

5. Have you detected the contradictory nature of your interests and desires? Can you offer an example? For example, have you been building a "burrow," like Frank did, only to find yourself trapped by the very things that offer you security?

6. Are you involved with some sort of "balancing act"? An example of a desperate effort at balance was my friend who sold insurance during the week and got drunk during the weekend. Another example at a terribly unbalanced effort at balance is the protagonist of the film, Looking for Mr. Goodbar (1977). It's about a dedicated schoolteacher who cruises bars in the evening.

7. Are you able to trace the negativity in your life back to problems with your answer to the question of how to be? I.E., have you ever wondered whether or not your vision of happiness and fulfillment may be flawed? Indeed, is there a flaw at the very heart of how you have been seeking to achieve selfhood?

8. Do you find yourself getting overwhelmed by life's negativities? Or are you able to balance the suffering that you experience with wonderment, amazement, awe and cosmic belly laughter?

9. Have you been living on autopilot? For example, have you merely acquired your social and political beliefs via indoctrination--from your parents, friends and professors? Are you, in other words, a child of the times? Or have you questioned your own beliefs, your assumptions about who you are and what you really wish to do with your life, as Ricky has started doing? Doing so opens the door to self-choice, real decisions, authentic living as well as to the unknown, to fate and perhaps the guiding hand of providence.

10. Do you share any of the problems and concerns that any of the characters, in these dialogues, have been experiencing?

Chapter IV
Unsettling Questions

A Dialogue in Four Acts

Dramatis Personœ:

    Frank--A recently retired owner of a record company, in his late fifties.

    Samantha--A shiatsu masseur, in her mid-fifties.

    Tim--Owner of a landscaping business, in his early forties.

    Ricky--A graduate student in music, plays in a rock band, in his mid twenties.

    Dorothy --A teacher of high school English, in her mid thirties.

    Mark--Philosopher, leader of this group, in my early to mid-fifties, at the time.

    Haley--A woman in her early twenties.

    Detective Mueller--A man in his thirties.

    Detective Clancy--A man in his late fifties.

Act I: A Contradiction that Tastes Like Amaretto

[Evening. A room with a couch and comfortable chairs. In one corner, there is a bookcase filled with books and a few sculptures. In another corner is a piano. There are paintings and photos on the wall. The room also contains small tables, assorted lamps, and plants. The various characters are sitting around the room.]

Mark

It looks like everyone's here. Did you have a chance to read the essays? Hmm, no answer. So, how is everyone to nigh...

Ricky

Lousy!

Mark

Why so, Ricky?

Ricky

It's my rock band. We've been making some very nice money, but we've lost our soul.

Mark

How can a band lose its soul? Is it metaphysically possible for there to be a group soul? Could you please elaborate?

Ricky

Our fans like us for who we're not. We play the music they want, mostly covers of popular songs, but we rarely get to do our own compositions. We get paid to put on an act.

Tim

An act? Isn't performing on stage a kind of like acting? Am I missing something here, Ricky?

Ricky

It's just that our agent insists that se act like we're having a good time.

Frank

Can you blame him?

Ricky

Well yeah, Frank. You see a real musical artist should be suffering. His soul should be tormented. He should be struggling. He should be straining. He should be …

Frank

Constipated?

Ricky

No! Not constipated! He should look like he's about to give birth to a higher realm of being, a new world order. How can we look cheerful when we're having labor pains?

Frank

Well, you got me there.

Ricky

Anyway, being happy go lucky is not who we are as a band. Yeah, we're faking it. We're frauds, phonies, imposters!

Samantha

What would happen if you did play the music that's you?

Ricky

Whenever we do, people lose interest, real fast. Our music is too far ahead of the times.

Tim

What type of music are you talking about? Is it avant-garde?... Post avant-garde?... Post, post, post, post, post, post avant-garde? Post modern? Post, post, post modern?

Ricky

No, not exactly. I'll give you an example. I've written a quadrille consisting of atonal harmonics.

Tim

A quadrille? Ha! Ha! Super-retro! The quadrille hasn't been in fashion since George and Martha Washington tripped the light fantastic.

Ricky

I'll play some of it for you.

>[Walks over to the piano, and sits down. He then begins to play a quadrille, then plays a rolling bass, which causes everyone to think that he it is going to accompany some blues, but instead it accompanies something very cacophonous.]

Pretty good, huh?

Tim

Definitely original.

Samantha

I never heard anything like it before, other than maybe in a previous lifetime.

Ricky

Well, it actually has gospel roots.

Mark

Since when have you become religious?

Ricky

Since last week, when you said that blessing over me.

Mark

Oh, so I'm responsible.

Ricky

Anyway, what I'm playing is designed to cause people to have an epileptic fit and then to cry out to Heaven for deliverance. But the guy who owns the club we're playing at says that he's not insured for that sort of thing. Is that unfair or what?

Tim

Well Ricky, most people come down to a club just to dance, to meet someone, to have a few drinks, not for a trauma, not to end up in the ER, followed by a religious experience.

Ricky

Anyway, the club owners see their patrons looking kind of bewildered. And so they tell us that we got to play what the audience wants to hear, oldies like:

[Singing and playing piano]

"And she'll have fun, fun, fun, Til her daddy takes her t-bird away." Or I'll sing: "Billie Jean is not my lover. She's just a girl who claims that I am the one. But the kid is not my son." Then the morons are back on the dance floor.

[Returns to his seat]

And everyone's happy, except for us.

Frank

Look kid, I've been in the music business myself, long before you were born. I was a singer and then I built my own recording company, which, as you know, I just sold. If you don't intend to play the stuff the schmucks like to hear, then you should get out of the entertainment racket. Yeah, why don't you find a job teaching music at a college? After a few years, you'll get tenure and then you can be as far out as you want, and maybe ten people a year will buy a CD of your inspired compositions.

Samantha

Gee, Frank, that's real encouraging!

Frank

I sold out. Elvis sold out. And as the immortal Dean Martin said [singing] "Everybody got to sell out sometime."

Samantha

Wait a second. He said that everybody loves somebody...

Frank

Look Ricky, the sellout train's leaving the station and you better get aboard or you're going to end up as a college professor, imprisoned in some ivory tower.

Ricky

Oh, yeah. Where's the train headed?

Frank

To the real world.

Samantha

Better bring along some medicine for migraines, ulcers and high blood pressure, because if you board that train, Ricky, you're going to get real sick. That's the price you pay for selling your soul!

Ricky

> [standing up]

I feel I'm being pulled in opposite directions. On the train, off the train, on, off, on, off!

Frank

All aboard! Choo! Choo! The trains about to pull out. Step lively Ricky. Watch the closing doors!

Ricky

I feel like I'm going to be split in two! This conversation is giving me a splitting headache! Maybe I ought to split! [Walks to the door.]

Samantha

No, stick around Ricky. I placed a pie in the oven, for everyone to eat during our coffee break, and Frank brought some cannoli's.

Mark

Yeah, stick around. We still need to get to the core of this inner conflict.

> [Ricky returns to seat]

Dorothy

Mark, isn't this an example of Pepsi flavored Coke! In your essay, you state that if we go too far in the direction of being the person the world wants--if we get aboard the sellout train--we'll be successful, but then we'll lose our soul, our identity, our essence. Yeah, you'll be like Pepsi flavored Coke.

Samantha

That's right. If you can't be your true self, you don't have anything.

Dorothy

Right Samantha... Look, I agree with Frank that we need to eat, which requires compromises of all sorts. And I can sympathize with Ricky that he needs to keep his integrity.

Tim

What a balancing act!

Dorothy

I try my best to reconcile these two dimensions of life--the practical and the ideal--making concessions here and there.

Samantha

How so?

Dorothy

Sure, I could pull an Emily Dickenson and not let what's best in me venture beyond the confines of my living room, but I chose to enter into the rude world of a high school. So, if I am going to expose young minds to the soul-enriching power of poetry, I must come to terms with the ignorance, narrow-mindedness and foolishness that I daily encounter. If I yell and scream and say that such foolishness shouldn't exist, I'll be out of a job.

Samantha

Well, Dorothy, they're only high school students, but I can't blame you for getting a bit frustrated with them.

Dorothy

I'm not talking about the students! I'm talking about my colleagues, the department head, the principle, the PTA, the parents, the teacher's unions, the school board, the New York State Regents and the Department of Education and a legion of other ignorant and officious administrators.

Tim

I have a question, Doc. Why are we divided this way? I mean, my Irish Setter, Slobbberchops, doesn't seem saddled with moral dilemmas. But human beings always have them. What's the story?

Mark

That's interesting. Slobbberchops has a single sense of self, if we could even call it a self, but we humans have at least two. One seems to relate to our physical existence and the other has to do with our ideals.

Tim

Why do we have ideals anyway? Of what practical value are they? It seems that they only cause us problems.

Samantha

Yeah, to hell with ideals. I'm with Slobbberchops.

Mark

Interesting Samantha. Anyway, good question, Tim. Well, let me ask you: what do ideals have that the real world lacks?

Dorothy

The real world is dark, chaotic, and confusing.

Samantha

Yeah, it's a mess.

Dorothy

But the ideal world, that's another story. It's light, ordered, coherent and meaningful.

Mark

Sounds like you've been reading Plato? He also has two worlds. There are dogs that physically exist, like Slobberchops, as well as...

Tim

Fido, Nikita, Augustus, Freeloader, Porkchops, and Dowser?

Mark

Right Tim. But Plato says that there also exists the Form, or Idea, of dog. Yes, Slobberchops is the physical manifestation of that eternal essence called Dog.

Samantha

Is there also an eternal essence of cat? Of pumpkin? Of jackass? Of slimeball?

Mark

Yes, Plato claims that there's a world of eternal Ideas. Slimeballs come and go, but the notion of slimeball is eternal. Anyway, Ricky has a conflict--I mean we all do--between the practical demands of this world and his ideals. Being that Ricky's an idealist, he seeks to implement his ideals, to change the world so that it conforms to his image of perfection, his vision of the way things should be.

Ricky

Oh, is that what I'm trying to do?

Mark

I guess in a way you are. After all, what are you trying to accomplish with your music? I know it's not just about giving your audience listening pleasure. It sounds like you have an altogether different agenda.

Ricky

Damn right! I'm trying to get people to see something important about themselves and about life. I want to reach their minds through their ears. I want them to hear the music of the heavenly spheres, to connect their minds to the absolute frequency. I want to transform the blockheads into spiritual beings. I mean, is that really too much to ask?

Frank

I'll say it is. You're some kind of wild-eyed revolutionary!

Samantha

Viva Ricky!

Ricky

But I never succeed. People don't hear a thing.

Mark

That's true, Ricky, they rarely hear anything... Tim, you said that the real world lacks unity. That it's a mess. What sort of unity would you like? Would you like everyone to wear the same outfit and chant together, like they did in Maoist China? Is that the unity you desire?

Tim

Noooo! I wouldn't want the unity to destroy individual differences.

Mark

What, then, did you have in mind?

Tim

[Mimes catching a ball and throwing it]

It would be like a baseball team. Each person has their own position--first base, pitcher, right field, short stop and so on. Yeah, they're all doing something different, but they all have the same goal, winning the game.

Ricky

Could it be like an orchestra? Everyone has his own part to play--the violins, the oboes, the clarinets, the drums and everyone else--but they all know the score and are following it.

Mark

Ah, so the score is the unifying factor. The score would be a synonym for the meaning.

Dorothy

What is the ultimate score?

Mark

The ultimate score?

Dorothy

Well, if I understand you correctly, the score is the meaning. I guess what I'm asking, then, is: What is the meaning of life?

Mark

Ah, that's the question! Some people claim to know the score. They insist that everyone follow their score. Then they fight with those who have a different understanding of the score.

Samantha

I'm not sure I'm following you.

Mark

For example, there are people who are communists. They insist that life is all about establishing equality. Then there are Islamic fundamentalists who insist that it's all about worshipping Allah and implementing Sharia law worldwide. So each would organize the world--or the orchestra, to use our metaphor--differently. And they would kill anyone who wanted to play a different melody.

Samantha

Last time I went to a classical concert, I saw this guy who played this big drum. I think it's called a...

Ricky

A tympani?

Samantha

Yeah, a tympani. Well the guy sits there and sits there. Everyone is playing, but the poor guy is just waiting and waiting. Finally, he gets his turn to play. And he just gets to bang the tympani five times. And I thought that if I were on stage I'd be banging away at the tympani all evening. Screw the first violin. To heck with the woodwinds, the brass section and everyone else. To hell with the score! I demand to be heard!

Mark

That's what's called individualism. Yeah, that's when everyone forgets about the score and does his own thing, producing the cacophony that we have today.

Dorothy

What if there isn't an ultimate score?

Mark

There are people who claim that too. They're skeptics, the relativists, the atheists, the Sartrean existentialists, the postmodernists. Jean-Paul Sartre says that each of us must create his or her own score. Yeah, I know it sounds whacky.

Dorothy

What if I could finally discover the true score, the ultimate meaning of life. Would I then find peace of mind?

Mark

Human beings are rebels. Dostoevsky said that human beings crave an ultimate meaning, but if they find it, they will fight against it, because it limits their freedom. They'd be like Samantha on the tympani.

Tim

Doc, is that an example of the contradiction between identity and freedom?

Mark

Damn straight it is! What we are calling the ultimate musical score, or meaning, is akin to an identity. But in this case it's not OUR identity we are seeking, but the identity of the world, the

Logos, it's true meaning, that which would bring everything into focus, as a unity.

Dorothy

But if there's no score for everyone to follow? If there's no ultimate meaning, then there's no real world, no unity, no wholeness. And if there's no world then what we inhabit is...

Frank

Chaos!

Mark

You got it Frank.

Ricky

So, if people are closed to my revolutionary musical ideas... No let me begin that again, Dr. Mark... If everyone is locked in his own world, there can't be a real world, as you're defining it, meaning one that has unity and wholeness. So, what's the solution?

Mark

There are a number of possibilities. For example, you could...

Frank

[to Ricky]

What you could do is to stop trying to get other people to see the world like you see it. Instead, you could find out how other people see the world and give them what they want. Yeah, you could exploit them and make a pretty penny in the process.

Mark

Well, that's certainly one sort of solution. I have no objection to giving people what they want, but I doubt that it's the path that Ricky's likely to take.

Ricky

What path do you think I'll take?

Mark

I suspect that you'll go on trying to get other people to see-- actually to hear--your vision of life, through your music.

Ricky

But that means a lifetime of failure and frustration.

Mark

It might or your music might catch on; who knows. In any case, there are other things that might emerge when we realize the ultimate discrepancy between your ideals and life's realities. For example, like I was telling Dorothy the other day, there exists ...

Dorothy

The comical? Humor? Laughter?

Mark

You beat me to the punch line, Dorothy. Examine anytime that you laughed and you'll discover it was based on your perceiving a contradiction of some sort. As we go through the day, we encounter all sorts of contradictions, one of which is the contradiction between the life's less than glorious realities and our ideals. And if we happen to get enough emotional distance from the contradiction, we laugh.

Ricky

Gee, I don't know that I see the joke yet.

Frank

That's because you take yourself too seriously kid.

Ricky

Then how should I view life? If it's a joke, it's a cruel one! A nasty one! A vicious one!

Mark

Do you like Beethoven?

Ricky

He was the greatest--greater than Wolfgang Amadeus Mozart, greater than Elvis Amadeus Presley, and greater than Johnny Rotten of the Sex Pistols. Yeah Ludwig was the greatest.

Mark

Well, what did Beethoven name the second movement of his Ninth Symphony? I'll tell you. He called it the *scherzo*.

Frank

Hey, that's Italian for joke.

Mark

That's right Frank. *Scherzo* means joke. Beethoven got the joke. He wrestled fate, but also laughed along with the gods. And the last thing he said on his deathbed was "Laugh friends, the comedy is over."

Ricky

Did Beethoven also experience the contradiction between the ideal and the real?

Mark

He certainly did. For example, he dedicated his *Third*

Symphony, the *Eroika,* to Napoleon Bonaparte because he saw him as a great liberator, but when Napoleon made himself into an emperor--into a dictator who had little respect for the ideals and institutions of democracy--the disillusioned and disgusted Beethoven retracted his dedication.

Ricky

Ah, like the song says "We won't get fooled again."

Frank

But we do get fooled again and again and again.

Mark

Yeah, history is what comedians call a running gag. Anyway, a *scherzo* is a joke, but Beethoven didn't consider it a cruel joke. There's plenty of sad passages in his music and angry one's too, but no bitterness.

Dorothy

You said last week that it's healthy to laugh about what you can't do much about.

Mark

That's very true Dorothy.

Dorothy

Hmm, at times I'm almost tempted to laugh.

Mark

Well, if you're not careful, you could crack up or, even worse, explode with laughter. My apartment renter's policy is not insured for that sort of thing.

Dorothy

Hmm, to laugh or not to laugh, that is the question. I think I'll play it safe for now and stay gloomy.

Mark

That's the spirit, Dorothy; misery is familiar and comforting. Anyway, Ricky, if you get some emotional distance from life's contradictions, the cosmic joke will emerge into view. Then life won't taste entirely bitter, but it won't taste like a cannoli either. Most likely, life will taste bittersweet, like...

Frank

Like amaretto?

Mark

Hmm, that's it Frank, like amaretto. Anyway, laugher is one way of dealing with the contradiction between life as we would want it to be, the ideal world, and life as it is, the real world. Any last thoughts, before we break for coffee and cannolis?

Tim

Yeah, how nice it would be to be like Slobbberchops, free of life's maddening contradictions... But then, again, he doesn't get to laugh like we do.

Dorothy

Ah, finally a consolation for being born a human.

Act II: Smoking, Drinking & Gambling to Infinity

Mark

It looks like everyone's back from the coffee break, except for Ricky.

Samantha

He said that he had to study for an exam. I'll lend him my tape-recording of tonight's discussion. And Tim's taking notes.

Mark

So let's turn to the dark side, for further clues to life's deepest mysteries.

Tim

The dark side! Woohoo!

Mark

I admire your infectious enthusiasm Tim, especially for all that's dark, grim and unholy.

Tim

> [Writing in his notebook, while speaking in a monstrous monotone]

Grim, dark and unholy. Must examine the deeper meaning of my fascination with these things.

Mark

Yes, that would be a splendid idea Tim... I thought that, tonight, we'd explore the deeper meaning of our vices. I suspect that even the most degenerate of them are an expression of... our longing for the infinite, the eternal--indeed for God!

Samantha

What type of vices? Do you mean like eating a gallon of ice cream at a single sitting? How about watching TV for over five hours a day?

Mark

No, nothing quite as serious as ice cream and TV! I was thinking more along the lines of smoking, drinking and gambling--that sort of thing.

Frank

Yeah, gambling! The article that you posted on your blog about the psychology of gambling really got me thinking. The other day I read it and it made me laugh.

Mark

Ah, the laughter of recognition. The laughter that comes from reading something and thinking to oneself, "Yes, how very true!"

Frank

No, not quite. I laughed because I found your analysis of gamblers to be absolutely idiotic.

Mark

Hmm, was there anything in particular that you found to...

Frank

Yeah, the notion that a gambler subconsciously wants to lose money. Ha! Ha! Ho! Ho! How, in the name of Nick the Greek, did you come up with anything so absurd?

Mark

Well, actually, it's an old idea, although I...

Frank

Look, I should know something about gambling. Since I've retired I've been gambling every week...

Samantha

Every week? Wow, Frank, I didn't know you were a compulsive gambler.

Frank

I'm not a compulsive gambler! Anyway, a few times a week...

Samantha

A few times a week! Where do you go? To the racetrack?

Frank

Yeah, but I also go on bus tours, with a group of friends. We go to the casinos, where I play blackjack and poker and other games. Then, about six times a year, we fly out to Vegas or some other city that has gambling or on a cruise ship. But it's not that I gamble everyday. And besides, I've been trying to spend more time at home.

Samantha

So that you can spend more quality time with your family?

Frank

No, so that I can concentrate on trading stocks online.

Mark

You never mentioned any of this to me.

Frank

Well now you know. Gambling is the only activity that gets my adrenalin going. It isn't just more of the same ho...

Samantha

Ho-humness? Blaséhood?

Tim

Gustolessness?

Frank

Yeah, those technical terms describe how I feel.

Mark

Well, that's not surprising, because in your everyday life you're drowning in finitude, that's why it seems blasé, or ho-hum. But gambling offers you an image of the infinite, which is why it's exciting.

Frank

The infinite? Is that what I'm searching for? Why, how very interesting, Doc! Nah, I'm in it for the money.

Mark

Yeah, infinite money.

Frank

Why would I want that? After all, I retired with plenty of money, more than I need to spoil the next seven generations of Franks and Frankettes.

Mark

Well, since you don't need the money, why do you gamble?

Frank

Hmm, I wish I knew and it would be nice if it were real soon, because I'm already down $85,000 for the year and I don't like losing money. It takes the fun out of gambling.

Mark

Isn't gambling the wish to get the good of life for free? And isn't the longing to live for free the longing for the infinite? As you know, Frank, there's nothing like labor to reveal to us that we aren't free. Rather, we're finite, limited beings, conditioned by circumstances. For everything we get in life, we must pay a price. Indeed, we must pay and pay and then pay some more, by the sweat of our brow. The allure of "for free" is a denial of the human condition. It's a longing to sneak back into Eden, before the fall. That's what I think is the basic appeal of gambling. Then there's the appeal that Lady Luck has chosen you alone--that's right, you alone, Frank--for this blessing, for this exemption from the human condition, because... Well because you're somehow blessed.

Samantha

What about my interest in bargains?

Mark

Very good Samantha! It's the same desire to get something for free. When a merchant advertises that an item is 10% off, it really means that it's 10% for free.

Samantha

OK, what about fat free?

Mark

It has this same appeal. It means that we can eat a certain tasty food, but without paying the price of hardening of the arteries. Anyway, Frank, the allure of money is that we can prevent the world from limiting your freedom. If, for example, you don't like what they serve at a particular restaurant, you can buy the place and hire your own chef.

Frank

I'd call it "Frankie's Place." Yeah, when you got money, it's kind of like having a magic wand. I understand your example, but I'm still not sure I'm getting your point about the infinite.

Mark

This is going to sound a bit philosophical. Are you ready?

Frank

I just had a strong cup of coffee and I'm sitting down, so please proceed Socrates.

Mark

OK, what is the ultimate source of limits, or finitude?

Frank

My wife?

Mark

I mean the *ultimate* source?

Frank

Hmm, I know that you want a philosophical answer. What could it be? What --could--it--be? Hmm,

> [Eyes open wide and speaks, as if in a hypnotic state]

I think therefore I am. I think therefore I am... I think therefore I am... Sorry, but I'm not connecting, Doc...

> [Drinks water]

Mark

OK. Here goes. At the moment that you become aware of yourself, you simultaneously become aware of the non-Frank.

Frank

> [Accidentally spits out water]

What the hell are you talking about?!

Mark

I'm talking about the subject/object distinction. At every moment, I'm aware of myself over against the world. I'm the subject and everything else is the object. That's what I meant when I said that there's the Frank and the non-Frank.

Frank

Who's the non-Frank? I haven't even met him, but I can already tell that I don't like the guy!

Samantha

Frank, if you and the non-Frank could chat over a few beers, I'm sure that the both of you would find that you really do have a lot in common. So many of life's misunderstandings are due to...

Mark

No! No! You're both misunderstanding me. The non-Frank is the world. At every moment the object, stands over against the subject, the world stands over against Frank.

Frank

[Talking like Tweety Bird]

Yeah, wittle Fwankie, the subject, over against the big bad wold.... So what's your point?

Mark

If you have the money, you know that you can purchase anything that you see. And if you can purchase anything, then it feels like the object, or the world, is no longer opposing you, because you can own it. In other words, money is a catalyst. It has the magic power of transforming the non-Frank, in other words the world, into the Frank.

Samantha

I'm not sure I'm following you.

Mark

Do you remember, a couple of years ago, you were telling me that you had just joined a health club and how alienated you felt. You didn't know any of the members.

Samantha

Eventually, I made friends, but I felt really strange, at the beginning. I felt like I didn't belong and I almost quit.

Mark

Well, imagine the same scenario, with one difference. Imagine that you had just purchased the health club. How would you have felt working out? Would the fact that you didn't know anybody have made a difference?

Samantha

If I were the new owner? I guess I would have felt totally different! Yeah, it's true that I still wouldn't have known anybody, but I would have had much more of a sense of belonging. So, if I understand your lingo, when I buy something I'm really transforming the object, or the world, into me, the subject. I'm transforming the non-Samantha into the Samantha. Did I get that right?

Mark

Sounds like you did.

Samantha

Is that why I like to go shopping when I'm feeling down?

Mark

Yes, that makes sense, because when you're depressed you feel alone and cut-off from the world. Shopping symbolically transforms the world into you. You are no longer alienated and no longer feeling down.

Samantha

Wow, so all this time shopping has been for me a form of therapy. I wonder if I could get my heath insurance company to pay for the items.

Mark

Anyway, if you were infinitely wealthy nothing, no material object, could oppose you the subject.

Samantha

I could go through expensive department stores, pointing to items, saying: "Mine, mine, mine," as my assistant followed me with a shopping cart. Eventually, I could transform the planet into Samantha-land. Yes, I would be infinite!

Frank

Hmm, I'm thinking of Irma, my mother-in-law.

Samantha

She also likes to shop?

Frank

Sometimes she does, but she always likes to eat. I wonder if she's trying to eat the world, so as to make it into Irma-land?

Mark

That's a great insight Frank! Yes, gluttony is a symbolic attempt to swallow the world, or the object, so as to make it into oneself. That's how Irma is seeking infinitude.

Tim

There's got to be a downside to all this craziness, I mean aside from the fact that Irma is overweight.

Mark

You're right. There is. For one thing, there's war, because everyone fights to make the world into him. Frank wants the world to be Frankland and Samantha wants it to be Samanthaland. And Tim wants to make it into Timland.

Tim

Ah, so each of us wants nothing less than the all, everything, to be infinite.

Mark

Yes, exactly, Tim. Furthermore, in the case of money, it is only an image of the infinite. After all, even if you possessed infinite wealth, you still wouldn't be infinite in other respects.

Tim

Like what other respects?

Mark

Like the fact that your life span would still be limited. And you still couldn't be two places at the same time. And you still wouldn't be able to flap your arms and fly through the air. And money can't buy love, as the song says? And your knowledge would still be limited. Many a billionaire is still perplexed about life, which isn't surprising since they've spent their days on the surface, never entering life's depths...

Tim

I hate to bring in Slobberchops again... he's finite, he's limited, but he isn't aware that he is. Is that why he romps around freely, without a care in the world?

Mark

Awareness would seem to make all the difference. Wouldn't it?

Tim

Is our problem, then, that we're aware we're finite? Or is self-awareness the source of our predicament, since if we didn't know we are finite, it wouldn't be a problem? Maybe Fyodor was right.

Mark

Maybe so, Tim. But how would we overcome self-awareness?

Tim

Through drink and drugs.

Mark

Yeah, that's what drinking and drugs are all about. It abolishes self-awareness, and with it our anxious sense of concern. For a time, we feel free of our responsibilities and all else that burdens us and limits our freedom.

Dorothy

You mentioned a friend of yours, from college. On weekends, he'd go on a drinking binge. You said that he was trying to balance his serious, ordered life as an insurance broker with Dionysian self-abandon. Well, when I was in my twenties, I spent about five years drinking a good deal more than I should have. Anyway, why then do some people gamble whereas others drink?

Mark

Good question. I don't really know why, Dorothy, but the two activities are very different. Gambling involves an assertion of ego, followed by expiation.

Dorothy

What do you mean assertion of ego, in regard to gambling?

Mark

A gambler believes that Lady Luck is shining on him. Winning the money is a way of proving that that is so. So, in gambling, the limits that a person experiences in life are overcome by overcoming other people, who are also claiming to be the one.

Frank

The one what?

Mark

The one who is king, the ultimate, unconditioned, God, that sort of thing. But only one person, at the gambling table, can attain that rank--after all, there can only be one king--and Lady Luck decides who it will be. Does this make sense to everyone?

Dorothy

It does, but something different is involved with drinking.

Mark

Yeah, gambling is about deciding who will be the one, the supreme ego, but drinking is about obliterating ego-awareness altogether. In gambling, the effort is to overcome limits by making the ego infinite, or absolute, but in drinking the effort is to overcome limits by making the ego not there at all. After all, if I'm not there for myself, if I'm unaware of myself, then I don't feel limited. Here, again, Tim's dog does not experience the limits we experience because he's not there in the first place.

Dorothy

Then the two vices are really opposite.

Mark

Yes, they point to the two fundamental ways to overcome limits... Frank, let me try to answer your earlier question about why a gambler would subconsciously wish to lose money.

Frank

Yeah, I've been waiting for that.

Mark

You've heard the expression "making a killing."

Frank

I've heard it at the casinos, but much more from my Wall Street cronies.

Mark

Well, the expression is pregnant with meaning. Let me then ask you: when you win, where does the money come from?

Frank

Either from other gamblers, the casino, the racetrack, or whatever. And when on those occasions when I make money in the stock market it's from the other speculators. Someone has to pay. It's certainly a not win/win situation. No, it's more like a live and let die situation.

Mark

That's what I'm saying.

Frank

But look, most of the people I'm playing against have enough money. If they lose, baby is still going to get a new pair of shoes and they'll still be able to make the monthly payments on their Mercedes.

Mark

Well, to wash away the fault involved with killing, the gambler then must take a bath. It's a kind of ritual purification, as in "Man, did I take a bath with that stock."

Frank

OK, then you're suggesting that losing money in the stock market or in the gambling casinos has to do with some sort of crazy, unconscious...

Mark

Expiation for guilt. Psychologically speaking, we have a sense that we should get what we pay for or else it's theft and murder.

Frank

Murder? Theft? Is that what I'm subconsciously doing? For a moment you had me worried that it might be something serious. I got to think about this more...

Samantha

Can we talk about another vice? I smoke four or five cigarettes a day. I'd like to quit. You said that a cigarette symbolizes the world and that smoking is an effort to destroy the world by sucking it in.

Mark

At least that's Sartre's analysis of it. If the world has, symbolically speaking, been sucked into the lungs of the subject, then the subject no longer feels limited by an opposing object. Actually, it's similar, in a certain respect, to eating crunchy foods, like potato chips or nuts. In that case, the chips represent the world, in all of its limits, which we then symbolically destroy by crunching away at it.

Tim

You said that we are likely to turn to crunchy foods when we feel frustrated. I think that that explains my addiction to corn chips, because I've been feeling very frustrated recently, particularly with some of my employees.

Mark

Do you feel free of the world's limits after crunching away at the corn chips?

Tim

Yes, I do, for about a minute.

Mark

That's longer than it is for most people!

Samantha

I understand Sartre's analysis. It makes sense. And yet, I still have a craving to smoke.

Mark

Have you ever given up for a few days?

Samantha

Yes, I have. I've even given it up for a week or two, but still returned to it.

Tim

The nicotine is said to stay in a person's body for only three days. Therefore, after quitting for more than three days, you couldn't have still been physically addicted.

Mark

Exactly Tim. The fact that Samantha still had a craving, after a week, must be because she was psychologically addicted. What's the psychological craving feel like?

Samantha

It's just a feeling of emptiness. It's not a terribly painful feeling. It's just that it's there all the time. And smoking seems the way to relieve it.

Tim

I smoked a pack a day, when I was in the Navy, and I can confirm what Samantha says. Even a few years after giving it up, I would have this restless hunger, this anxious sense. Yeah, it wasn't a physical pain, but a kind of… spiritual craving.

Mark

That makes sense and it leads to a larger question about addictions. You see, all addictions are answers to a question that life asks us.

Dorothy

So, it's really an answer to a question that we're addicted to?

Mark

Yes, Dorothy, and what makes certain answers--such as drinking, gambling, smoking, consuming a gallon of ice-cream, watching TV, playing video games, viewing pornography, or checking one's e-mail--addictive is that we have not come up with a better answer to the question. Consequently, when we experience that hunger for an answer, we return to the same answer that we already know doesn't work. That's what addiction is all about.

Dorothy

OK, what is this question that life asks us?

Mark

There are many ways to state the question. But, more or less, life asks you: how can you be real?

Dorothy

But I am real. I mean I physically exist.

Mark

But then life says to you: "It's not enough, dear Dorothy, for you to physically exist to be real." And then you say to life: "Oh yeah, is there another criterion to which I subscribe?" And then life answers back: "Apparently there is, Dorothy. Were you to examine all of your interests and desires, you take what's real to be what's infinite, unconditioned, absolute, eternal, unlimited--that sort of thing." And then you say: "Oy, no wonder I'm feeling unreal." And then life says: "So, it looks like you haven't successfully answered the question of how to be real."

Dorothy

Wow, I don't remember having this dialogue with life!

Mark

It all takes place unconsciously. I'm merely dramatizing it.

Dorothy

Well, when did it take place?

Mark

It takes place at every moment.

Frank

And so gambling is my answer to the question of how to be free of limits? Is that how I'm seeking to be real?

Mark

Yes, it is. And then you ask life: "Did I pass the exam?" And life responds: "No Frank, you failed. Gambling won't free you from life's limits. So go to jail. Do not pass go. Do not collect $200. You're still unreal."

Frank

Well, how can I tell if my answer to life's questions are right or wrong?

Mark

If it's the wrong answer, life let's you know right away. You suffer. Yes, suffering is the penalty for a wrong answer.

Dorothy

I'm thinking about what happened to me when I gave up drinking. It was like I had broken up with somebody I loved. So, I went a real long time feeling that hunger, that emptiness that you described when you were talking to Samantha about giving up smoking. I wonder, then, if the emptiness is the same, no matter what the habit is.

Mark

I would think it is. It's the same emptiness, or hunger, that's not only there for people who give up addiction, but for everyone. Anyway, did the emptiness finally leave you?

Dorothy

Yeah, it did when I got married.

Mark

Well, that's because it became another answer to the question about how to be in the world--in other words, how not to experience limits. You had another person telling you that you're the one, you're everything to him. "Everything" is another term for the infinite.

Dorothy

That answer sure had a short shelf life.

Samantha

I have a question. It seems that we stumble through life, from answer to answer. Do we ever stumble upon the right answer?

Mark

No, but what could happen is that we get clearer on the question. It's an amazing thing to discover the questions. Few people do.

Tim

Why don't they discover the questions?

Mark

That's because they're too intently absorbed in working out their answers.

Tim

Is that the value of suffering? I mean, I wouldn't have examined anything if my answers hadn't failed.

Mark

Exactly, Tim. The value of suffering is that it causes us to examine our answers, thus leading us back to the hidden questions. Yes, that's what we're doing here. There is, though, one last thing to consider. If you give up an answer, the question might appear, but so will the hunger for a new answer. If you give up smoking, drinking, gambling, watching TV, eating gallon tubs of ice cream or any other addiction, that hunger for an answer will be there with a vengeance.

Tim

It sounds like the conservation of suffering. Only in this case, it's an answer that has to fill the void.

Mark

Nice analogy. Just be very careful that the new answer doesn't let you forget the question. Anything else, before we take a break?

Frank

Just a correction. I said that gambling is the only activity that gets my adrenalin pumping. Well, that's not really true. These meetings also do! I never know what I'm going to discover and that's the scary part. I mean, I could choose door number three and out pops the non-Frank... Do you know what the funny part is?

Samantha

Tell us Frank.

Frank

When I'm here I'm still gambling, but there's something other than money at stake. I'm not sure what to call it.

Dorothy

Your soul? Is that what's at stake? Is that what's on the line?

Frank

Yeah, Dorothy, my soul.

Dorothy

Your mind?

Frank

Certainly, my mind.

Dorothy

Your sanity? Is that what's on the line? I know it's on the line for me, Frank.

Frank

Yeah, whatever sanity I have left is on the line.

Dorothy

How about, your psyche?! Your spirit?! Your destiny?! Your life?!

Frank

Yeah, Dorothy! All the above! All the above! Everything's on the goddamn line!

Tim

Wow, the man won't even hedge his bet! What cahones!

Frank

Anyway, playing for such high stakes gives me this gut-wrenching feeling, like I just walked out of Frankie's place, only to run smack into a tornado.

Tim

Whoa! Nauseating, dizzying, disorienting. The scariest rides at Coney Island raised to the 100th power!

Frank

That's what it's like, Tim. The truth of the matter is that I actually crave the thrill that I get from being here. Yeah, I wouldn't miss this discussion group for anything. I'm eternally grateful Doc.

Mark

Don't mention it.

Tim

Hey Frank, you wouldn't even miss this group for the Kentucky Derby?

Frank

Not even for...

Tim

Not even for the Super Bowl? Not even if...

Act III: I Woke Up to Find My Tattoos Had Gone

[Ricky has returned to the meeting, with Haley, a woman his age.]

Mark [To Ricky]

So you've returned. And I see that we have a visitor.

Ricky

We've been studying together for our midterms, which are tomorrow. Sorry about missing the last hour, Doc.

Mark

No problem.

Ricky

Do you remember when I asked if I could bring Haley to one of our sessions? Well, here she is.

Haley

Hi y'all!

Ricky

Haley talks that way because she's from down south. She's studying to be a biochemist.

Samantha

I like your tattoos.

Haley

Thank you. Funny you should mention them.

Ricky

Haley is saying that your essay on tattoos is what got her interested in attending tonight's discussion.

Mark

Ricky, it's a good thing that you're here to translate. Otherwise we'd be completely lost.

[To Haley]

Anyway, Haley, did the essay make sense?

Haley

It was as clear as the waters that flow along Kentucky's Green River, near the Cumberland Falls.

Frank

More like the East River, when it flows past Canarsie's sewage treatment facility.

Haley

But your essay left me with more questions than I began with. They've multiplied like rabbits!

Mark

Questions are funny that way.

Dorothy

Speaking of questions, I have one myself, about something you wrote

[Reading from essay]

"The ease with which we can divest ourselves of our sense of our identity and put on a new identity, through a simple change of clothing, has its appeal. It is the appeal of freedom from the limits of a fixed identity." You're saying, then, that the reason that I like to change my outfits...

Samantha

And your hair styles too, Dorothy...

Dorothy

...is so that I can, symbolically speaking, put on and take off all sorts of identities, but in doing so I'm never limited by any one of them.

Mark

It would seem to be so. Isn't that the appeal? It's a feminine image of infinite, unlimited being.

Dorothy

OK, but here's where you say that there's a problem. [Reading]: *"Like water, an identity predicated on appearances never becomes anything solid. The contemporary interest in becoming tattooed is indicative of a craving for a permanent and abiding identity."* First you say that we don't want to be limited by any sort of permanent identity, because if I'm this I can't be that.

Mark

Yes, because then you'd lose the infinitude of possibility. And who'd want to lose that?

Samantha

Heck, I wouldn't!

Dorothy

But then you say that we wish to have a permanent and abiding identity. And, if I understand you correctly, a meaning or a purpose would be an example of an identity.

Mark

I guess that's right.

Dorothy

Well how can we wish to be free of the limits of identity and simultaneously seek to have an enduring identity? It's another one of your goddamn contradictions!

Mark

I didn't invent these contradictions. I'm just pointing them out. Anyway, I think that you're now getting the point of the weekly discussions we've been having. We want opposite things. On the one hand, we need identity, form, limit, direction, focus.

Samantha

Why do we need that?

Mark

Because, without a form, shape, identity, limit, we're nothing at all.

Samantha

Yeah, tell me about it. That was my life for a long time. It was a chaotic and disunified mess. And, if I don't watch myself and maintain focus, I veer towards shapeless chaos. My husband says that I have a tendency to be all over the place, with my ideas, interests and activities. He's always telling me that I need to prioritize.

Mark

Yes, Samantha, focus is also in the identity family. So is having a direction. Anyway, we seek give our life shape, focus, direction and identity. But we also seek to be free of identity, form and limit.

Samantha

Why do we seek to be free of identity, form, focus and limit? I mean, I like the idea of having a meaning or purpose.

Mark

That's a good question. Let me ask you. Do you like the idea of being limited?

Samantha

Well, certainly not!

Mark

Why not?

Samantha

Well, isn't it obvious? D'oh! It's because... It's because... I don't really know why I don't want limits. I just don't want them! I need to think about it.

Mark

Sometimes, what seems most obvious, shining forth in broad daylight, is also the most mysterious.

Tim

So, if I'm following this conversation, we seek an identity, but we don't wish to be limited by that identity.

Mark

That's right, Tim. It would be a contradiction.

Frank

OK, that explains it. That explains it!

Tim

Explains what, Frank?

Frank

It explains why we're nuts.

Mark

Exactly Frank. The fact that we seek opposite things--and at the same time--explains why human beings are fundamentally insane.

Dorothy

Wow! In that case, my inability to achieve happiness is not just a personal failing.

Mark

That's right. It's nothing that you've done wrong, other than being born a human being. Are you relieved?

Dorothy

Hmm, yes and no. On the one hand, there's no reason to have an inferiority complex. I don't need to feel that I've missed the boat to the land of connubial bliss. Yeah, I don't need to envy my friend Myra or anyone else.

Tim

And I don't need to feel like the boxer in the Brando film, the one who's got a one-way ticket to Louisville... Ah, I mean Palookaville.

Mark

Yeah, in truth all trains go to Palookaville, because the object of desire is a contradiction of terms. Anyway, if being liberated from a sense of personal failure is the good news, then what's the bad?

Dorothy

The bad news? If what we're really seeking in life were contradictory, then it would seem that we all have a rendezvous with despair.

Mark

There's a route beyond existentialist despair, beyond life's contradictions, beyond the conservation of suffering.

Samantha

We should really call you Dr. Beyond.

Tim

> We have faith that you, our Sherpa, is familiar with that route beyond despair.

Mark

> The route consists in attaining absolute clarity about everything we do. All of the dark corners of our life must be illuminated.

Frank

> All the dark corners? First you take the joy out of gambling, by telling me that I have a secret wish to lose.

Mark

> I didn't ruin gambling. I merely sought to illuminate it.

Frank

> I'll bet you did. What's next? My golf game? Are you going to illuminate that too? Is nothing sacred? Will somebody stop this madman before he analyzes everything to death!

Mark

> Well Frank, I can understand your feelings and I sympathize, for I too...

Frank

> There's only one reason why I'm still here, after three years, and I suspect you know what it is.

Mark

> I think I know the reason. You can't help opening the door that says, "Warning! Do not open!"

Frank

> That's exactly it! Each time a voice screams at me, "Sei Pazzo? Are you off your rocker? For the love of God, Frank, don't open the door!" But this insatiable curiosity, of mine, always gets the

better of me and compels me not just to open the door, but to walk into the room.

Mark

Well Frank, I always knew you had the markings of true philosopher.

Frank

You mean that I've always had the markings of a lunatic. Well, I'm done, for now. I accept my fate. It looks like Haley has a question.

Haley

Thanks Frank. Dr. Dillof, you wrote something about how in our modern world we had become abstract. I didn't really have a question about it. It's just that I'm scared that I've become more and more that way since moving up to New York and going to college here. I was hoping that you might discuss it.

Dorothy

Mark, if it's all right with you, I'd like to read aloud the section that I think Haley's referring to.

Mark

Sure, go ahead.

Dorothy

[Reading]

"Previous generations of Americans had a strong identification with being American. Similarly, they identified with the region of the country in which they lived. They identified with their family, with their profession, with their interests, and all else."

Mark

Make sense?

Haley

I notice the difference when I visit my folks down in Charleston South Carolina.

Mark

Please read on, Dorothy. I think you're getting to the part about abstractness.

Dorothy

"But ours is an abstract age, in which the very notion of having a strong sense of identity is judged to be naïve. Or else, it is viewed as dangerous, for it is believed that such identifications are divisive and lead to conflicts and to wars."

Haley

That's it. Most of my graduate school friends, at Binghamton University, are really interesting. They're so cosmopolitan. They can talk about everything. They've been there and done that. It's just that... Well, I was reading about Abraham Lincoln.

Samantha

Oh, are your people still angry with him?

Haley

Angry with Abraham Lincoln? Ha! Ha! Ho! Ho! Certainly not!

Ricky

Haley's is trying to say that where she's from they've taken down the rebel flag and put up the Stars and Stripes.

Mark

Thanks for the clarification Ricky. What would I do without you?

Haley

Well, anyway, I was reading that someone, in Congress, had once asked Abraham Lincoln how long a man's legs should be. And

Old Abe replied, "Long enough so that they touch the ground."

Samantha

What an interesting comment! Could Lincoln have been a Zen master?

Haley

I guess what I'm trying to say is that some of my graduate school friends have legs that don't seem to quite touch the ground. Now, don't get me wrong, I'm really fond of the friends I've made here. But they sometimes seem so darn abstract.

Ricky

Hmm, I wonder if my legs touch the ground.

Frank

No, but your hands do. But that's OK because you're an entertainer.

Haley

Well anyway, one day--when I was feeling really worried that I was becoming like them, like I was becoming totally ungrounded, like I was losing my identity, like I was having a panic attack--I decided to get some tattoos.

Samantha

They look like buildings, like some sort of city. Let me guess. Are those tattoos on your arms scenes from Charleston South Carolina?

Haley

You just scored a bull's-eye, honey! When I'm feeling like I'm losing my identity, I take a look at my tattoos and I think, "OK, I guess I'm from Charleston. That's my identity." And then the world stops spinning out of control.

Mark

All that makes wonderful sense.

Dorothy

Can we read on a bit more?

Mark

Go ahead.

Dorothy

"Without a sense of identity, people feel lost, disconnected from life, like Camus' stranger. It would appear, then, that the present faddish interest in tattoos is indicative of a craving for identity. But, from a psychological perspective, there seems to be something desperate about needing a tattoo to have an identity."

Mark

What do you have to say about that, Haley?

Haley

That's what worries me. I think I've become a desperate woman.

Frank

Is there any other kind?

Dorothy

OK, I'll read on. *"Why does the Bible prohibit tattoos? It's because if one's identity is to be legitimate, it must come from God. Rather than being on the mere surface, one's true identity must reach the depths of one's soul. It is expressed in all that ones does, in one's entire way of life, from morning till night. An identity bereft of inwardness, i.e., a identity that is merely on the surface i.e., on one skin, is mere idol worship. Hence, the biblical prohibition. Although relatively permanent, it is as superficial as declaring one's identity by wearing a tee-shirt that has on it the insignia of a company, a clothing designer, a certain city, etc."*

Tim

Are you recommending that we seek to return to an earlier sense of personal identity?

Mark

No, not at all. I don't really think that we be able to return to what we've lost, even if we wanted to. The gates of Eden are closed... Let us take a short break. By the way, I smell something burning. What's all this smoke? Samantha, what temperature did you put the over on, for that pie?

Samantha

Ah! I can't believe I forgot all about the pie.

Act IV: Two Detectives Inquire into a Metaphysical Conspiracy

Mark

It looks like Rickey and Haley are gone again.

Dorothy

They said that they had to study for their exams.

[A knock is heard. Mark walks to the door.]

Samantha

Maybe they decided to return.

[Mark opens the door. Standing there are Detectives Clancy and Mueller.]

Mark

Uh oh!

Detective Clancy

Hello Professor. We've met before. We're with the New York State Police. I'm Detective Clancy and this is Detective Mueller. Can we come in?

Mark

Sure, but what impeccable timing. You always arrive when I'm conducting my philosophical counseling group.

Clancy

We wont be too long. Do you mind if we look around?

Mark

Go ahead, but I'd like to accompany you.

[The detectives and Mark leave to enter the kitchen.]

Dorothy

I wonder what they're looking for.

Samantha

Probably broomsticks. Didn't I tell you that they thought we practiced witchcraft?

[The detective's and Mark return to the living room.]

Detective Clancy

Sorry folks. Several of your neighbors reported that you were a witch's coven and that you were burning someone as part of a ritual sacrifice. But it would appear that what was sacrificed was an apple strudel pie. That's too bad, since I really like apple strudel, especially with cinnamon! Anyway, we're very sorry folks. Your neighbors are, shall we say, cranks? We won't bother you ever again.

Mark

No problem. Next time we heat up a pie, we'll keep the oven somewhere between low and medium.

Detective Clancy [to Frank]

By the way, you look familiar.

Frank

I didn't do it officer. I swear! I was framed!

Detective Clancy

Hmm, I still think that I know you from somewhere.

Frank

Would you like a clue?

Detective Clancy

Sure, detectives love clues.

Frank

[standing and singing]

"Oh Danny boy, the pipes, the pipes are calling
From glen to glen, and down the mountain side
The summer's gone, and all the flowers are dying
Tis you, 'tis you must go and I must bide."

Detective Clancy

Wait a second... You sang at our charity fundraiser picnic last year. What a melodious set of pipes you have! Hey, you're... Frank...

Frank

Guilty as charged.

Detective Mueller

Just one question before we leave. I hope that you don't mind me asking you, but is this a cult? It's OK if it is. There's no law against it. I'm just curious.

Mark

Do I look like a cult leader?

Detective Mueller

No, not really. I figured a cult leader to look more... charismatic.

Samantha [to Mark]

I told you that you should try to look more charismatic. You need to dress trendier. You're too traditional, too button-down, too Brooks Brothers.

Mark

I'm not wearing a pointed hat with stars and moons!

Detective Mueller

Well, let me ask you, what do you folks talk about anyway?

Mark

Real philosophy, and I don't mean the academic stuff they teach in college. You'll find the real thing here, detective. I mean thinking that transforms our being.

Detective Mueller

I gather, that you charge money. Right?

Mark

I do. Can't you just tell by my luxurious apartment in Binghamton that I'm rolling in the dough?

Detective Mueller

Well, Socrates never charged money. That makes you a sophist, doesn't it?

Mark

Look, Socrates had a wife who worked and she wasn't too happy about the arrangement. She became a real shrew. Did you know that she once dumped the contents of a chamber pot on top of him? And can you blame her?

Samantha

I can't blame her. Can you blame her detective?

Detective Mueller

Hmm, I'll need to give the question some thought. Well, what type of philosophy do you do here anyway?

Tim

Actually, we try to solve mysteries. Doc here is the chief detective.

Detective Mueller

What sort of mysteries?

Tim

The great enigmas of human existence--that sort of thing.

Detective Mueller

Look, Dr. Dillof, I'm sorry if I was a bit gruff with you.

Detective Clancy

My colleague here flunked out of police charm school three times in a row, so they made him a detective. You can't blame him, though, since he has almost as many holes in him, as I do, which can often cause a sour disposition.

Mark

Do you mean holes, as in philosophical arguments or do you mean the holes that are at the very core of our being, the inner nothingness, which Jean-Paul Sartre...

Detective Clancy

No, I mean bullet holes. We're both lucky to be alive. And I'll be even luckier if I make it to retirement in two years.

Mark

Well, I wish you both all Godspeed on the road that still lies ahead.

Detective Mueller

Look, Dr. Dillof, the truth of the matter is that mysteries are my passion, which is why I became a detective.

Samantha

You must have read mystery stories, as a kid.

Detective Mueller

Ah, but being a detective is a far cry from Sherlock Holmes. It's mostly dealing with lowlife criminals. There's no mystery there. But philosophical mysteries, I like that!

Mark

OK, now that you haven't found any evidence of witchcraft, why not sit down for a spell...

Detective Clancy

A spell? What type of spell?

Mark

Poor choice of words, on my part. What I meant to say was that we'd be honored to have you philosophize with us.

Detective Clancy

Hmm, my feet do hurt and that couch looks rather comfortable. OK, but we'll need to leave in fifteen minutes.

[They both take a seat.]

Mark [to Detective Mueller]

You look like you have a question.

Detective Mueller

Actually, I do. Look, I took a philosophy course in college, and there was something that always puzzled me: Why did they kill Socrates?

Mark

They didn't just kill him. A jury condemned him to death for corrupting the youth of Athens, with his philosophical ideas. Yeah, he was accused of making young people think.

Samantha

What's wrong with getting young people to think?

Mark

I suppose that thinking causes people to fall into doubt. And when they fall into doubt, they might become iconoclasts, questioning the established institutions of their society and the powers that be.

Detective Clancy

Interesting. Sometimes, when we're after someone with power and money––and that could be anyone from a politician to a businessman to a Mafioso––we find that someone starts discouraging us from continuing with our investigation. Yeah, some higher up in the department starts telling us that asking too many questions could be deleterious to our career advancement, like the time we went after the governor for seeing prostitutes. Man, did we feel the heat.

Mark

Well, detective, asking questions has always been a risky business, both today and in times past. Personally, I think that Socrates was on to something. And that may have been why they condemned him to death.

Detective Mueller

Do you mean a conspiracy!

Mark

Exactly. I mean a metaphysical conspiracy.

Detective Mueller

Oh, like in the film "The Matrix!"

Mark

Sort of like that. And way before that there was Plato's *Allegory of the Cave*.

Samantha

What the heck is a metaphysical conspiracy?

Mark

It's the conspiracy to keep us from finding out what life is all about. I think that there exists a force in the universe intent on keeping us ignorant.

Samantha

Why would the universe want to keep us from knowing its secrets? I don't get it.

Mark

Well, it's kind of complicated. Sharon once told me that... Well, what I'm trying to say is that it's because the world, in all of its familiarity, is predicated on an illusion. When we discern the truth, the world collapses... Detective Clancy, did you ever have your world collapse?

Detective Clancy

Ha! Ha! I should hope not!

Mark

Are you sure? Of course, if you'd rather not talk about it, that's perfectly...

Detective Clancy

Uh, I'm not sure what you're getting at professor, but maybe my world did collapse about twenty years ago. I found out that my wife was cheating on me, with my partner, another detective. Yeah, for four years I was living the illusion that my wife was loyal and that my partner was my best friend. When I found out, it really did seem that my world collapsed. It had no more substance than one of those soap bubbles and then it burst.

Samantha

Gee, that's really too bad. You didn't deserve that.

Detective Clancy

I appreciate that. Well, I got remarried to a really wonderful woman and so it was a blessing in disguise.

Mark

Thanks for sharing that with us, detective. The illusions that we're talking about go much deeper than personal illusions. What if the very notion of a separate ego was an illusion? What if the very distinction of self and world was an illusion? What if our notions of happiness, success and fulfillment are illusions? What if time and space are illusions?

Samantha

Well, what if?

Mark

If everyone realized that it's all an illusion, the world, as we know it, would collapse, just like the detective's world collapsed when he discovered his ex-wife's infidelity, only to far greater extent. There would appear, then, to be some force in the universe intent on maintaining the illusion that we call our world.

Samantha

How does this force, as you call it, maintain the illusion?

Mark

Good question, Samantha. It maintains the illusion by keeping us in the dark. The world we experience is predicated on our ignorance. So this dark force does all it can to keep us dreaming and deluded, and distracted too. Yeah, it's hell-bent on keeping us ignorant.

Tim

So maybe Socrates became the man who knew too much.

Dorothy

And those on the jury, who voted to have him executed, were servants of the dark force that keeps us ignorant!

Detective Mueller

I'm really fascinated by what you're saying, Dr. Dillof, but in all due respect, it doesn't sound very scientific. I mean, I took a physics course in college and I never heard of a force like the one you're describing.

Mark

No, you won't find any of this in a science textbook, for it's from a different realm, but one that exists all the same. I really don't know what to call this force, but for want of a better term, I call it "Mr. Big." Yeah, Mr. Big is the grand deceiver that maintains the cosmic illusion.

Tim

Mr. Big? Isn't Mr. Big the supervillain in all the gangster movies, the one who's really behind it all? And isn't he Professor Moriarty, Sherlock Holmes' archenemy? And isn't he also that villain Blofeld, James Bond's arch enemy?

Frank

And don't forget Mrs. Big. I mean my mother-in-law.

Mark

Well, Tim, those are just Hollywood images of Mr. Big. In any case, Tim, most people spend their lives battling Mr. Big's henchmen, but never encounter Mr. Big.

Detective Mueller

Henchmen? The guy's got henchmen? Who are his henchmen?

Mark

Mr. Big's henchmen would be all the many problems that we face in life. We can exhaust ourselves trying to solve life's problems, never getting to the real roots of those problems. Let's say, for example, that you are encountering difficulties in a relationship. Now, your first instinct would be either to blame your partner or yourself or both.

Dorothy

Well, it has to be someone's fault? No?

Mark

If you stay on that level, you are only dealing with Mr. Big's henchmen. But, you might be tempted to ask a deeper question. You might inquire into how you relate to the opposite sex, no matter who your partner is. You might then inquire into the nature of romantic love in general.

Tim

Wow, Doc, that would seem to be a more ultimate question.

Mark

Yes, it is Tim. Then, even apart from relationships, you might inquire into what it was that you were ultimately seeking in life. Yes, each level of inquiry is more ultimate than the last, and more dangerous, because you're really challenging certain fundamental assumptions, one's that are the basis of your world. You would realize, in other words, that life's problems run much more deeply than you had initially expected.

Tim

I gather that these higher-level problems are no longer Mr. Big's henchmen.

Mark

That's right Tim. They're his various lieutenants.

Detective Mueller

We're talking organized crime here!

Detective Clancy

Maybe we should call for backup. Yeah, why don't you call the chief and tell him that we're after Mr. Big. And let me know what he says.

Mark

Finally, if you look deeply enough into the mystery of human dissatisfaction, you reach the level of the ultimate contradictions that constitute the warp and woof of our existence. Kant calls them the antinomies. Then you realize that selfhood is predicated on contradictory requirements.

Detective Mueller

Selfhood is contradictory? I'm not exactly sure what you mean by that, but I'm beginning to suspect that there's serious trouble in Riverside City.

Mark

Well, detective, please remember that I'm using Mr. Big as a metaphor to describe a certain force that maintains the illusion that we call our world.

Detective Mueller

Got you. It's just a metaphor.

Mark

Anyway, if you manage to survive each question, you enter into the most dangerous region, a place where no ordinary mortal dares set foot. You enter the inner sanctum of Mr. Big, or to use a more classical analogy, into the center of the maze, where you encounter the Minotaur.

Dorothy

So Mr. Big is the Minotaur?

Mark

Again, we're using metaphors, symbols or myths here, but yes. Anyway, if you survive this encounter, you will finally have solved the mystery of human suffering and will know what life's all about.

Detective Clancy

[Standing up]

Well, thanks for the free session. We really appreciate it. Next time we'll bring over some apple strudel.

[Both detectives walk to the door.]

Detective Mueller

I may be back, but next time as a civilian; I mean as a student, a client, a disciple, whatever. I really need to find out more about this Mr. Big.

Mark

Stay on his tail, detective.

[Both detectives leave.]

Tim

Doc, what's it with your neighbors? I mean calling the police. That's really insane.

Mark

Well the neighbors suspect that there's something funny's going on here and they're right. They intuitively know that it's dangerous to ask deep questions.

Tim

Why's that Doc?

Mark

It might evoke the uncanny. If that happens, everything that had been familiar begins to look strange and unfamiliar.

Tim

That sounds pretty scary.

Mark

It is. Freud said that the uncanny is the sense of not being at home, even though one is at home. He said that nothing is more terrifying.

Dorothy

Ah, to be Myra!

Tim

Ah to be Slobbberchops!

Mark

Oh, I almost forgot. I have a homework assignment for everybody. Try to find something that embodies your mode of being.

Samantha

I know you've used that term before, but what do you mean by a "mode of being?"

Mark

Well, we've explored the various requirements for what it means for us to be. Naturally, to be is to exist. But we also need to have a shape or form, an identity. And it seems that we long for the infinite, the absolute, the unconditioned.

Samantha

OK, I've with you so far. But what's the thing with the mode?

Mark

The mode of being would be the particular way in which you try to satisfy those being requirements, in your own life. For example, for one person an activity like smoking is a way to be and for someone else it would be running for office. So try to find something in your life, something that you like or do, that seems to capture your particular mode of being.

Chapter V
Second Philosophical Intermission

Let's take a look at the second dialogue, the one from the previous chapter, called "Unsettling Perplexities." Let's see if we can further explore some of the questions and major contradictions that we daily encounter as human beings.

Act I: *A Contradiction that Tastes Like Amaretto*

The first act begins where Ricky has left off, in a previous dialogue, with his quest for authenticity. Ricky and his band would like to play their own creations, but the club owners would like them to play the type of music that their patrons would enjoy. At the root of Ricky's conflict lies a contradiction between one's ideals and the real world. If we wish to eat, we must compromise our ideals, but if we so, we then feel like we have lost our very soul. As we go through life, we find balances of sort, various compromises, but such balances are usually tenuous.

Tim observes that his dog, Slobbberchops, is not divided that way, but human beings are. The question then arises as to what the real world lacks, such that we seek an ideal realm? The real world lacks unity and clarity. It's the longing for intelligibility--the need to give a recognizable shape to the chaos that we encounter--that makes philosophers posit an intelligible realm. As to whether there exists such a realm, like Plato contends, is another matter.

We then explored the sort of unity we might wish to establish. What place would there be for the individuals comprising this new world? A totalitarian state brings everyone into a unity, but individualism is crushed. Tim then suggests that the unity that he would like would be like that of a baseball game or an orchestra. In those cases, each person's unique position is important to the team or to the musical score.

The musical score, as Dorothy points out, is akin to the meaning. This leads her to pose an ultimate questions: "What is the meaning of life?" No matter what people take to be the ultimate meaning, it negates our individualism. Certainly, Samantha doesn't cherish this negation, which is why she finds it objectionable that the person who plays the tympani doesn't get to express himself very much. She calls to mind the narrator of Dostoevsky's "Notes from Underground," who contends that human beings are creatures of contradiction. They crave an ultimate meaning, but if they find a meaning, they will view it to be a straightjacket and will rebel against it.

A relevant example of that contradiction involves making a schedule for oneself. In the evening, we might think that our life is badly in need of order and organization. So, we make a schedule of things that we must do. We'll get up early in the morning and do exercises, followed by various chores, and so on. But when we awaken the next morning and look at the schedule, we might immediately toss the paper on which the schedule is written in our wastebasket. (The same is true, if we wish to go on a diet.) That is because we are in a different state of awareness in the morning then in the evening. In the evening, we wished for order and in the morning we find any sort of discipline to be limiting to our freedom. So it is, as Dostoevsky argues, that we are creatures of contradiction.

Then we returned to Ricky's question. He's concerned about the contradiction between his ideals and the need to make a living, which means compromising those ideals. I recommend that he seek to acquire some emotional distance from that contradiction. A contradiction viewed at a distance leads to laughter. Gaining the right amount of emotional distance might require that a certain amount of time transpire before we can experience an earlier setback objectively, and even laugh about it. Were we, indeed, to examine any joke or anything else that was humorous--including those things, in our life, that we've come to view as humorous--we would discern a contradiction. Discerning this contradiction makes our life, with all of our sorrows, taste bittersweet, like the taste of amaretto.

Of course, it is not easy taking life less seriously than we do. It takes a lot of practice. In one of my essays, I recommended a kind of crutch, bringing along a tape of a laugh track. It could be recorded to an I-Pod. Then, each time we experienced something unpleasant--like a rude waiter--we could play the laughter sound track to ourselves, as if we were in a situation comedy, which we are.

Before leaving our analysis of Act I, I'd like to mention that, in a subsequent group meeting, which isn't recorded here, we analyzed Ricky's rather unusual musical composition. Why was this rock musician suddenly interested in quadrille's and other musical styles from previous ages? It emerged that Ricky was searching for something that he felt must lie in the past, but what was it?

In what might confirm C.G. Jung's notion of synchronicity, Ricky brought with him, one day, an item that offered us a clue, a bottle of Coca-Cola. He said that that he had just switched from Pepsi. What, on the surface, might seem like lighthearted banter had a deeper meaning! Let us explore what it is. The life we live, as human beings, is finite and transient. Unwilling to tolerate this condition, we assume that if true reality--which has the marks of infinitude and eternality--is not to be found in the present, then it must be found either in the past or in the future.

Coke claims that reality is to be found in the past. It is the "real thing" because the formula for Coke is a timeless, mysterious secret, like a law of nature. Its newer slogan is "Always Coca Cola!" The word, "always" is a synonym for the everlasting. Coke is appealing to the mystique of origins, to the myth of the golden age. This is the mythical timeless period before time began. Plato's eternal Ideas likewise reside there. Naturally, the ads stress tradition, calling their product "Coke Classic." Similar are the ads for Dewar's Whisky, which also capitalize on our longing for traditional values, for heritage, such as camaraderie between father and son. For a while, their slogan was, "The good things in life stay that way." The interest that many people have in antiques similarly derives from the belief that true reality, eternity, is to be found in the past.

Pepsi, on the other hand, claims the value, not of the past, but of the future, with its mystique of progress, science, and technology. The metaphysics of progress began to be popular in the middle of the 19th century. Philosophers like Hegel believed that reality is not to be found at the beginning, but only at the end of time and history. Pepsi's ads, with their emphasis on youth, "choice of a new generation," "for those who think young," and "Generation Next," reflect this ontology.

Ricky's change of beverages, from Pepsi to Coke, and his interest in antiquated musical styles, like the quadrille, would indicate that what was at issue for him was nothing less than a shift in ontologies, from Hegelian to the Platonic. Of course, it wasn't as simple as that, for Ricky wasn't just interested in old musical styles, but in drawing out the essence of these styles from their original contexts, and he did this by retaining certain melodies and rhythms, but changing all else.

Ricky's project is similar, in a certain sense, to those who wish to extract a certain truth from its incarnation in a certain cultural context. For example, there are those who have sought to extract the essential truth of Zen Buddhism from its connection to Japanese culture. Thus instead of wearing traditional robes, while meditating, they dress in contemporary western garb.

I wonder if I had been intuiting Ricky's shift to a Platonic ontology. Perhaps that's why, in the earlier dialogue, the one in which Ricky requests that I offer him a blessing, I evoke the spirit of an ancient philosopher, Pythagoras.

Act II: *Smoking, Drinking and Gambling to Infinity*

We next took a look at some of the popular vices--smoking, drinking, and gambling--to see if we could discern their deeper meaning. We began with gambling. Frank was annoyed by the notion that a gambler deliberately wishes to lose, for it denies the notion that we are rational beings and that we have freewill, in regard to our actions. He was also somewhat resistant to my notion that the various vices are really a longing for the infinite, and for God. Frank

Second Philosophical Intermission

would agree, though, that there is something deficient in his life--it seems blasé and unexciting--such that he needs to gamble to get his adrenalin going. Samantha agrees that having money is magical, in so far as it has the power to transform the object (the world) into the subject.

Tim then brings up his dog, Slobberchops, again. It would appear that it's our self-awareness that makes us feel limited. Since, dogs are not self-aware--at least as far as we can determine--they do not feel limited as we do. That's where drinking and drugs figures in. We use these substances in an effort to abolish self-awareness, and thus annul our sense of limits and finitude.

We then discussed smoking. Sometimes a comedian is able to bring out the oddity of an activity. Bob Newhart, the comedian, did a routine called "Origins of Tobacco," in which Sir Walter Raleigh-- the man who, among other things, exported the tobacco plant from the American colonies to England, where it has been unknown. Sir Walter tries to describe cigarette smoking to the head of the East Indian Trading Company, who never heard of such an activity. He comes to question Sir Walter's sanity, for it seems ridiculous that someone would roll some tobacco leaves together, light them on fire, and then suck in the burning fumes. When an activity--in this case, smoking-- is separated from its symbolic meaning, it causes us to wonder about that symbolic meaning. We might have an intuitive sense of it, but we cannot articulate what it is.

What, then, is the meaning of smoking? I introduced Sartre's analysis, from *Being and Nothingness*. Sartre contends that smoking involves the symbolic effort to suck in the world, which we find so limiting. Tim rightly contends that smoking has the same symbolic destructive appeal as eating crunchy foods.

Tim also points out that there is a certain restless hunger that precedes the urge to smoke. Actually that hunger--which is really a spiritual craving--is there for everyone. It's the physical concomitant of a philosophical question that life asks each of us, at every moment. The question is, "How can you be real?" Then we seek to answer that question. An addiction is an answer to that question that we continually return to, even though we know it can't work. Dorothy's addiction to drinking ended when she got married. It would seem, then, that she substituted one answer to the question of how to be for another answer.

Samantha then asks a very good question, "Do we ever stumble upon the right answer to life's ultimate questions?" In point of fact, we never do, but we do become clearer on the question that life is continually asking us. When we get very clear on what the question is, it could happen that we paradoxically answer the question. It may sound mystical, but the one who is searching is not the one who we thought was searching. It is not Frank, or Dorothy or Mark or anyone else. If we find out who it is who has been searching, all along, then the mystery is solved.

Finally, Frank points out that gambling is not the only activity that gets his adrenalin going. The pursuit of life's deepest questions is really far more thrilling, for it's a bet, a Pascalian Wager, in which one's life, soul and sanity are up for grabs.

Act III: *I Woke Up to Find My Tattoos Had Gone*

As Dorothy rightly observes, if we are creatures of contradiction, then our inability to achieve happiness is not just a personal failing. That is why the type of investigation in which we've been engaging, in this group, is not psychotherapy, but rather philosophical counseling, for the problems that we are facing are not just a matter of personal conflicts or inadequacies, but rather ultimate contradictions, which all human beings face. In any case, there is, a route beyond life's ultimate contradictions and so beyond despair. It requires that we attain complete clarity over what we are seeking to accomplish in all of our interests, desires and activities.

We then discussed Haley's tattoo, which is a cityscape of Charlestown, South Carolina. As she explains it, whenever she feels disoriented, like she doesn't know who she is--and perhaps having a panic attack in regard to that--she looks at her tattoo and that seems to grounds her. (I'm reminded of a fellow, I once knew, who had a picture of his grandfather tattooed on his arm. His grandfather embodied certain traditional values that this fellow found to be important, and which served to orient him in times of stress.) Perhaps, we live in an age of panic attacks, due to the fact that modern life doesn't allow the roots of connectedness to grow. Alas, there is no returning to simpler times.

Act IV: *Two Detectives Inquire into a Metaphysical Conspiracy*

This last act of the dialogue is about a metaphysical conspiracy. Sometimes, it seems that there is a certain force in the universe hell-bent on keeping us in the dark about life's deeper mysteries. For want of a better name, the daemon Sharon refers to that force as "Mr. Big." Here is the thing: we rarely pursue the ultimate questions. Instead, we pursue Mr. Big's soldiers, meaning that we spend our energies dealing with life's many problems, rather than investigating the ultimate source of those problems.

By nature, we are pusillanimous, turning away from the more ultimate ground of our problems, and rightfully so. For example, if we are experiencing a relationship conflict, we might hope that a minor adjustment, in how we relate to our partner, will do. Or we might think that we need to find another partner. But if the problem that we are encountering is ultimately due to the nature of relationships--if there exists a contradiction, at the very heart of the masculine/feminine enterprise--then we have a far more serious problem on our hands, than we initially realized.

Indeed, we have an intuitive sense that we should not ask too many questions or look too deeply into anything, or else we might become the man or the woman--like in the cinema noir detective stories-- who knows too much. That is why it takes a certain type of courage, a kind of daring, to look beneath the surface and to ask more ultimate questions. Perhaps, as I suggest to the two detectives, Socrates was a man who knew too much, which is why the Athenians had to kill him.

It turns out that my neighbors alerted the police about our group. They intuited, and rightly so, that there was something dangerous about the enterprise in which we were engaging, but had no other way to conceptualize it, other than to say that it was witchcraft. Indeed, asking deep questions is fraught with peril. In addition to opening up a ten thousand pound can of worms, asking deep questions can evoke the uncanny. That's the terrifying sense that everything that seemed familiar is unfamiliar. It always was unfamiliar; it's just that we had mistakenly believed that we knew what it was about.

More Questions for Readers to Explore

How did you do with the first group of questions? Answer these next ten to win a free trip, aboard Plato's chariot, around the world of eternal Forms! All entries must be postmarked before June 1, 2150.

1. Examine several jokes and see if you can find the contradiction at their core. An example would be the line from Henny Youngman, "I miss my wife's cooking… as frequently as possible." Here we have a contradiction between tender affection and the often-dyspeptic realities of marriage and life. If you need another example, take a look at the essay, included here, which explores the Dr. Epstein joke.

2. How does the contradiction between the real and the ideal play out in your own life? What sort of compromises, if any, have you had to make?

3. In the previous dialogue, there was some discussion of a certain restless emotional hunger that precedes desire. The hunger is the psychophysical concomitant of a question. The question could be formulated as, "What is lacking at this moment?" Or perhaps as, "How could I be real as a self, i.e., attain selfhood?" Then various answers to these questions appear. A habit is an answer that appears repeatedly in lieu of a satisfying answer. Can you connect to that emotional hunger, that feeling of lack? When do you experience it? What do you do to then end that hunger? For example, do you turn on the TV? Go to the refrigerator? Check your e-mail?

4. If you could take a pill that would allow you to instantly attain

Second Philosophical Intermission

the relatively unconscious state of Tim's dog, Slobberchops--and the peaceful freedom from human concerns that went with it--would you do so? Or would you feel that there is something was missing in a dog's state of consciousness? If there is something missing, what is it? (Don't rush through this profound question; a facile answer won't do. If the question starts pursuing you, then you know you're really thinking.)

5. Examine the clothing that you wear. Does it express your identity? If so, what does the type of clothes that you wear say about you? Examine also your haircut, your car, your home, and your workspace. What do these things say about you?

6. Have you ever had a habit, a vice, or simply a passion? Can you discern its symbolic meaning and see it as an inadequate answer to a deeper question?

7. In my conversation with Frank about gambling and with Samantha about shopping, I suggesting that the appeal of gambling and of bargains was the desire to get something for free. That desire is an expression the more fundamental longing to be free of conditions and limiting circumstances, to be unconditioned, infinite and absolute. Spend a week looking at ads, in magazines, as well as on the radio and TV. Observe the many ways in which advertisers appeal to our longing to be free and unlimited. An automobile, for example, is a practical invention, but they are often named after animals of speed or daring (Impala, Cougar, Mustang, Pinto, Jaguar, etc.) We also see commercial in which an automobile travels through rugged terrain, jungles and all the rest, suggesting freedom from conditions. Another industry that appeals that longing is travel and tourism. The ads promise that we can magically be transported beyond the limits that belong to our present situation in life. What other examples can you find of ads that appeal to our longing for freedom from conditions?

8. The longing to be unlimited isn't the only appeal of advertisements. For example, the car named "Acura," which sounds like accurate, evokes the mystique of science and technology, with its notion that true reality lies in the future. The old Saturn ads used to appeal to the longing to be part of something larger than oneself and of being taken care of because of it. That's why they spoke of "the Saturn family." Then there's the appeal of security, as we might find in the classic ad from Prudential Insurance Company, which features, as its logo, a gigantic rock, undisturbed by the crashing waves of the sea.

   A lot of advertising appeals to the desire not just to be free, but free as a rugged individual. The old Marlboro ads, which showed a cowboy, out on the range, were classic examples of that appeal. A lot of ads appeal to individuality, in the form of nonconformity. Jean companies, for example, make the risible claim that if you purchase a pair of certain type of Jean, for example Levi Straus' *501 Jeans*--despite the fact that millions of other people war them--you're a freewheeling individualist. Similarly, we find the appeal to individuality in the classic *Burger King* ad, "Have it your way." There used to be an ad for *Saab* that stated, "Find your own road." The ad appealed to people seeking an iconoclastic, not conformist style of individuality.

   Spend another week or two gathering examples of advertisements that offer a variety of ontological appeals. Also, consider how the various appeals--for a new tomorrow brought about by science and technology, as well as the desire for security, for freedom, for individuality, etc.--are but a species of the more fundamental longing to be real, for selfhood. Furthermore, look at the products that you purchased and consider whether you purchased them based on their having a certain ontological appeal.

9. Look at the problems that you are dealing with in life, whether they are at work, in your marriage, or anywhere

else. How deep has been your analysis of the problem that you are facing? (In the dialogue, we used the example of relationships.) I.E., are you dealing with one of Mr. Big's henchmen, or soldiers, one of his lieutenants, his underboss, or with Mr. Big himself?

10. Are there deep questions that you fear asking? Or have you already become the man or the woman who knows too much? How has your journey into life's depths affected your relations to other people?

Chapter VI
Dangerous Questions

A Dialogue in Five Acts

Dramatis Personœ:

Frank––A recently retired owner of a record company, in his late fifties.

Samantha––A shiatsu masseur, in her mid-fifties.

Tim––Owner of a landscaping business, in his early forties.

Ricky––A graduate student in music, plays in a rock band, in his mid twenties.

Dorothy ––A teacher of high school English, in her mid thirties.

Mark––Philosopher, leader of this group, in my early to mid-fifties, at the time.

Haley––A woman in her early twenties.

Detective Mueller––A man in his thirties.

Waiter––from the restaurant

Act I: A Yogi Becomes Consumed by Road Rage

Scene: [A private room, in an elegant restaurant]

Ricky

Wow, this is like that film I saw in college, "My Dinner with Andre."

Frank

More like, my dinner with Satan.

Mark

Hmm, why is everybody looking at me? Did I do something wicked?

Dorothy

Yeah, you opened the box and let out the dangerous questions!

Mark

Maybe so. Well, do you all of you think of me as Satan?

Haley

Wait till I tell the folks back home, in Charleston, that I had dinner with the devil!

Mark

Whose idiotic idea was it to have this third anniversary dinner?

Samantha

I think that it was your idea, Mark.

Mark

Hmm, maybe so.

Tim

Doc, I've been looking over my notebooks, for the past three years, and I've detected a disturbing trend. It seems that so many of our conversations, lately, drive and drive, until they reach the same point.

Samantha

What point is that, Tim?

Tim

It seems that all roads lead to the edge of a cliff. What I'm trying to say is that just about all our conversations here end when we've arrived at a contradiction, which in turn leads us to realize that a fundamental way of living fails to give us the happiness and fulfillment that we seek. Did I get that right Doc?

Mark

Yes, precisely Tim.

Dorothy

Aha! That's the thing with these damn discussions, and it's why I often drive home shaken. It's like I'm running through a giant maze, desperately trying to find an exit.

Mark

I guess life is, indeed, like a gigantic maze. It's pretty *amazing*, huh?

Dorothy

Yeah, each week I discover that what I thought was a pathway out of the maze is actually a dead end.

Mark

Well, that's making progress.

Dorothy

I'm trapped! We're all trapped! There's no way out of this infernal maze! I'm trapped here, with my fellow idiots, almost seven billion of them, including my boss! I want out!

Ricky

[Standing up on his chair]

Dorothy's right! We're doomed! We're doomed!

Mark

More of or less, but here's the good news...

Waiter

[Rushing into the room]

Is there anything wrong folks? Is everything OK?

Frank

Yeah everything just fine. The food's delicious. Ricky here was just telling a funny joke, about a lunatic who stands on chairs, so that he can reach great heights.

Ricky

Yeah, a really funny joke. Ha! Ha! Ho! Ho!

[Sits down]

Waiter

No problem. If there's anything I can get you, please let me know.

[Waiter leaves.]

Tim

Let me ask you, Doc: What's the value of seeing that what I'm really attempting to do is contradictory and therefore impossible?

Mark

It actually opens the door to new possibilities, of a different order.

Samantha

What do you mean "of a different order?"

Mark

Well, our life's journey is not just horizontal. It's not that we're always doing more of the same. It's also vertical, so to speak. We reach new elevations. It's sort of like mountain climbing, in that respect. The awareness of the impossible is what drives us higher up the mountain, where we encounter...

Dorothy

Mr. Big?

Mark

Uh, yeah.

Samantha

Oh, him again.

Tim

Tell me if I'm wrong, Doc, but I see that you've first discussed the contradiction between security and adventure with Frank.

Frank

It's Mr. Moleman to you Tim.

Tim

And you mentioned your college friend, the insurance agent, who would get drunk on weekends. You said that it represented the contradiction between the desire for order and the desire to be free of order, to the point of embracing chaos.

Mark

That sounds right.

Tim

And then you got into the contradiction between identity and freedom. Last week, we discussed the contradiction between the real and the ideal and now you're back to identity and freedom. Are there others that we haven't discussed?

Mark

Yes, quite a few Tim. We'll really see contradictions when we discuss masculine and feminine relationships.

Samantha

There's something that's been bothering me. I think it may involve a contradiction. So I'd like to explore it, unless Tim had other questions.

Tim

No, not at all. Please go ahead, Samantha.

Samantha

OK, I spent part of my last vacation at a yoga and meditation retreat. I was hoping to integrate the inner peace that I gained there, into my everyday life.

Mark

Were you able to achieve your goal?

Samantha

Not for very long! On the ride home, some jackass apparently thinks I'm driving too slowly. So he cuts me off and honks his horn at me. It really pissed me off.

Mark

Ah, but then you quickly returned to your state of inner peace and tranquility. Right? The petty annoyance just washed over you, like water off a duck's back. Right? You saw the other driver as a fellow, suffering sentient being who was just deluded and so you just smiled beatifically. Right?

Samantha

Wrong! I gave the schmuck the finger and honked back at him.

Mark

Well, we all have our lapses. Were, you able to return to your meditative calm for the rest of the ride home?

Samantha

No, not really. The whole goddamn incident really perplexed me. On the ride home, I kept on wondering, what the hell was I defending?

Mark

Hmm, one day, you decide that you want to be free of the very thing that you spent your life defending, namely your ego. Why? Because instead of being enamored with yourself, you now experience who you are as a limit, a burden, an albatross and so you want to be free of yourself.

Samantha

Yeah, Mark, it's ironic when you put it that way... That's why I was so damn perplexed about giving the finger to the rude driver. I mean, here it is that I attend the yoga and meditation retreat to attain selflessness and then, on the way home, some guy cuts me off and honks at me and I'm immediately back to being the old Samantha, defending who I am from some minor assault to my pride.

Mark

Why do you think that you so quickly returned to being your old self?

Samantha

I really don't know.

Mark

> You want to affirm your identity, i.e., as Samantha. And there is a great mystery here, as to why each of us clings to the burdensome and constricted sense of self, known as our ego. It's the mystery of attachment. But, on the other hand, you want to be free of your identity with your ego. Or maybe, it wants to be free of you.

Haley

> Lordy be! Human beings sure have their conflicts!

Mark

> By the way, Haley, we haven't been talking about neurotic conflicts. These are just the normal conflicts endemic to all human beings. And another thing, I used the word "conflict," but maybe these longings really point to an ultimate and irresolvable contradiction--in other words, an antinomy--at the heart of who we are.

Ricky

> An antinomy? That doesn't sound good. Well, I had a feeling that we were in big trouble. Hmm, maybe I'll compose an ode to the antinomies, or maybe a dirge to...

Mark

> Ah, but there is a good side to all of this, Ricky. In time, you realize that you are neither side of a contradiction, nor are you both sides of the contradiction. You are the *awareness* of the contradiction. That awareness is your true self. So maybe you could compose a cheerful dirge, if there's such a thing.

Dorothy

> OK, you're not talking about balancing life's opposites. You're talking about being beyond them, in some way.

Mark

> That's right.

Dorothy

And you're not talking about integrating, oh, let's say, yin and yang. You're talking about some third thing emerging. So, what is this mysterious third?

Frank

[Imitating an Indian mystic]

Ah, the eternal question, young grasshopper: who's on third?

Mark

Good question Frank. It's not a thing, like Dorothy called it, but simply awareness.

Dorothy

Samantha said that on the way home from the yoga retreat she wanted to be selfless, but life, in the form of a rude driver, put her to the test and...Well, I'd also like to be selfless, but it's not when I'm driving that the rubber meets the road... so to speak. It's when I have to give a speech, and I often do for work and for the professional organizations to which I belong.

Mark

There is something curious about the dread of public speaking. There's more to it than meets the eye.

Dorothy

I'd like to know why I'm so damn anxious. It's really perplexing.

Mark

How so?

Dorothy

It would make sense that I'd be nervous, if I were making some grand claim about myself, if I were trying to convince people that I'm an important person. But my speeches are merely intended to convey helpful information to other people.

Samantha

Maybe you lack self-confidence.

Dorothy

Not really, Samantha. In the other areas of my life, I'm not a fearful person...

Samantha

Are you sure that it's not due to a lack of self-esteem?

Mark

I don't think that Dorothy's anxiety, when giving a speech, is due to an inferiority complex or a poor self-image or a lack of self-esteem. Many people who fear public speaking are confident in every other aspect of their lives.

Samantha

Then this is a mystery.

Dorothy

It certainly is, for I don't see a logical reason why I should be nervous and yet I am. So, put that in your pipe and smoke it, inspector Dillof.

Mark

OK, let's try to figure this out. First of all, logic has nothing to do with this. Our emotions operate on the level of symbolism and myth. And symbolically speaking, you are making a claim, one that might not seem to you to be a legitimate claim.

Dorothy

What sort of claim?

Mark

You are claiming that you know more about some aspect of a particular subject than your audience.

Dorothy

Well I do.

Mark

I'm sure that it's a valid claim. You may, indeed, be the world's foremost expert on your subject matter. There's nothing wrong, at all, with making a valid claim. Indeed, it is very important to educate our fellow citizens and to disseminate the truth. But you can still feel anxious about doing so. It can be experienced as an act of pride, of hubris.

Dorothy

Pride? Hubris? I never thought of it that way, but maybe I do on an emotional level... It may sound odd, but when I speak it seems like the audience can see right through me.

Mark

And what do they see, when they look through you?

Dorothy

This is going to sound bizarre, but this is how I feel: They judge that I'm a fraud, an imposter, a fool pretending to be wise, and a knave pretending to be moral.

Mark

This troubles you, especially since you are acting in all good faith. You're speaking for a good cause. And you are, for the most part, not egotistically motivated. You, therefore, feel perplexed. You wonder why you're being assaulted by these troubling feelings of illegitimacy.

Dorothy

You suggested that it had to do with a sense of fault.

Mark

Yes, but to make sense of it, you must understand the symbolic resonances involved with the claim to know something. If you are addressing a group of people about a particular subject, it can feel as if you are claiming to know absolutely everything.

Dorothy

But that seems absurd!

Mark

Yes, it's odd that a claim to know--for example, how to play a better game of bridge--can seem no different, psychologically speaking, from a claim to comprehend the alpha and omega of the universe.

Dorothy

I'll grant you that my emotional life operates by a different set of laws than does my rational mind.

Mark

That's true. Our emotional life operates by strange laws, one of which is that one thing can feel life everything. In this case, the one thing you are claiming to know (how to play better bridge) represents all knowledge. The fear, once again, is that everyone will see through your claim to omniscience, find it to be outrageous, and accuse you of arrogant pride, or hubris. What we really fear, then, when we are at the podium, is the punishing forces of Nemesis.

Dorothy

Well if I do have a sense of fault, wouldn't it be due to something that I did?

Mark

Here, then, is the oddity of it all: the sense of hubris and nemesis can derive not from what you did or didn't do, but simply from the fact that you exist. To say, for example, "I am Dorothy," is itself, in the eyes of the gods, a falsehood, a deception. It must be punished, if the order of the universe is to be restored, after your claim to be who you are threw it into disarray. The sense of fault is not merely personal. It's ontological.

Dorothy

This is intriguing.

Mark

I remember reading somewhere--I'm pretty sure that it was in a book by Alan Watts--that ordinary questions often have a far deeper import than we usually realize. A question that comes to mind is "Who do you think you are?!"

Tim

Yeah, whenever my parents or teachers were angry with me, they would ask me: "Timothy! Who do you think you are?"

Mark

Very good Tim. That gives me an idea. Let's all engage in a bit of psychodrama. Here is the imaginary dialogue from my essay on public speaking.

[Hands out the scripts to everyone.]

I've actually meant to hand these out to last week, to perform. Tim, you'll play the part of Bernard. Ricky, you play the president of the company. Frank, you play the CEO. Samantha, you play the vice-president. And Haley, you play the COO. And everyone will play the Greek chorus, in other words, the board of directors. I've made copies for each of you.

Dorothy

Hey, what's my part?

Mark

Someone has to be the audience.

Dorothy

So, what do I do? Just applaud?

Mark

No, applause is not enough. Your job, Dorothy, is to become illuminated and transformed from what you witness on stage, such that your dread of public speaking can begin to dissolve. OK, if everyone is ready, we shall begin.

President of company

I'd like to turn the meeting over to our illustrious sales manager, Bernard Smith. He has devised a new website marketing strategy that is going to really knock your socks off!

Board of Directors

(shouting in unison)

Ooh-rah! Ooh-rah!! Ooh-rah!!!

Bernard

I have devised a new website marketing strategy that promises to...

CEO

Who do you think you are?!

Bernard Smith

I'm sales manager for...

CEO

Who do you REALLY think you are?!

Bernard

Bernard Smith?

Vice President

We all know that personal identity is really what Zen masters call a mask, out of which the spirit speaks. Ever watch a Japanese Noh play, Mr. Smith?

Bernard

No...

Vice President

That's right, a Noh play.

Bernard

I mean no, I haven't seen any lately.

Vice President

Are you familiar with Jungian psychology, Mr. Smith? Are you aware that Jung refers to our personality as merely a persona, and that this persona is just a social fiction?

Bernard

I took a psych elective, as part of my marketing degree...

COO

OK, then, who do you think you really are?

Bernard

The other day, my girlfriend called me a rascal...

President

Being a rascal might be part of your persona, Bernard, but it's not the real you. Let's put the question this way--what was your face before you were born?

Bernard

OK, I give up, I don't know who I really am...

Board of Directors

[chanting in unison, like a Greek chorus]

We can see by the way your palms sweat, the way your legs shake, and from the butterflies in your stomach, that you are concerned with knowing yourself. Then go find yourself, your true self, and when you think you know who you are report back to us to tell us what you found. Until then, you are banished and please leave your key to the executive bathroom, with the receptionist, on your way out!

[Everyone places down their scripts.]

Dorothy

Are you saying, then, that this is, more of less, the scenario, the silent script that I hear when I get up to speak?

Mark

Yes, Dorothy, more or less it's what every anxious person hears when they get up to give a speech. If Watts is correct, the question--"Who do you think you are? --resonates with ontological meaning. This is because the question is really asking about who we take ourselves to be, and whether our sense of self is a valid one. So, here it is that we are giving a speech and we hear that question, silently asked, by every member of the audience, "Who, the heck, do you think you are?!" That is the subtext we hear, more or less. It all takes place, in a split second, as we stand up to deliver our speech.

Dorothy

Maybe, then, that is what I'm silently hearing. If so, I really don't have an answer to the question.

Mark

If you did have an answer to the question, you wouldn't be anxious anymore. I'll add that the question, "Who do you think you are?" isn't only there when we get up to give a speech, but it's always there. For example, let's take the example of a person driving home from a yoga and meditation retreat.

Samantha

I wonder who that might be?!

Mark

Well, we'll change the script, just a bit, for dramatic effect and to protect the innocent or the guilty... OK here goes... You're driving along, when a rude driver cuts you off and calls you a moron. You then think to yourself: "How dare you call me a moron! I know who I am. I'm Samantha. Hell, I graduated from Radcliff and I drive a Lexus! That's right buster. Furthermore, I listen to tapes of new age books, while I drive. But even if I were a moron, which I'm not, you have no right calling me one! Who the heck do you think you are putting me into self-doubt?

Samantha

Although I wouldn't use those exact words, that dialogue is disturbingly familiar.

Mark

Therefore, the person who has not answered the question--"Who do you think you are?"--can have the question emerge at any time, usually unannounced. The dread of public speaking and road-rage are only two of numerous possible instances.

Dorothy

Then the cure is...

Mark

> The cure is to know oneself. And when you do, you'll find that you're not the person you think you are. You are still Dorothy or Samantha or Ricky or Tim or Frank or Mark, or Haley, but you are also the spirit that speaks through one of these masks. Then, when you walk up to the podium, there will be no fear, for you see that the members of your audience are but fellow performers in the Noh play called life.

Haley

> Then, if I got to truly know who I am, I wouldn't need my tattoos.

Mark

> That's right Haley. You'd lose your tattoos and your name and you'd be free.

Act II: To Hell with the Infinite

> **Scene:** [The same private room, in the elegant restaurant]

Mark

Did you do your homework? Did you find something that embodies your mode of being?... It looks like everybody's nodding "yes." Very nice... Ricky, you look rather anxious, or should we say eager, so why don't you begin.

Ricky

As you know, I can't decide anything. I can't even decide what to order in a restaurant. That's why I love to eat at buffets, especially at Chinese restaurants. At a buffet, I get to have it all. Yeah, that's the connection I made. My undergraduate course advisor said that I even tried to make college into a buffet.

Mark

How did you do that?

Ricky

I tried to convince the dean that I should be allowed to major in everything, but he wouldn't let me do that. He said that I had to choose only one subject as a major.

Mark

Hmm, it's surprising that you're able to do anything, for every action involves a decision, even what shoe to tie first.

Ricky

Well, Dr. Mark, actually, I can decide if I think to myself that my decision is only temporary, that it can always be undone.

Mark

I see, sort of like getting married, but being able to have it annulled at any moment. Well, that's not a real decision. Kierkegaard would say that you suffer from the despair of possibility.

Tim

The despair of possibility? Sounds scary! What's it mean Doc?

Mark

It is scary, Tim. Look at it this way: we all crave the infinite, that which is without limit, the unconditioned, the absolute.

Samantha

OK, so no one wants to be limited. Well, I could have told you that.

Mark

Well, you probably will, Samantha, when we explore how you seek to be unlimited or infinite, but let's first see how Ricky seeks to do that. Anyway, possibility is an image of the infinite, because it hasn't become anything yet.

Ricky

Ah, I love the infinite, beautiful infinite, darling infinite, tasty infinite!

Mark

Ah, but if you try to actualize any one of those infinite possibilities, you then need to limit yourself. You can't, for example, play both the piano and the oboe and the drums, at least not at the same time. In any case, the despair of possibility consists in never realizing actuality.

Tim

Realizing actuality?

Mark

Imagine, Tim, that you have a piece of clay. You struggle with it, but at the end of the day you still haven't formed it into anything recognizable. It's just a formless blob. That's the thing. We have these criteria or what's real. Infinitude is one of the criteria. But identity, or having a form, is another criteria.

Ricky

Gee I wouldn't want to be a blob. I mean, maybe in the morning it would be OK, but not at the end of the day.

Mark

Rightly so. Imagine, then, that your life has ended. It's your funeral and the minister gives his eulogy: "Ricky never really became anything, never amounted to anything. He was full of all sorts of fascinating possibilities, but never actualized any of them, because he couldn't chose one of them, for he wanted to stay infinite."

Ricky

Gee, Dr. Mark, I'm not too keen on the idea of being dead to begin with, but you're making it like I died without ever having lived.

Mark

And then, Ricky, the woman you never married...

Ricky

Who is this woman and why didn't I marry her?

Mark

Well, you would have had to choose only one of the many women out there. Anyway, this hypothetical woman walks over to the pulpit to give her speech about you. She then turns to the casket, where you lie, and concludes tearfully with, "Farewell, sweet blob!"

Ricky

To hell with the infinite! I don't want to die a blob! I want to become something!

Frank

You're something, all right.

Mark

This is the thing, Ricky, if you remain in possibility, you'll be in despair. You'll suffer from the vertigo of infinity.

Ricky

[Standing up and swaying to and fro]

Vertigo of infinity? I don't know exactly what that means, Dr. Mark, but it's making my head spin! [Dancing like a madman]: I mean I'm here. No. I'm there. But maybe I'm really here. No, maybe I'm really there. Where am I? Man, the vertigo of infinity is making me want to throw up!

Frank

[Moving to the side]

Not on me, you don't!

[Ricky collapses in chair.]

Mark

The vertigo of infinity is a term that Jean-Paul Sartre coined. It means that staying in possibility can be disorienting. That's why, a few weeks ago, you felt like you were losing your mind. In any case, maybe you need a practice.

Ricky

A practice?

Mark

Yes, a practice is an activity that can help you overcome your mode of being in the world. I'd recommend no more Chinese buffets for you, for a year. Next time you go to a Chinese restaurant, decide on only one of the menu options. And as you have the one item, try to explore what it means to shift from possibility to actuality, in other words, to decide something.

Rickey

I think that I understand my mission.

Mark

OK Samantha, you look like you're chomping at the bit, so let's hear what you discovered.

Samantha

Coincidentally, the connection I found also has to do with eating. But, in my case, I noticed... well, to be honest, I didn't notice it, Dorothy did.

Mark

That's OK. In either case, someone noticed something. Very good. What was it?

Dorothy

I noticed something odd, whenever I have lunch with Samantha. She will take a large plate of rice, pasta, or even salad and first gather all the food together into a large circular clump on her plate. Then, with her fork, she will make a whole in the center of the food, so that it looks sort of like a donut.

Samantha

That's really true! I keep the whole in the center of my food, until I've finished the dish. If, for example, it's a rice dish, I'll always begin by eating the rice at the outer edges of the dish. Round and round I'll go, as the dish of rice gets smaller and smaller, all the while keeping the hole in the center, until it disappears, at the very end.

Mark

That's one of the strangest eating rituals I've ever heard of! Have you always eaten this way?

Samantha

Hmm, let me think... wait a second. For many years, I was bordering on being an anorexic. I ate practically nothing. I was real skinny. I think that it was just about when I began putting the hole in my plate of food that I stopped eating like an anorexic. I started eating normal and started gaining weight.

Mark

So the end of your anorexic eating was coincident with the development of your eating ritual. Wow, this is intriguing!

Samantha

What do you think it means? I realize that we were supposed to make a connection, but I really can't think of what it says about the rest of my life.

Mark

Obviously, there's something about the hole in the center that has a symbolic meaning for you.

Samantha

Hmm, there's something real nice about an empty space, something appealing about the nothingness of that whole. When I gaze upon it, I forget that I'm eating.

Dorothy

Why would you want to forget that you're eating?

Samantha

I've always felt somewhat guilty about eating. I was even a vegetarian for a number of years. The whole thing with killing other beings so that I can eat was getting to me. I felt kind of... egotistical. Even the slightest amount of fat, on my body, seemed to be evidence of my murderous misdeeds. That's what got me interested in eastern religion and mysticism. I like the idea of not being there, of being free of desire, of becoming one with the void.

Mark

There may be a connection here between your eating ritual and what you do for a living. Let me ask you, Samantha: What do you think that you're really trying to accomplish in your work as a Shiatsu masseur?

Samantha

I'm trying to free people from the blockages in their flow of energy. The blockages show up as tensions. Gee, I guess I'm really trying to free people from themselves.

Tim

Free people from themselves? Hmm, I'm not sure I get it Samantha.

Samantha

I see a person's ego, their very individuality, as a limit.

Tim

What is it a limit of?

Mark

That's a good question Tim. Let me know if I'm right, Samantha, but I think ego, identity, and individuality limits the pure wholeness, the oneness of the void, which you represent symbolically as the hole in your dish of food.

Samantha

My head is spinning from thinking about this for the first time, but it sounds about right.

Mark

Do you actually succeed in freeing people from limits, I mean from being who they are? Or maybe I should ask: Do you succeed in freeing the void of its limits?

Samantha

No, once the massage is over they immediately return to being their obnoxious selves, only a bit more relaxed for about a half-hour. That's the sad truth of the matter. My efforts are futile.

Mark

It seems, then, that what you are trying to accomplish as a masseur is represented by the whole in your plate of food. The donut hole is a symbolic image of true reality, the pure trackless void, free of the shapes, forms and limits that people bring to it. And you can only eat, in so far as you have that whole in the center. It protects you noticing that you, too, are there as a being in the world.

Samantha

It all sounds outrageous and yet what you say resonates with me, in some strange way. Yeah, I think it's true.

Mark

Let's return, for a moment, to your work as a masseur. Even if you could free a particular person of his or her individuality, there would still be five billion other people out there blocking true reality, the limitless void from reemerging.

Samantha

Yes, if only I could nuke all of them, melt down their individuality, without killing them, of course. I just want to free the hole, the void from their individuality. And, in so far as I am the void, I want to free myself from them.

Frank

That's assuming that a person's wants to be free of his individuality. I don't think that I'll be voting for you for world dictator this year.

Mark

Frank has a point. Not everyone has Samantha's particular ontology, her particular vision of truth and reality. For some people, human beings and their individuality are essential for the emergence of true reality. For those people, identity, form and individuality are not something to get rid of.

Frank

Yeah, Doc, that's what I meant to say.

Dorothy

Should Samantha eat without the whole in the center of her plate of food? Would that be her practice?

Mark

I suppose, Dorothy, it would be a practice for Samantha, but the key would be for her to do so without shifting back to the anorexia that she had before developing her eating ritual. She couldn't even be a vegetarian, for that too would deny the harsh truth that we eat other beings.

Samantha

How could I eat without a sense of fault, without feeling guilty?

Mark

You associate eating with fault, with sin, but if eating were justified in some way, then you wouldn't have a sense of fault about it. That's what you need to explore.

Samantha

Could you give me a clue where to start?

Mark

Hmm, maybe it would be good to read Aristotle. He justifies eating other beings. And the Bible implicitly does so too, when God gives man dominion over the animals. But if you try to bring morality into the domain of eating, while rejecting the belief in human exceptionalism, then you got problems. Then you can't eat.

Dorothy

Are you referring to Samantha's rejection of speciesism?

Mark

Speciesism? I'm forgetting what that word means.

Tim

If you believe that human beings are more important to the scheme of things than wolves, crocodiles or even bedbugs, then you are guilty of speciesism.

Mark

Hmm, I guess I am guilty, Tim. Yes, there are those who reject the notion that humans are justified in eating other beings.

Tim

It sounds like those who worship nature have been watching too many Walt Disney movies. Nature's really all about bigger things eating littler things.

Mark

I agree with you Tim. It's just romanticizing nature. Those who reject hierarchy end up worshipping nature as sacred and human beings as defilers of its purity. They would have us relocate to the moon, so as to return nature to its pristine state of being.

Samantha

Well, what sort of justification could there be for eating animals?

Mark

Using plants and animals to serve a higher purpose is the only real justification for eating them. We must serve that higher purpose, by how we live our lives. Then our eating is justified and sanctified.

Samantha

What is that higher purpose?

Mark

Some have said that we are the eyes of the universe. It's through us that the universe knows itself. Anyway, Samantha, why don't you and Dorothy meet for lunch to discuss these ideas, and then we can explore it more next time. Tim, you're on.

Tim

I had some insights about my work I do; I mean landscaping. I think that I'm beginning to understand its real appeal of landscaping for me. Man, it hit me like a bolt of lightning!

Mark

Let's hear it Tim.

Tim

As you know, Binghamton is full of hills, which is perfect because I specialize in hillside landscaping. That's why much of the landscape designing I do deals with the dynamic of vertical and horizontal.

Samantha

Vertical and horizontal?

Tim

Yeah, sometimes the land is relatively flat. Sometimes it ascends, sometimes descends. It's rarely an even grade. That's what really intrigues me.

Samantha

So why does it intrigue you?

Tim

OK, I'll explain, Samantha. I bought a book, the other day, on hillside landscaping, by a woman named Hazel White. Well, Ms. White claims, if I remember correctly, that vertical is exciting and dramatic and that horizontal is soothing and meditative. I think that she's right. But I think there's more to it for me. As you know, there is a side of me that has a passion for just living and doing so intensely. But there's another side of me--some would call it the spiritual dimension--that seeks to transcend life.

Mark

Am I correct in assuming that the horizontal symbolizes being in the world, and that the vertical symbolizes transcendence?

Tim

Exactly, Doc. I'm torn by these two longings. Maybe, there's some sort of contradiction here.

Dorothy

Would it be akin to feminine and masculine?

Mark

Let's see, Dorothy. Feminine and masculine, Earth and Heaven--yes, it does relate to horizontal and vertical, to the longing to find earthy fulfillment versus heavenly transcendence. Do you remember that line from Goethe's Faust? It goes, "Two souls within my breast dwell apart." Tim, with his dual longings, is Faustian, in that regard.

Dorothy

I think that I am too.

Mark

Maybe we all are, more or less. But for you, Dorothy, the conflict seems to be more emotionally intense. Tim, on the other hand, seems to have found some sort of channel for it.

Tim

OK, if I understand correctly, what interests me about landscape gardening is working out a dynamic tension between opposing longings, the earthly and the heavenly. I feel they need to be in some sort of relation to each other and so each hill that I work on becomes my laboratory, where I try to find a solution. That is, if I able find a solution.

Samantha

Why shouldn't you be able to find a solution?

Tim

Well, the problem isn't only the land, the varying soils, settings, gradients and the building materials. That makes for enough of a challenge. The real problem is that the fact that it's not my own landscape that I'm designing. I'm always designing it for a customer. What emerges is that the customer has his own vision of things.

Dorothy

Are you saying that your customers have their own relation to the horizontal and vertical?

Tim

Exactly. And then there are the many other symbolic meanings involved with landscaping a hill, such as waterfalls. Even a retaining wall has a certain meaning.

Frank

Isn't a retaining wall just a practical matter?

Mark

It certainly is practical Frank, but I imagine that the type of retaining walls that Tim builds, alongside hillside paths, have an aesthetic and symbolic meaning. As a matter of fact, I think that the word "paradise" comes from the word meaning "a wall."

Frank

Hmm, maybe the wall's there to keep guys like me from barging in.

Tim

Anyway, each customer I have has his or her own vision of life. That's where it gets difficult, if not downright impossible.

Samantha

Can't you figure it out by talking with them?

Tim

Sometimes I can and it's mind-blowing. But very often they don't want to be bothered. They say to me, "Tim, just show me a nice design." And so I guess what they might like. Then, when their hillside has been created, I try to explain to them what I've done, I mean from a deeper perspective. But I may as well be talking to a wall or a rock. They couldn't give a hoot about the solution I've created for them.

Samantha

Do they need to understand what you've done?

Tim

I'm not sure why, but I have this need for them to understand it. Maybe I need for them to rejoice with me in the custom designed unity of Heaven and Earth that I've created, but they don't. And so it makes me feel... lonely. I need to think about this more.

Mark

Maybe it's the loneliness of participating in a certain symbolic meaning that other people don't share with you. Here it is that, in your mind, you've brought together Earth and Heaven--wow!--But all they care about is that their landscape looks attractive.

Tim

That could be it. Doc, I understand your analysis, but it still doesn't change the fact that I'm trying to do something with hillside landscaping that can't be achieved.

Mark

That's true. Yes, hillside landscaping doesn't succeed as an answer to the question, but it does succeed in making you clearer on the question.

Dorothy

What's the question?

Mark

Well, maybe there are two questions for Tim. One has to do with how to integrate his longing to achieve the fullness of existence with his longing for spiritual transcendence.

Tim

That sure is one hell of a question for me.

Mark

Yes, it is. But there's another question for you, Tim. I think that you're trying to communicate with people on a certain level. Maybe *commune* is the right word. You're trying to share with them certain truths about life, but they aren't receptive to it. They're not interested in exploring your profound question with you.

Samantha

Well, why the need to share the question with other people?

Mark

Now that itself is a good question, Samantha. It could be that we must be seen, known or understood to be real. If we're unseen, we feel invisible and unreal.

Dorothy

That reminds me of this British fellow I read about when I took a college philosophy class. He said that to be seen is to be real.

Mark

Yes, it was Berkeley. I'm just elaborating on his idea. Could being seen be a basic requirement for selfhood? Do we need to have other people see or recognize, in some fundamental way, the person we really are? If other people don't grasp the meaning of Tim's hillside creations, then he feels invisible, unreal.

Samantha

Maybe so. When I'm with people who don't know the real me, I feel like the invisible woman. Hmm, maybe that's why I come here. It's the only time all week that I don't feel invisible. OK, what's Tim to do?

Frank

He could cry all the way to the bank, along with Ricky.

Mark

Maybe so, Frank. Artists, including landscape gardeners, have always been misunderstood or misinterpreted. Maybe the truth needs to be expressed simply for truths sake, whether or not other people grasp it, and if they're fortunate enough to sell their paintings or landscape designs, then they can cry all the way to the bank.

Haley

Then who grasps it, Dr. D.? Does God grasp it? Does the universe grasp it? Future generations?

Mark

Good question...

Ricky

I don't think that I like this idea of being invisible. And I don't like being unreal. Even if just one other person could grasp the meaning behind one of my musical compositions, it would make all the difference in the world.

Mark

That is an interesting observation, Ricky. As to whether we are seen by God, the universe or some all-knowing eye is something I can't answer... And so, at the end of the project, the artist, composer or landscape creator, in Tim's case, collects his money from the customer and leaves it at that. And yet, there still exists that longing to communicate the deeper question. We'll leave Tim to think about it more. Dorothy, you're next. But let's first pay the bill and meet at my philosophical counseling room.

Samantha

Philosophical counseling room?

Mark

OK, the dank and dusty living room of my apartment in Binghamton.

Samantha

Got it.

Act III: Wading Through the Water

> **Scene:** [Mark's philosophical counseling living room]

Mark

OK, let's continue our exploration of the connections we've made to our mode of being. Dorothy, you're on.

Dorothy

It's actually a dream I've been having, a recurring one. I think might connect to some question that I have. Anyway, I've been dreaming that I'm walking around underwater, at the bottom a lake or the ocean. And I can breathe underwater!

Mark

How do you feel when you realize that you have this ability?

Dorothy

It feels exhilarating, joyous. Beautiful tropical fish swim past me, in clear waters. It's wonderful!

Samantha

Wow, my friend the mermaid!

Mark

Can you guess why you've been having this dream?

Dorothy

I'm not really sure, but I remember telling you that I often feel like a bar of Ivory soap floating to surface. You said that I was coming up for air, which you said was symbolic of my need for consciousness.

Mark

That's a good clue!

Dorothy

Well, what if the bar of soap could stay down, traveling though the waters, without drowning? I mean, what if, somehow or other, I could be in the midst of various activities––really engrossed in them––while still, paradoxically, being self-aware? And what if I could just be flowing along, in my feelings, without drowning in them, because I'm able to maintain self-awareness? Then I would have brought air into the water, in other words, consciousness into life.

Mark

It would appear, then, that your dream is telling you what you need to do to achieve reality as a self. The dream is very useful in that regard, but it offers a kind of mythic or mystical solution. It suggests that such a state of being is possible, but it doesn't tell you how to attain it.

Dorothy

Well, what good is that?! So how am I to achieve this mystical solution?

Mark

That's difficult to say. You'll need to experiment with being in the midst of activities, while maintaining a peripheral, backburner self-awareness. If you go too far in the direction of awareness, or transcendence, you will lose the imminence that you need to be in the activity. But if you lose your awareness, or transcendence, you will drown.

Dorothy

Ah, so where do I begin?

Mark

Start with simple activities. See if you can eat, while fully enjoying every bite of the food on your plate, while maintaining a peripheral self-awareness. Actually, it might be a good idea to first try to lose yourself completely in your eating. When you feel that you are able to maintain this dual awareness while eating, then experiment other activities. That will be your practice.

Ricky

Dr. Mark, can we all try this?

Mark

By all means, try to maintain a dual awareness, Ricky, while playing the piano, conducting or doing anything. The truth of the matter is that in order to attain insights into our emotions we need to maintain that dual awareness.

Tim

How's that Doc?

Mark

Well, if we are totally in our feelings, then there's no one there to look and to see anything. But if we are totally on the side of looking, of being an observer, then there aren't any feelings to look at.

Ricky

Wait a second, Dr. Mark. How can I be in two places at the same time?

Mark

Yes, I realize that it sounds like a contradiction, but in truth it's a paradox. That's why it's paradoxical, which is why it's sort of a mystical solution, for it is, in point of fact, possible, even though it doesn't sound like it is. That's why insight into oneself requires that twofold awareness. It's quite a balancing act.... OK, let' hear from Haley.

Haley

I also have a dream that I think is significant.

Mark

Let's here it.

Haley

Well, coincidentally, it also has to do with water. But it's not at all a pleasant dream like Dorothy's been having. No sir, Dr. Dillof, nothing sweet about it at all. It's really a recurring nightmare. I dream that I'm on an island and the surrounding waters start threatening to engulf the island and drown me. Oh Lord, it's terrifying. I've been having this darn scary nightmare for almost two years now. The dream totally perplexes me, because I don't live on an island. And I'm not afraid of water, since I'm a real good swimmer.

Mark

That seems to be a common dream of women your age. It usually means that life is telling you that a certain type of life that you've been living is over for you.

Haley

What type of life might that be, sir?

Mark

The life of feelings and emotions.

Haley

Are you saying that I'm drowning in them?

Mark

I'm not saying that you are. But a dream like the one you've been having often indicates that you feel that there's a danger that you can drown in feelings.

Haley

Darn! If only I could learn to walk under water like Dorothy does in her dream, but I guess that's not my dream... Well, Doc, I've been fine till now. How come, all of a sudden, I'm scared of the power of my emotions?

Mark

That's a good question, Haley. It seems that the identity requirement increases, over time. At a certain point, your ego, your identity, emerges out of the watery depths of the unconscious. And when it does, you no longer identify with the waters, but with the emerging island of consciousness. And when you begin identifying with the island of consciousness--sitting there in the vast sea of unconscious emotion--you naturally fear that it can become overrun by the emotions, and so return to the sea.

Dorothy

Are you saying that emotions are dark and dangerous? Were I a feminist, I'd say that that was just your male, logocentric bias!

Samantha

Logocentric?

Dorothy

Yes, the supremacy of male reason over feminine feeling.

Mark

Oops, sorry, Ms. Friedan!

Dorothy

Well, fortunately for you I'm not a feminist. As a matter of fact, I have always feared, more than anything else, being overwhelmed by anger, rage, jealousy, desire, dread, all of the emotions. And yes, drowning is the right word, for that's what it would feel like. I mean, when I'm in a dark mood, it feels like me, Dorothy, is gone.

Haley

Oh, Lord, that's how I feel! And that explains my nightmare. I'm scared of my own fury! I'm scared that it will drown me!

Ricky

And drown me too!

Tim

Drown you too? Huh?

Haley

I guess I can explain what Ricky means. I've been having some emotional outbursts, when we've been together. He said that sometimes he feels like he's being pulled into a vortex of emotion.

Ricky

Being that I'm an emotional guy, to begin with, it's not easy for me to stay balanced. It's like trying to surf a tidal wave.

Tim

Wow, Ricky, what an image!

Haley

And I'm that tidal wave?

Ricky

I just meant that...

Haley

That's all right. I know I am.

Mark

Has something developed between you two?

Haley

Well, sir, it's been about two months since stupid cupid shot his arrows at us. It's just that certain conflicts have begun to emerge.

Ricky

Conflicts? Try World War III.

Haley

I was originally attracted to Ricky because he seemed so wild and free. Sweet Wildman Ricky, I'd call him. But, after a time, I began to criticize him for it.

Mark

What did you find objectionable about Ricky being wild and free?

Haley

Well, we both can't be wild and free or we'll both drown. I mean, someone has to be the responsible one. Someone has to count the chickens; I mean be able to balance the checkbook.

Mark

I'm guessing who that one is going to be, Ricky... In any case, Haley, it would make sense that you would turn to Ricky, or a relationship in general, in an effort to resolve this conflict.

Haley

What sort of conflict do you mean, Dr. D.?

Mark

Do you remember, before our break, we were talking about our longing for the infinite and Ricky finally cursed out the infinite? He did so because he also needed to be somebody. Well, here too is the same problem. As feminine, you might identify with the infinite waters, in their fluidity, their ability to change, just like Tiamat, the Babylonian goddess of the sea.

Haley

How is a woman's identity fluid?

Ricky

I can answer that one. Every time I see Haley, her hair is different and she has on a new outfit. And I never know what mood she'll be in.

Mark

Nice example, Ricky! Yes, Haley, that's your way of being fluid, never being a single identity, but being the infinite waters that take on and lose different identities, but is never just any single one of them.

Haley

Hmm, I never thought of it that way, but I suppose that would be me, and it would also connect up to what you said the other day about my tattoo. Hmm, I wish to be free of identities, but I also seem to need an identity.

Samantha

Don't feel too bad. We're all up to our "you--know--what" in contradictions.

Haley

Ha! Ha! That sounds like that perfume Ricky gave me for a present, "Contradiction."

Mark

Huh?

Dorothy

Calvin Klein makes it.

Mark

Wow! Now that's an interesting name for perfume. And it's even more interesting that Ricky got it for you. Well, we'll need to discuss the deeper meaning of Mr. Klein's perfume and the real reason why Ricky got it for you. Let's do so next Monday.

Ricky

Uh oh!

Haley

Is there a practice that you'd recommend for me, Dr. Dillof?

Mark

Hmm, I'll need to think more about that Haley. For one thing, it would be very useful if you and Ricky, in your conversations, and in your arguments, could try to discern the dynamics of identity and freedom. Notice the seesaw effect, how when one person is one way, the other person is the opposite. Apart from your relationship to Ricky, you might focus on the question of how to become centered, without losing your feminine energy. Just as there exist higher levels of the masculine, so it is that there exist higher levels of the feminine, like...

Samantha

Like Sharon?

Mark

Ah, yes, certainly Sharon, but also Sophia. Also, see if you can find some books by Erich Neumann. He has some very insightful things to say about the psychological development of the feminine.

Haley

OK, sir, will do.

Mark

Finally, it's Frank's turn. Any epiphanies, Frank?

Frank

I had one, the other day, while playing golf with my buddies. It was on Sunday. The day began with me getting into a bit of an squabble with my wife and mother-in-law, right before leaving for the greens. They were trying to convince me join them in church.

Mark

Did you join them in church?

Frank

No. I went off to play golf with my buddies. Anyway, I'm playing golf and, at one point, I get the golf ball stuck in the sand trap. I'm about to take a swing, when my friend Jake, who used to be a gold pro, says, "Wait a second Frank. You always dig yourself in deeper! Don't do it this time." When I heard that, something went off in my head. Yeah, that's often my problem and I'm not talking about golf here. I'm talking about people. The more I try to have a reasonable conversation with certain people, the more I get myself dug in deeper into the sand trap, till it ends up that we're arguing about our argument.

Samantha

I think I know what you mean, Frank, but can you give an example?

Frank

Yeah, I say something and then my wife says, "Why did you raise your voice at me?!" And then I say, "You always try to change the subject, when you're losing, by complaining about my voice volume." And on and on the argument goes.

Tim

Man, that's a sticky wicket.

Samantha

Well, what can you do? Not say anything?

Frank

Yeah, silence is golden, but sometimes people get angry if they feel that I'm ignoring them. I can pretend to agree with someone.

But that, too, doesn't always work, especially when I'm arguing with people who know me well. They can see right through me. So what's a fellow to do?

Mark

What do you do on the golf course, when you get the ball stuck in the sand trap?

Frank

I take out my trusty sand wedge.

Mark

And then what?

Frank

Well, what Jake says that I should do is to hit the ball just enough to get it out of the trap, without getting it dug in.

Mark

There must be something comparable, when it comes to having a difficult conversation.

Frank

A conversational sand wedge? Hmm, I wonder what that would be.

Mark

It might be a remark, maybe a witticism, maybe a wisecrack, but whatever it is, it would serve to illuminate the disagreement between you and the other person. It would serve to free you and the other person from the argument, or conversational sand trap, in which the two of you are stuck. Actually, Frank, being that you have a keen sense of humor, you are quite capable of couching a liberating insight in a witticism.

Frank

I am? That's intriguing. Hey, let me ask you. Is everything about golf significant?

Mark

Do you mean symbolic?

Frank

Yeah, isn't a golf ball ever just a golf ball?

Samantha

You already know what Mark is going to say to that one.

Frank

Damn!

Mark

In one respect, at least, golf is like baseball. With baseball, we start out from home, from home plate. Golf, too, involves a circular journey--from home, through life, with its adventures and misadventures--and then back home again. That's why they call it a round of golf. It's a circle. In baseball, one travels around the bases, but in golf one makes a circular journey from the first tee, traveling throughout the green, until one finally returns, upon completion of the eighteenth. So here we see a symbolic rendition of our journey through life in search of... in search of ourselves.

Tim

Why do we have to leave home in order to return home? Is it just that like in the "Wizard of Oz," we come to appreciate that there's no place like home? Is there some deeper meaning to it?

Mark

Yes, there is. What are those lines from T.S. Eliot? We shall not cease from searching... Hmm, is there an English teacher in the house?

Dorothy

They're from Eliot's "Four Quartets" and it goes, "We shall not cease from exploration, And the end of all our exploring, Will be to arrive at where we started, And know the place for the first time."

Mark

You see, Tim, that's the reason for the journey. We get to know the place, meaning that we get to know ourselves, for the first time. That's what's meant by self-realization. And so, this journey of self-discovery, and all the obstacles along the way, is symbolized by these sports.

Frank

OK, let's talk obstacles. More particularly, I have a most unfortunate habit of hitting the ball into a lake or other body of water, so much so that I wear my waterproof fly-fishing pants on the golf course, because I never know when I'm going to wade into the water.

Mark

Haley, you and Dorothy have now become experts on water symbolism. What do you think it means to have a golf ball under water?

Haley

Is it about finding oneself in the depths unconscious feeling? Is a golfer required to drive the ball, meaning himself, out of his feelings and on to dry land?

Mark

That sounds right, Haley. Also, Frank, consider why they call it a fairway. It suggests that the journey through life must be in accord with the straight and narrow; I mean that one must live morally or else one is penalized...

Frank

Yes, cheaters are penalized... if they're caught moving the ball. [Makes motion with his foot, as if moving the ball, while whistling.]

Mark

Ever read Michael Murphy's book "Golf in the Kingdom." Murphy has his own really intriguing insights into the symbolic meaning of golf. He suggests--or I should say that his teacher, Shivas Irons, suggests--that the golf ball is akin to the philosopher Parmenides' notion that being, or reality, is actually a rounded sphere.

Frank

Reality is a golf ball? It figured as much.

Mark

No, reality isn't a golf ball, but the roundness of the golf ball is an image of being, at least for Parmenides it was. The golf ball would, therefore, seem to symbolize absolute fullness, in contrast to Samantha's image of that round whole, which she creates in the center of her dish of food, which suggests absolute emptiness.

Samantha

Fullness, emptiness, wow, my head is spinning. Which is better?

Mark

Neither is better. Ever look at those paintings they have on the wall, at the Indian restaurant downtown? The paintings suggest the mystical fullness of existence. It's overflowing with life's creations, which I suppose are various incarnations of Vishnu. The paintings evoke a sense of plenitude. Contrast that with the aesthetics of emptiness that belong to Zen art. Neither is better. They're just based on different ways of seeing the world, different visions of reality. Anyway, we got into this because Frank said that he had an insight about golf and I suggested that golf is a sport rich with symbolism.

Frank

I know I've asked you this question before, Doc, but what is the value of discovering the secret symbolic meaning of everything we do or like?

Mark

Well, Frank, by illuminating our everyday interests and activities, we get to see what it is that we are really seeking for in life. And I mean really seeking. Then you have a chance of finding it.

Frank

OK, then all along I've been in search of the mystical golf ball, I mean myself. And so that's how I'll spend my retirement, journeying though the links of life, finally making the return journey back home.

Mark

Sounds like a plan, Frank! And I'll be joining you on the cosmic golf green, digging up the divots and maybe the truth, as well. Any last questions, before we take a break?

Ricky

No but I'd like to dedicate a song, actually a spiritual, to Frank and his game of golf. Is that OK Frank?

Frank

Hmm, sounds dubious but go ahead.

[Ricky walks over to the electric piano and starts playing.]

Ricky

[Singing]

"Wade in the water.
Wade in the water, children."
Wade in the water.
God's going to trouble the water."

Frank

Wise guy!

Mark

OK, let's take a short break. Oh, and by the way, Detective Mueller called me to let me know he may stop down.

Samantha

On official business? We must really be in trouble.

Mark

No, he's the one in trouble. He's recently been assaulted by some formidable questions.

Samantha

Oh, that sort of trouble.

Act IV: What Gets You Through the Day?

>**Scene:** [Mark's philosophical counseling room]

Mark

I've been thinking; most people philosophize because they find it interesting.

Samantha

Brilliant! Absolutely brilliant, Mark!

Mark

I detect a slight note of sarcasm.

Samantha

Well, why else would a person philosophize? Because it's boring? Look, sorry for being sarcastic, but am I missing something here?

Mark

Philosophizing might have nothing to do with interesting or boring. On the contrary, a person might philosophize because it's a matter of life and death!

Ricky

Yes, someone might pull a gun on you, Samantha, and say: "You philosophize or I kill you!"

Frank

That would be one tough philosophy professor. Well, students need discipline.

Mark

I think you're all missing my point. What I mean is that our very existence, well-being, and sanity could be at stake. And, if one were religious, one's soul might hang in the balance, awaiting an answer to a certain ultimate question. That's why one would philosophize. It has nothing to do with whether or not it's interesting. Anyway, I mention this because our friend here has a philosophical question, indeed an urgent one. So, Detective Mueller, why don't you state what it is.

Detective Mueller

I've been reading Nietzsche. He's the ass-kicking gentleman who wrote, "God is dead." I realize it's not completely true. Just driving around Binghamton today, I noticed that there sure are a lot of churches. Somebody's got to be attending them. Yeah, Americans are basically religious. So here I am searching for the perp, when the supposed victim may still be alive, although in a weakened state.

Dorothy

The perp? What's a perp?

Detective Mueller

Perp as in perpetrator. I mean, if God is dead, somebody had to kill him, but God might not be dead. In that case, we can still haul the perp in, only this time for attempted murder.

Dorothy

Then who's the perp? I mean who tried to kill God?

Detective Mueller

That's what I'd like to know!

Samantha

Are you religious?

Detective Mueller

I'm an agnostic. I'm really not sure whether or not God even exists. For me, it's still an unsolved mystery. Man, being an agnostic is difficult enough.

Samantha

What do you mean by "difficult enough?"

Detective Mueller

My brother-in-law, Jerry, is a college chemistry professor. He's also an atheist. I'm trying to figure out how Jerry's able to make it through the day. Now, there's a mystery.

Tim

Do you mean, without a belief in God?

Detective Mueller

Yeah, more and more I'm finding that I need something to believe in, but other people seem OK without God.

Tim

Well, they say that there are no atheists in foxholes.

Detective Mueller

Exactly Tim, which brings me to my point: what's an atheist do when his best friend gets killed in the line of duty? Or when his wife cheats on him, like happened to my partner? Or when his daughter becomes a drug addict? Or his son comes back from the war in a coffin? How do those guys make sense of it all? Where do they find solace? I'd like to know so that I can do what they do.

Samantha

So you're talking about dealing with tragedy.

Detective Mueller

I guess so, Samantha, but not always that extreme; sometimes just the stresses and strains of everyday life, whether at the workplace or at home. I awaken, every morning, not knowing what awaits me. Oh, I do have many a pleasant day, but I'm greeted, all too often, by insults and painful misunderstandings, ingratitude and slander.

Tim

We all have days like that.

Detective Mueller

Yeah, but here's the funny part: I used to think that once I became a detective, I would have only the bad guys, the criminals, to contend with. Wow, was I wrong! Now I realize that it's the good guys--my friends, family, fellow detectives, the chief, the lawyers, judges, the DA, and the people I'm trying to help--who cause me the most aggravation. Yeah, it's the good guys, not the criminals, who may yet send me to an early grave. That's why I admire my partner; he's got only a few years till retirement.

Mark

It makes sense, detective. People being as they are...

Detective Mueller

I can't even trust my friends.

Mark

Who was it that said, "God save me from my friends"?

Frank

OK, this time I'm pretty sure that it was Dean Martin.

Mark

That's a very good guess, Frank, since Dean Martin did have some real problems with his partner Jerry Lewis, and an occasional disagreement with Frank Sinatra and the other members of the "Rat Pack," but actually I think that the quotation is from the philosopher Voltaire... But, back to your question, detective.

Detective Mueller

Well, I just wonder how other people, those who lack a sustaining faith, make sense of it all. I wonder how they make it through the day, because it's becoming increasingly more exhausting for me to do so. That's why I'm looking forward to retirement; I'm hoping that it will offer me some relief.

Frank

I wouldn't depend on it.

Mark

So you're asking what sustains people without faith. If it's not some belief in God or some deeper meaning, it would have to be something else that fits the bill, something that seems to be infinite, absolute, eternal.

Dorothy

Why would it need to have those qualities?

Mark

Hmm, those are the qualities commonly attributed to God, or that which seems to be ultimate. Of course that's begging the question, for one could ask, why does God have to have those qualities? In any case, we long for true reality, and for something to be truly real, it must it be ultimate, absolute, unlimited, infinite and...

Dorothy

Well, something that seems ultimate, but really isn't ultimate, would seem to be an idol. No?

Mark

Maybe so. Do you remember when we were reading Saint Augustine and he writes that there's a God-shaped hole in each of us?

Samantha

Yeah, you said that I was attempting to fill that God-shaped hole with chocolate chip cookies.

Mark

Yes, I do remember. The sweetness we crave, so lacking amidst the heavy burdens we bear, the anxieties and self-doubts, the wearisome conflicts--both inner and outer--that darken our days. By contrast, the sweetness seems like heavenly bliss, the Promised Land... So how's those chocolate chips been working out for you?

Samantha

I guess that if cookies were really God, I wouldn't be here searching for a better answer. And I don't mean fudge brownies either.

Detective Mueller

So, when Nietzsche said that God is dead, the reason why people haven't been jumping off the cliff is because they went out and bought themselves a bag of chocolate cookies? Is that what fills the void for them? Is that their M.O?

Mark

Food is definitely one answer. Yes, it does seem to be a surrogate for meaning and purpose in life. There are, of course, many other answers, many other things that fill the void.

Frank

Yeah, don't say it. I know, gambling and golf, for example.

Mark

Yes, indeed, Frank. But can the cosmic golf ball ever fill the hole at the core of our being?

Samantha

Wow! Sounds like a Zen koan.

Frank

Right now, I'd prefer an ice cream koan.

Mark

Hey, let me ask you, have you read Tolstoy's *Confessions*? Well, you know, in midlife Tolstoy was threatened by the specter of mortality and meaninglessness.

Tim

Mortality and meaninglessness? What's the connection?

Mark

Tolstoy figured that if we die anyway, what good is it what we do while alive? He was threatened by nihilism and even contemplated suicide. So Tolstoy began to examine how other people live, in the face of the ultimate questions. Ignorance was one way that people survive. Some people are simply ignorant of the absurdity of life. Then there are those who are epicureans.

Frank

I've been accused of being that one.

Mark

Epicureans seem to be unaware of what the Buddha taught about life being about sickness, old age and death. Finally, Tolstoy chooses to believe in God, as an answer to the question of ultimate meaning. I'm not sure, though, whether or not Tolstoy's answer is satisfying to most people.

Samantha

Aren't there other answers or did Tolstoy run the gamut?

Ricky

Yeah, what about music?

Mark

Music does give shape and form to the chaos of our lives. In that sense it is a surrogate for meaning.

Samantha

What if music could improve people in some way? What if it could bring about a better world?

Mark

If that were what you believe, then you'd be a humanist.

Samantha

A humanist? I like the sound of the word, but I'm not sure exactly what it would mean for me.

Mark

It's the vision of many scientists, of Marxists, and of Utopians in general. It's the belief that human being themselves can bring about the millennium, the perfect world, Paradise. And that they can do it without God's help. A certain type of humanist worships science. They believe that science will one day bring about a Utopia.

Samantha

Gee, I don't know if I want to be a humanist.

Mark

Why not?

Samantha

Because I do have a spiritual side, as you know.

Mark

Hmm, I didn't know that you were religious.

Samantha

Well, I'm not because, for one thing, I don't believe in God.

Mark

Then how are you spiritual?

Samantha

I worship nature. I view it as divine.

Mark

I wonder, then, if you're a pantheist. I mean it sounds like you do have a notion of God, the absolute, the infinite and the eternal. It's just that, for you, God is not separate from the world. He's not up there is the Heaven's. He's not transcendent. And He's not even a he. Rather, God is the world. Yes, for pantheists the world--particularly the realm of nature--is God.

Samantha

Wow, so I'm a pantheist. That sounds even better than being a humanist!

Mark

I just have one little, bity question for you Samantha.

Samantha

Uh, oh! I worry when you say that you have one little, bity question. OK, what's your question, Inspector Columbo?

Mark

Isn't nature the realm of death and destruction? I mean isn't it about killing other creatures for...

Samantha

No! That's a lie! How dare you say that! I worship nature. I revere nature! Nature is the realm of life, of new creations! Nature is healing; it's forever; it's eternal! It's wonderful! Nature is... what do you mean that it's the realm of death and destruction?

Mark

I simply mean that things are born and then they die. Yes, the circle of life: birth, then playing around a bit, as a young cub.

And, if one is a carnivore, killing other creatures. A painful struggle for survival, then mating, followed by more painful struggle for survival, then a painful death, in which one may be killed and eaten by another creature, finally having one's bones picked dry by vultures. That's the cycle. That's the circle of life.

Frank

[singing in a nasal falsetto]

"Till we find our place, On the path unwinding, In the circle, the circle of life."[4]

Samantha

Yes, but nature itself is eternal. It never dies.

Mark

I suppose that's why some people chose to worship it. In some societies, people worship the Great Mother. They regard nature as the mother. Her creations, I mean her children, emerge from her and then return to her.

Samantha

Ah, returning to Mother Nature. It seems very comforting.

Mark

Yes, in respect to that mythic notion called "Mother Nature." But in respect to each suffering creature that is being eaten by another creature, it's not so comforting. And that leads us to the notion of justice. I mean, aren't you always decrying the world's injustices? But nothing could be more unjust than nature, which is all animals eating other animals. It's all about the more powerful ripping their teeth into the guts of the less powerful. Where's the justice there? Where's the fairness?

Samantha

Well, for example... there is...uh...

---

4 *"The Circle of Life." Music by Elton John. Lyrics by Tim Rice. 1994: "The Lion King."*

Mark

If there's any justice at all, it's solely in the human realm.

Dorothy

OK, Samantha's pantheism is hopelessly riddled with problems.

Samantha

Gee, Dorothy, I knew that I could depend on you for support!

Dorothy

What if, instead, we say that God is separate from the world, that he's transcendent? Is that a viable alternative?

Mark

No, it has serious problems of it's own, such as the problem of relation.

Dorothy

What's the problem of relation?

Mark

How does God relate to his creation? Has God simply created the world and then abandoned it? That's what Aristotle argued.

Samantha

Kind of like an absentee landlord. I think that would be kind of irresponsible, don't you think?

Frank

Yeah, I'd move out!

Mark

Or does God participate in human affairs and if so, how? Is he responsible for human suffering? If he isn't responsible, then his power is limited, and who worships a limited being? After all, we worship the infinite. But if God is responsible for human suffering, then he's evil. Anyway, there are 101 problems with trying to make sense of how God relates to the world. That's always the problem with Western religions, like Judaism, Christianity and Islam.

Haley

Dr. D., you had been talking earlier about our search for the absolute and you mentioned idolatry. What about when two people get sweet on each other? Wouldn't they be idolaters?

Mark

I suppose that they would. After all, the expression "You mean everything to me" does suggest a kind of idolatry, since "everything" is a synonym for the absolute, and idolatry is all about worshipping something as absolute, rather than God as absolute.

Haley

I was looking at your book, and remember you saying that there can't be two absolutes. That can create one heck of a lot of problems, if both he and she want to be the absolute.

Samantha

Of course, that's only in the honeymoon stage. After getting married, it's nothing but clay feet.

Dorothy

Some people worship a movie star. Isn't that a sort of substitute for God?

Mark

I suppose it is, Dorothy. Yes, I guess that's why they call them "stars," for they seem to have the aspect of eternity, even though they are actually ordinary mortal beings. But to answer your question, Haley, no there can't be two absolutes, which leads to the problem that...

Tim

Doc, I think that I had been following the thread of this conversation for a while, but now I'm not sure.

Mark

Well, Tim, we've been exploring the question of what gets us through the day, because no one can be continually inundated with limits of all sort, finitude and transiency.

Samantha

And why not?

Mark

It's because human beings seem to take that which is truly real to be that which seems absolute, infinite, eternal, and so on. Religious people believe that God has those qualities. Idolization consists in taking other things--from movie stars to science, from certain foods to a relationship--as being absolute, infinite and eternal.

Detective Mueller

So, if I understand you, Sherlock, this is the problem: When Nietzsche wrote, "God is dead," he thought that without God that people just couldn't go on. Maybe Nietzsche didn't realize that people would find all sorts of substitutes for God.

Mark

That's right, detective. Nietzsche never anticipated that even chocolate chip cookies would be a substitute for God, or a relationship, or a movie star, or a political leader, or a thousand and one other images of God.

Detective Mueller

But if I can neither find God nor use the type of substitutions that people use, then I'm in trouble. I mean then there's no way for me to escape what you call finitude, transiency, meaninglessness and death. Did I get that right?

Mark

That sounds right. Yes, detective, existentially speaking it sounds like you're in a scary place. Like Wile E. Coyote, you've ran over the edge of the cliff and you've looked down, only to realize that you're not standing on anything and are about to plunge into the abyss. What seems to be getting you through the day, then, is the faith that you will be able to find an answer to this perplexity, which you will if you...

Detective Mueller

Goddamn, my beeper went just went off. I got to go. I think it's another homicide. Yeah, apparently some guy thought that another guy had been blocking him on the road to happiness and fulfillment. If only, he had read Kant's ethics, but I guess he can borrow it from the prison library and he'll have plenty of time to read it. Anyway, thanks Doc. Thanks everyone. So long folks. [He leaves.]

Mark

Gee, I was hoping to add one last thing. Well, the detective can listen to the tape. I was going to add that it's important to find out what exactly it is that get's you through the day. It could be something seemingly trivial, such as a donut in the morning or some TV show in the evening. The amazing thing is that it doesn't take much.

Dorothy

Why's it important?

Mark

So that you can rid yourself of those things in your life.

Samantha

What?! No donuts? Have you no decency?! I'd be left with nothing, without support, without foundation, wandering. I'd be lost without Duncan, the holy donut!

Mark

Exactly! When you rid yourself of false absolutes, your inadequate answers to the question of how to live life, the big questions will return in full force, as they seem to have returned for our detective friend. And when the questions return, you open yourself up to life-transforming, liberating insight.

Samantha

Here we go again with the life transforming insights.

Mark

So make a list of everything that gets you through the day, all those little things, the false idols, and rid yourself of them.

Tim

Anything else before we take our break?

Mark

Yeah, if you do discern what gets you though the day and no longer do those things, you should be prepared for an onslaught of anxiety.

Tim

Whoa! Thanks for the heads-up Doc!

Act V: Are You Ready?

> **Scene:** [Mark's philosophical counseling room]

Tim

Doc, I have a little question to ask you.

Mark

Let's here it.

Tim

How should one live?

Mark

That's a tsunami of a question, Tim! After a lifetime of painful misadventures, I'm still trying to figure that one out myself. Can you elaborate a bit?

Tim

I mean, how should one live in the face of the silence of God, the apparent absurdity of the universe, and the inability of human beings to give an ultimate shape to the chaos within and without? I mean, I've been considering Tolstoy's question and the answers he offers. So, should I chose what's behind doors A,B,C, or D? Well, which is the right answer?

Ricky

I'm with Tim. What's the right answer, Dr. Mark?

Mark

Who says any of them are right? Tolstoy was a deep thinker, but he had his limits. Maybe the real question is: how to live, if we wish to gain clues to this amazing mystery story called life?

Tim

OK, that's my question.

Mark

Yes, how to be receptive to clues?

Tim

I'm writing that down.... Uh, how can we be receptive to clues?

Mark

The clues are there for everyone to see, but most people are too obtuse or distracted or involved with getting and spending. They're right in front of their eyes, but they don't see a thing. That's what's strange about it. That's why it's a mystery in broad daylight.

Tim

OK, we should live a certain way, in order to see the clues, but how exactly?

Samantha

Pin him down, Tim. Don't let Mark worm his way out of this one.

Mark

Tim, you told me once that you were a Boy Scout. Well, their motto is "Be Prepared." Prepared for what?

Tim

To do the right thing, based on the requirements of a particular situation? To do one's duty, to rise to the occasion?

Samantha

To be prepared for new opportunities?

Frank

Prepared for investment opportunities?

Mark

Yes, all the above.

Frank

Everyone's a winner!

Mark

The founder of the Boy Scouts, Baden Powell, was no wimp. That's for sure. He said that a Boy Scout should live such that, if the occasion calls for it, that he will be ready to face death itself, if necessary, fearlessly and peacefully... And what does Hamlet say to his friend Horatio... readiness is all. Readiness to face death.

Frank

[Using oriental accent]

Ah, to die fearlessly, like a Samurai.

Mark

Yes, like a Samurai. I think that there exists a related type of readiness, involving being open to insights about yourself and about life.

Dorothy

How's it related to death?

Mark

Insights always involve dying. They may be liberating, but they're dangerous. There's no going back, no returning home, after you've seen certain things.

Frank

No return flights? Huh.

Mark

Yeah, just one-way tickets. The thing is that if you live a certain way, such insights will ambush you, often when you least expect it. You had better be ready for them.

Dorothy

And if one isn't ready?

Mark

Then such insights can be devastating, shattering, destructive and deadly.

Samantha

You were talking about clues before. How can I tell that something's a real clue?

Mark

Well, Samantha, if you're doing something or desiring something and it doesn't make any sense on a practical level, then you know that there's something funny going on. You know that what you're doing has a certain symbolic meaning for you. And when you decipher the symbolic meaning, you get a valuable clue to the mystery of life.

Samantha

Got it. If it's not practical it must be symbolic. And if it's symbolic, it offers a clue. Hmm, a lot of activities are symbolic.

Frank

Unlike gambling, which is a practical activity! Yes, gambling away one's hard-earned money is very practical.

Haley

So is wearing tattoos. Oh, so practical!

Mark

Yes, they're symbolic. And they do offer us clues to the obscure object of desire.

Tim

Aha! Doc, I've got a question about the obscure object of desire. I've been reading over my notes, the other day, about contradictions. Damn! A whole lot of contradictions going on.

Mark

Well sure, the world is composed of contradictions.

Tim

So I'm just wondering, what if we this obscure object of desire involves a contradiction of some sort? I mean, what if we actually desire contradictory things?

Mark

Yes indeed! I'm thinking, Tim, did you ever play of those games where you had to get everything in order, all the numbers or all of the colors, in a certain sequence?

Ricky

Like Rubik's Cube?

Mark

Yeah, that's what I'm thinking of Ricky, Rubik's Cube. Well, let's just say that you're given a kind of puzzle like that at birth, whether it consists of ten numbers, four colors, or maybe the four elements--earth, air, fire, or water--or whatever. You're told that if you can figure out the puzzle that you can achieve happiness and fulfillment.

Dorothy

I'm presuming that it's possible to solve the puzzle. Right?

Mark

Ah, very good Dorothy. Yes, everyone tells you that the puzzle can be solved. Your parents, your teachers, your pastor, the announcers on TV commercials, motivational speakers, politicians, psychotherapists and of course your friends--they all tell you that the puzzle has a solution.

Dorothy

My friends tell me that? I don't remember...

Mark

Yeah, especially Myra. She tells you that. She thinks she's very close to finding a solution to the puzzle of human existence, even though she hasn't found one yet... And each form of psychotherapy promises a different solution to the puzzle. Let's just suppose, though, that everyone is mistaken. And it's not just that they're mistaken about their particular solution to the puzzle of existence. They're mistaken that there even exists a solution. They're mistaken that it's even possible.

Samantha

Mistaken? What the hell! Mark is this your idea of a practical joke?!

Mark

No it's life's idea of a practical joke.

Ricky

Ah, despair. I shall shoot myself today. No wait, I think I'll compose a requiem to lost hope. Yeah, maybe I can use it for my independent study project!

Dorothy

OK, let's say, then, that we're involved with an impossible project, that the puzzle can't be solved. Then what to do?

Frank

I say chuck the damn puzzle. Take it for a drive to the end of the world and then toss it into the abyss.

Tim

Interesting possibility, Frank! Can we just chuck the puzzle, Doc?

Mark

That's the question. Can you just let go of the effort to get it together, assuming that you know it can't be done?

Tim

Just the thought of no longer laboring at what's impossible--what a relief!

Mark

Yes, it would be a great relief. It would be the same as waking up from a long, long dream. Yes, it's what the Buddhists call awakening, or enlightenment. Paradoxically, it's when you realize that the puzzle can't be solved that you discover who you really are.

Frank

Please don't tell me it's the non-Frank.

Mark

No, not the non-Frank. Nor the non-Mark. Nor even the non-Dean Martin.

Frank

That's a relief!

Mark

Chucking the puzzle, Tim, doesn't mean that you can now live like Slobberchops, who never examined the puzzle, because seeing your true self changes everything.

Frank

No dog biscuit for you, Tim.

Mark

> Anyway, letting go of the puzzle is easier said than done. Maybe it begins at certain moments. Maybe laughter derives from a perception that the puzzle can't be done, so maybe it's an intimation of mystical release. But there exist moments of a much different type that also may involve a kind of letting go of the impossible puzzle.

Samantha

What about timeless moments?

Mark

Have you experienced a timeless moment?

Samantha

Yes, on September the 18th, at 7:20AM, Eastern Standard Time! Hmm, it does sound absurd to have had a timeless moment occur at a certain time.

Frank

> [in an Indian accent]

Swami say the truth is often paradoxical.

Samantha

Well, what about living in the present. Yeah, I want to be here now! That's my goal.

Mark

Why haven't you been able to do so thus far?

Samantha

I don't really know.

Mark

Maybe there's something lacking in the present moment.

Samantha

To be honest, I always feel that something's lacking.

Mark

What do you feel is lacking at this very moment?

Samantha

Hmm, I really don't know what's lacking. All I know is that something's missing. That's why I make plans for the future. It's as if I'm trying to make up for the lack, even though I don't know what it is that's lacking.

Mark

Yes, something is always missing, always lacking. The question of what is lacking is a profound mystery. It's really a doorway, down the rabbit hole, into the depths. It's certainly worth pursuing that question.

Dorothy

Well, are there ever any moments when we do live fully in the present? I mean, when nothing is lacking?

Mark

Such moments do exist. We're unable, though, to simply will them to appear, for they seem to come of their own accord, through a kind of divine grace. I was once exploring how the experience of danger and doom can invite such moments.

Tim

You called them "strawberry moments."

Mark

Yes, I had been thinking about the Buddhist story of the man hanging over a cliff by a vine. How'd that story go?

Tim

I remember it. Wow, what a story! There's a tiger on top of the cliff and there's a tiger on the bottom of the cliff. And if that wasn't bad enough, there's a mouse gnawing away at the vine that the man is holding on to. The man realizes that he's clearly doomed. But at that moment he sees a strawberry hanging from the side of the cliff. He plucks the strawberry and bites into it, and then says how delicious it is.

Mark

OK, that's the strawberry moment.

Tim

And then you related it to a certain moment in Quentin Tarantino's film, *Inglorious Bastards*. It's the moment when the English lieutenant, Archie Hicox, realizes that he may be doomed. He's sitting at a table, across from a Nazi officer, who has uncovered Hicox' disguise and has a gun pointed at him. At that moment, Lt. Hicox comments on the excellent quality of the scotch that he's drinking.

Frank

I saw the film. Actually, Lt. Hicox asks the Nazi officer if he would mind if he finished his Scotch. The Nazi agrees to let the lieutenant finish it. Lt. Hicox then says "There's a special place in hell reserved for people who waste perfectly good Scotch."

Mark

Yes, that was a strawberry moment, when Lt. Hicox was fully in the present.

Frank

Yeah, but not for very long.

Dorothy

Do we always have to be doomed like that, in order for us to be in the present?

Frank

You want something for nothing?

Mark

Good point Frank. I suppose there always is a price to be paid. Anyway, Dorothy, we'd been talking about "readiness is all." Maybe "readiness" means always living in the light of truth.

Dorothy

Hopefully, though, I won't be hanging from a vine.

Tim

But I thought that the point of the story, Dorothy, is that we're always hanging from a vine, whether or not we realize it. Isn't that our existential condition?

Mark

You're right, Tim. We're always hanging from a vine. The truth of the matter is that we're all doomed, in the long run. Remembering our mortality puts everything in a sobering light. And so, whatever circumstances dictate, we should always live in the light of truth, open to the blessed moment of grace, when eternity appears in time.

Ricky

That's quite a moment, Dr. Mark. It sounds mysterious.

Mark

Actually, Ricky, at that moment, we stand in the presence of the Great Mystery.

Dorothy

And we solve the mystery?

Mark

Yes and no. We come to know something awesome, but what we

come to know lies beyond understanding. Anyway, the question for us right now is, are we ready? ... Dorothy, are you ready?

Dorothy

I've been dragging my feet for the longest time. But now I'm ready.

Chapter VII
Reflections on the Third Dialogue

Let's take a look at the third and final dialogue, the one from the previous chapter. It begins, in the restaurant, with Frank suggesting that I'm Satan, or the devil. It's been said that many a true word is said in jest. After all, Lucifer--one of the names for the devil--literally means "bringer of light." Knowledge, i.e., light, destroys innocence, calling everything into doubt. It's not surprising, then, that my neighbors detected something threatening to them and notified the proper authorities.

In any case, as the dialogue proceeds, Dorothy and Ricky have something akin to a panic attack. Self-knowledge is ultimately liberating, but first we must realize that we're trapped in a maze of unworkable solutions to life's perplexing problems.

Act I: *A Yogi Becomes Consumed by Road Rage*

What then follows is a review of some of the fundamental contradictions that the group had been exploring. Samantha proceeds to discuss her yoga and meditation retreat. She is concerned over her failure to integrate the elevated consciousness--which found expression as loving kindness, centeredness, and peace that she experienced, at the retreat--into her everyday life. It all began on her drive home from the retreat. Some "jackass" honked his horn at Samantha, causing her to lose her temper. Gone was her inner peace and tranquility.

Ah, but what an interesting question Samantha raised, "On the ride home, I kept on wondering, what the hell was I defending?" Here, indeed, is an inner conflict that almost everyone experiences. On the one hand, we will defend ourselves to the death, sometimes even against the slightest affront to our dignity. On the other hand, we find having to be ourselves--with all the limits intrinsic to whom we are--to be a terribly oppressive burden. Thus we might seek the egolessness that spiritual pursuits promise. So it raised a question, for Samantha and for everyone else: what is this thing called ego, such that we cling to it and yet are burdened by it? It's a certainly an enigma!

Dorothy then states that she's perplexed as to why she dreads public speaking. It's quite mysterious, for Dorothy is not a fearful person. Her dread of public speaking can only be understood by illuminating its symbolic meaning. When we are up there, in front of an audience, we are making a claim to know something. It could be about anything, from how to play better bridge to why students need a new social studies curriculum. But a limited claim of that sort can seem like a claim to know everything! And so, we experience a sense that we are guilty of hubris, of overweening pride--and that everyone in the audience can see this--and then we fear the force of nemesis. That is what we really fear when making a speech.

The group and I then acted out an imaginary dialogue to illustrate a person's fear of public speaking. We discover that the fearful speaker really fears that her or she is being asked a metaphysical question: "Who do you think you are?" If we did have an answer to that question, we wouldn't be anxious anymore when addressing an audience, we wouldn't be too offended by other people's animadversions and we wouldn't fall into self-doubt.

The thing to do, then, is to find our true self, and so to provide the correct answer to the question, "Who do you think you are?" If we were to discover our true self, we would see that the person who we have always taken ourselves to be is akin to a mask that the Self plays in a kind of divine drama.

How, then, to discover our true self? We might discover it while meditating, but it would be better if, in the midst life's turbulence--such as when another person's remarks causes us to fall into self-doubt--that we ask the question, "Who am I?" Yes, who am I such that I am capable of feeling injured and insulted? What exactly am I defending? If, at some point--in the very midst of a difficult situation, such as an altercation or a speech--we begin to laugh, it's because we're beginning to suspect that we might not be who we think we are. It's really not the little ego, but the true self that is laughing at its absurd predicament.

Act II: *To Hell with the Infinite*

I had given everyone an assignment. They had to find something that embodied their mode of being, their way of seeking selfhood, or reality as a self, in the world. It is interesting that selfhood is something that we are continually seeking. It is what really makes the world go round.

We began with Ricky, who offers an example of his refusal to decide upon anything, thus his attraction to buffets, where he gets to eat everything, rather than having to narrow his choice down to merely one selection. What Ricky is seeking is the infinite, and he is pursuing it in the form of the infinitude of possibility. Actuality, on the other hand is always limited. The problem though--as Kierkegaard points out--is that living in possibility is a form of despair, for our life can seem unreal, like an imaginary life. Also, by remaining in the realm of possibility, our life lacks a determinate shape. We are no more than an indeterminate blob. Ricky discovers lack of identity to be the dark side of remaining in possibility.

I must confess that I've had my own long flirtation with possibility. A certain magic trick has always appealed to me for that reason. It's the one in which the magician apparently cuts a rope in half. Presto Chango! The rope remains uncut. Again the magician apparently cuts the rope and once again it is restored to wholeness. To appreciate the symbolic appeal of the trick, we should realize that the word "decide" means to cut. There's something ultimate about deciding, just as there's something ultimate about cutting a rope. Thus the appeal of the trick is that one can make a decision and yet have it magically undone. Thus actuality need not negate the infinitude of possibility. Alas, it's only an illusion. It's akin to a marriage that has been annulled, as if it never happened. Of course, as William James pointed out, not to decide is itself a decision.

Samantha then offers an example of what she has discovered about her mode of being, or at least what Dorothy has discovered. It involves a strange eating ritual, in which Samantha creates a hole in the center of her plate of food, which symbolizes, to her, the infinitude of the void. She is able to eat, and avoid becoming anorexic, by focusing on the hole. We then relate Samantha's wish to be free of limits to her wish to free other people of their limits. She seeks to do this as a Shiatsu masseur. It really intrigues people when they are able to see, in all aspects of their lives, the same mode of being. Samantha is certainly surprised that their exists that connection between her work and her eating. Were she to examine the other aspects of her life, she would discover that same mode of being.

This then leads us to explore the metaphysical grounds of Samantha's eating ritual. Like a lot of people today, she lacks a justification for eating. Consequently, she is beset by a sense of fault. The sense of fault stems from the fact that our meal is at another creature's expense. C.G. Jung has said that when the great symbols, myths, and rituals disappeared from people's consciousness, they became replaced by various neurotic symptoms, all of which are symbolic, like Samantha's eating ritual. The value of our discussion was that it raised questions that Samantha didn't even realize she had.

We then explored Tim interest in hillside landscaping. He is fascinated by the possibility of unifying the horizontal (feminine, earthly) and the vertical (masculine, heavenly) dimensions of existence. Tim views each job that that he and his crew do as an experiment. Will he be able to unify these two great polarities of existence, and thus create a cosmos?

There arose, though, for Tim a number of problems, in his symbolic effort to effectuate this unity. For one thing, if he is landscaping a particular piece of land, Tim's customer might have his or her sense of how the horizontal should be unified with the vertical. Thus Tim does not just wish to offer his own solution, but wishes to intuit what his customer's solution might be. But most of Tim's customers have no interest in exploring, with him, these deeper concerns. They just want a nice looking garden. Consequently, Tim feels that his particular solution to the integration of the horizontal and the vertical is not being appreciated by most of his customers. As such, he feels invisible.

We then explored Tim's sense of invisibility. It led us to consider whether being seen, or understood, is actually a criterion for what it means to be real, and therefore a requirement for selfhood. The British empiricist, Berkeley, had said "to be real is to be seen." Thus if we are not seen, or understood, we feel invisible, like we don't exist.

Throughout these dialogues, we have suggested that exists certain criteria, in which we judge ourselves, to determine whether or not we are real, as a self. The most obvious criterion is spatiotemporal existence. In other words, we must physically exist to be real. We cannot possess an imaginary, or virtual existence. Thus Ricky, if he is to feel real, cannot remain in the realm of possibility.

But there are other criteria by which we judge reality, whether or not we realize it. We have seen, repeatedly, that we hunger for the infinite, unlimited, absolute, and unconditioned. There are a great many ways in which we seek to satisfy that criterion of reality. We might, like Frank, be attracted to the infinite in the form of infinite riches. That would explain his interest in gambling. We also saw, for example, that Samantha's curious eating ritual, with the hole in the center of her food, involved an effort to satisfy the criterion of infinitude.

Another criterion for reality and, therefore, for selfhood, is identity, focus and unity. If we do not give shape, focus, or unity to our life, we will feel like we are nothing at all, a mere formless blob. Our earlier discussion of Plato focused on the identity criteria, for Plato's Ideas, or Forms, conform to the criterion of self-identity.

Finally, we considered whether there is yet a forth criterion or reality and, therefore, of selfhood. To be real, as Tim brought out, is to be seen. The question, then, arises, if these are the four criteria by which we unconsciously use to determine whether or not anything is real, including ourselves, can we satisfy we satisfy all four criteria? Could it be that these criteria of what it means to be real are such that if we satisfy one, we must fail to satisfy another? In other words, are the criteria contradictory?

If so, that might explain why there exists a conservation of suffering. I.E., it could be that we must always leaving out one of the criteria, of reality and therefore of selfhood. Therefore, we can never be fully real. Hence we suffer and seek new solutions. But if we could see that the whole game is impossible, we might let go of it. That would correspond to the moment of awakening.

Act III: *Wading Through the Water*

Upon returning from the restaurant, to my counseling center, Dorothy told us her dream, in which she had the ability to breathe underwater. She makes an insightful connection to what she had expressed several weeks earlier, that she feels like a bar of Ivory soap, floating to the surface of life, coming up for air. The dream image of breathing under water suggests to Dorothy that it might be possible for her to be fully in the midst of an activity and yet still self-aware. Similarly, it might be possible to be in our feelings while simultaneously being able to observe them.

The value of being able to be both in and out, simultaneously, is that we can see who we are. Real insight requires that we are being ourselves while seeing it, at the same moment. For a moment of insight to occur, the light of self-awareness must be there, but not be overpowering.

It's recommended that readers experiment with the right balance, walking along this "razor's edge" between immanence, or immediacy (being in feelings) and transcendence (looking at their feelings). Readers will learn if they are too much on either side. Achieving that balance takes practice. Curiously enough, romantic relationships are often a surrogate for that inner balance. It is very common, in other words, for one person to be in their feelings and the other to be distant, and then to fight it out. Both parties in a relationship need the other side, but wish to make their side--immanence or transcendence--primary. Immanence and transcendence corresponds to feminine and masculine, even though in a relationship a man can sometimes be the immanent one and the woman the transcendent one.

I might add that several months latter the group and I discussed another symbolism that relates to this question of breathing underwater. Ricky came in, one day, with another carbonated which led us to explore the symbolism of soda pop. I remember discussing this symbolism with a teacher of mine, back in college. He astutely suggested that since soda has air trapped in water, the unconscious paradoxically contains consciousness. This is paradoxical because consciousness displaces unconsciousness, just as thinking and reason displaces feelings, and just as air displaces water.

If you become self-conscious, you can no longer be in your feelings; you can no longer go with the flow. Then you are hamstrung by self-doubt. Unselfconscious feeling and conscious deliberation are mutually exclusive, like water and air. The carbonated beverage symbolizes the impossible state of the two polarities of human reality existing together, of being unselfconscious without the danger of drowning. No wonder carbonated beverages are so popular, particularly among the young, who so strongly fear self-consciousness on the one hand, and the power of their dangerous emotions on the other. Carbonated beverages are the magical elixir that gets them through the day.

Haley's dream is apropos, for it deals with the increasing fear of the destructive power of the emotions. It's the one in which she's on an island and the rising waters are threatening to drown her. It signals that the life of feelings and emotions needs to come to an end, or else she will drown in those feelings and emotions. And it indicates that Haley has begun to side with her identity--and with the psychic stability necessary to maintain one's identity--over the emotions.

This leads us to briefly discuss the relationship that has developed between Haley and Ricky. The key to all relationships is grasping how the two people parcel out, amongst themselves, the two sides of a contradiction. For example, we cannot simultaneously be both carefree and serious. But we can agree that one person will be carefree and the other serious. Then the two sides fight it out between themselves, as do Haley and Rickey. (For more on this, please see my book *"Awakening with the Enemy: The Origin and End of Male/Female Conflict."*)

A few weeks latter, we did discuss the perfume that Ricky bought for her, "Contradiction," by Calvin Klein. It's interesting that, for the first time in history, many people are beginning to suspect what the existentialists have known for a long time, that selfhood is riddled with contradictions. For example:

a. We wish to be innocent, immediate and spontaneous, but we also want to be emotionally controlled, self-aware and hip.

b. We wish to have our problems taken care of by another person or by society in general, but we also wish to be self-reliant.

c. We wish to be carefree, but we also wish to be responsible.

d. We wish to be emotionally involved with other people, but we also wish to be independent.

e. We wish to live for the present, but we also wish to be goal-directed and live for the future.

f. We wish to choose a direction, but keep our options open.

g. We wish to take risks, but also wish to play it safe.

And so on. In the past, people parceled out the polar opposites in an institution called marriage. But it is a strong trend of our zeitgeist that each of us seeks to embody all of the polar opposites. Of course, it's no more possible to embody polar opposites than it is possible to make a left turn and a right turn simultaneously. It has been dawning on us that we are caught up in an impossible effort. And so, now there appears on the market a true sign of the times--a woman's perfume, and a men's cologne, by Calvin Klein, with the name, "Contradiction."

The implication of "Contradiction" is that although the effort to achieve selfhood is contradictory, it's OK. The ad suggests that being riddled with contradiction makes us all the more mysterious, ungraspable and fascinating! The fact that Ricky purchased it for Haley is significant. It suggests that his attraction to Haley was founded on the hope that she could embody what he himself couldn't, namely conflicting and contradictory ways of being. Of course, Haley also hoped that Ricky could embody contradictory ways of being. This effort, to have the other person effectuate in his or her life, a unity of life's opposites--and then to relate oneself to this complete being, this syzygy, as Jung call it--is a fundamental source of romantic attraction.

We next discussed Frank's epiphanies about his game of golf. I wont repeat here our analysis of golf. But it's important to consider, again, a question that Frank asks: "...what is the value of discovering the secret symbolic meaning of everything we do or like?" As I told Frank, by illuminating the symbolic meaning of our various interests and pursuits, we can come to discover what it is that we are really seeking for in life. By knowing what we are searching for, we have a much better chance of finding it.

Frank expressed a fear that many people have, that if he discovers the real meaning of an interest or activity that he will lose interest in it. Sometimes, that indeed does happen, and it's a good thing, for our energy is instead channeled into pursuing the real object of desire. But, from my own experience, discerning the symbolic meaning of most interests and activities doesn't necessarily diminish their pleasure.

On the other hand, discerning that baseball is about the journey through life and home again tells us that we cannot undertake that journey on a baseball field, but can only do so in real life, which is a lot more arduous an enterprise than a sport like baseball, and requires a lot more fortitude. There's certainly nothing wrong with playing a game of baseball or watching it on TV, unless of course baseball becomes a surrogate for the real journey through life. Not to undertake that journey means failing to fulfill our destiny. Alas, many people never even make it to first base.

Some months after these dialogues took place, Frank did undergo an attitudinal shift, in regard to the symbolic dimension of everyday life: It really began to fascinate him. What precipitated this shift was returning from a sky trip with one of his legs in a cast. During the months Frank spent recuperating, he devoted his time catching up with the long list of books that I had recommended. There are theologians who speak of the *felix culpa,* or fortunate fall, in regard to the fall of Adam and Eve. Although I'm completely misusing the term, "fortunate fall," it comes to mind when I think of Frank's skiing accident. So it is that when accidents, illnesses and other disasters stop us in our tracks, it often causes our energies to retreat from the world and to turn inward. That inward turning can cause new capacities to emerge, as it did for Frank.

Act IV: *What Gets You Through the Day?*

We began our discussion by distinguishing an aesthetic from an existential relation to knowledge. An aesthete is a person who is always in search of the interesting. Philosophy can, indeed, be very interesting, but if our philosophical search is really a matter of life and death, it's not simply interesting. If we are to get anywhere, we must pursue these life's deeper questions with a do or die attitude.

As it turns out, Detective Mueller has an existential question. It's about the existence of God. How do so many people, who don't believe in God, seem to make it through the day? Obviously, they must have something else that they believe in, that they regard as absolute, or which--on some symbolic level--acts as the ultimate ground of their existence. This is because no one can endure finitude, transiency and mortality for very long. We long for the transcendent and for meaning. Indeed, Saint Augustine writes about the "God-shaped hole" in each of us. As Samantha realizes, she attempts to fill that hole, with all sorts of things, including cookies. Readers should consider what gets them through the day, and if their answer is really adequate or not.

We then explored the metaphysical problems with Samantha's pantheism, the notion that God is the world. On the other hand, the dualistic notion that God is separate from the world leads to the problem of God's connection to the world. Does God participate in the affairs of man, as the theists contend? If so, is he responsible for evil that we encounter? If God is responsible, it leads to some serious theological problems. Or has God merely created the world, as the deists contend? There are serious problems there too. Unfortunately, Detective Mueller had to leave to investigate a murder, but we continued our discussion with him, on a subsequent evening.

Act V: *Are You Ready?*

Tim asks the question: "How should we live?" I suggested that we should live such that we are open to clues to life's mysteries. Not everyone regards life as a mystery story. That is unfortunate, for life's a lot more interesting and exciting if we realize that it's a mystery story beyond all measure, the greatest of detective adventures.

A related answer to the question of how to live is the notion of readiness, which we find to be both Hamlet's answer and that of the Boy Scouts, with their notion of being prepared. Readiness for what? In the context of the current enterprise, it means readiness to encounter major insights, which can often be devastating.

Samantha then asks a rather important question: "You were talking about clues before. How can I tell that something's a real clue?" If we can't determine that something we're desiring or doing has a practical value, then it probably has a symbolic significance. It's important to decipher our symbolic interests and activities, for they can offer us clues to the obscure object of human desire. This prompts Tim to ask whether it may be the case that the obscure object of desire involves a desire for contradictory things. The answer to that is yes and no. The effort to grasp the obscure object of human desire leads to contradiction.

The dialogue ends with the question of what it would mean to live fully in the present moment, indeed to live so intensively that we do not suffer from our ever-present sense of lack. If we experience such a full moment--I called it a strawberry moment--it seems to arrive as a moment of grace. What, though, can precipitate that moment of grace? Living in the full awareness of our existential plight is the best that we can do to invite strawberry moments.

Mind-blowing Questions for Readers to Explore

Here are ten more questions to put in your pipe and smoke. If you channel all of your energy into answering a good many of the questions that appear in this book, the resulting inner illumination will transform your world.

1. As Samantha realized, on the way home from the yoga center, consciousness is labile. In other words, it won't stay in one place, but shifts up and down. Alas, mostly it comes down to a lower level, after we have had a moment of insight. Why do you think that we have trouble staying at a higher level? What sort of practices might be done to elevate your consciousness back up to higher levels?

2. Consider a time when someone offended you and you became angry. What exactly were you defending? How is it that someone was able to put you into enough self-doubt such that you needed to defend who you are?

3. Consider the question that we explored, in relation to Dorothy's fear of public speaking, "Who do you think you are?" Consider that you've been asked that question. Seriously contemplate it and then attempt to answer it.

4. In the last dialogue, both Ricky and Samantha express themselves and their problems through their eating. Ricky does so through his preference for buffets and Samantha does so through her odd eating ritual, in which she creates a hole in the center of her dish of food. Examine closely your own eating. Think about your food preferences, as well as any foods that you dislike. What does it say about you? (You might find it useful to have someone videotape one of your typical meals.)

5. What was the scariest nightmare you've ever had? Even if it occurred long ago, it might still bear on your present concerns. What might be its significance?

6. We discussed Samantha's work as a masseur and Tim's work as a landscape gardener. Both activities proved to have a certain symbolic significance for them. Now reflect upon the work that you've done. Can you discern that it has had a

certain symbolic interest for you? It could be that what drew you to the work was symbolic, but once you engaged in the actual work, it proved to be bereft of the symbolic meaning that drew you to it, which resulted in disillusionment and a loss of energy.

7. In this book's introduction, I had suggested that any seemingly little thing--such as lost golf ball or a toasted corn muffin--can be a doorway into the deepest questions and can lead to wisdom and enlightenment. Indeed, it's possible to analyze that we do to reach the most fundamental questions. It's possible because everything about us expresses the entirety of who we are. That's why a perceptive actor or a film director can capture a characters entire way of being through only a single gesture--the way he or she holds a cigarette, enters through a door, or straightens a hat. Start with anything that you observe about yourself and analyze it as far as you can, in terms of the fundamental criteria of what it means to be real. Then attempt the same with something else that you observe about yourself.

8. Our talk with Detective Mueller led us to ask, "What get's you through the day?" How do you seek to overcome life's finitude and transiency? I.E., how do you attempt to fill the God-shaped hole that St. Augustine says is in each of us?

9. Are you a monist? A dualist? A pluralist? A pantheist? A theist? A deist? An atheist? An agnostic? How has your theological views influenced other areas of your life? How is it that you arrived at your view? Through reason? Through a leap of faith? Or maybe your views are the product of dark, unilluminated, psychological motives.

10. In the last act, we explored the question of readiness, which both Hamlet and the Boy Scouts share, in the form of preparedness. (And the Girl Scouts too.) And so the question is: Are you, dear reader, ready?

Part II

Essays Found at the Bottom of a Cocktail Glass

Thanks to recent technological advances, I (or a virtual Mark Dillof) may soon be able to pop out of the book that you hold in your hands. Then, as you peruse certain passages, I, the author, could grab you, the reader, by your collar, slam you against the wall, and say, "Hey, I'm talking to you! What's your answer to the deep questions I've raised? And don't jive me about your being just a casual reader or a book reviewer. OK, buddy, lets start with a simple question: What's your answer to the riddle of existence?"

In lieu of interrogating you myself, I've created questions following each reading. To truly answer them, you must enter your soul's interior space, where your inner light hangs harshly overhead, as the dread spirit prepares to grill you. "Wait a second, Dr. Dillof," you say. "I was expecting a pleasant, feel-good, self-help book. Interrogation? Why, this is an outrage! I demand to have my lawyer present!" If your lust for life is intense enough, you'll give your inner lawyer the boot and engage in some serious existential cogitations. The dialogues, essays and the questions following each will shed light on your basic plan to achieve happiness and fulfillment. You may soon be able to discern whether or not it's even viable. (Vegas will give you 1000 to 1 odds that it isn't.)

In any case, each essay is a doorway into the depths. The first is about the conservation of suffering. It's a propitious place to begin, for it opens the door to the enigma of human dissatisfaction, leading us to wonder what we're really seeking in life. What, then, is the obscure object of human desire?

The Conservation of Suffering Principle

"What is it about life that there always seems to be something missing?"

-- Epicurus

The ten-thousand forms of human suffering are but the transformations of a single dark force. Endlessly it displays itself, and yet it remains unknown! At times its existence may be suspected. Surmount any of life's difficulties and another one takes its place. Overcome that problem, and a new problem arises. Human suffering is truly the most elusive of shape-shifters.

In its plasticity, suffering bears a curious resemblance to matter. Like matter, it can be neither created nor destroyed. Efforts to eradicate it succeed only in changing its form. We free ourselves from anxiety but now feel bored. We are no longer lonely but now suffer from conflicts with others. Within these transformations, the magnitude of suffering remains constant. Consequently, no matter what we do to find fulfillment, we still find that our world is "out of joint," that something is lacking. The law guiding these changes is, "The Conservation of Suffering Principle."

The Premise of Life's Comedy

Man's guiding star is his belief that changes can make him happier. He dreams, "My life will improve after I move into the new house, receive a promotion, retire from work. Or after I have something to eat, buy a car or win the contract. Or after my children are grown, the new president takes office, the snow melts, the heat wave ends, we win the war..."

Endless are the images of freedom and fulfillment that captivate us, feeding our hope that tomorrow can be better than today. We are easily mesmerized by the advertiser's siren song, "It's new and improved!" If our faith lies in the new and improved, we have not yet grasped The Conservation of Suffering Principle.

You may protest, "It's obvious that changes do make a difference! If I win the lottery, I won't have to work for my demanding boss. If I move, I'll be free of my noisy neighbors. Progress is possible!" Yes, a change improves our lives in a relative sense, by ending a particular hardship. But here is the rub. We satisfy a desire, or overcome a difficulty, and almost immediately the familiar hunger for "we know not what" returns.

This hunger does not linger, for a mental image soon appears and declares: "I'm really what you're looking for!" Hopeful, we search for what corresponds to the image. Our search might lead us to the distant corners of the globe or perhaps no further than the inner recesses of our kitchen refrigerator. We obtain our desideratum, but immediately our lack returns. Our imagination then cooks up a new magical image.

The cycle of frustrated hunger begins in childhood. The joyous excitement of Christmas Eve is followed by, "Okay. What's next?" after we open the presents. In school, we long to be free of exams. But when summer arrives, we are pursued by the demon of boredom. We grow up, and drunk with love's promise, we are soon sobered by family responsibilities. We look forward to retirement, but when it arrives...

Why Do the New Episodes Seem Like Reruns?

Perhaps you have reached the point in life where you have no expectations. You no longer believe in those magical images that you formerly thought could satisfy you. You are disillusioned. It comes about because you increasingly grasp the identity, or sameness factor, amid a host of differences. You perceive that the changes that occur are merely variations on an all too familiar theme. Consequently, before embarking on the evening's entertainment, you already have anticipated the ensuing "lack." You know, before meeting him, that husband number four will not be essentially different from the first three. On an intuitive level, you apprehend the conservation of suffering.

Disillusionment is potentially a very good thing; it can be the route to spiritual awakening. But unless accompanied by a deeper understanding of life, it usually leads to a spiritual malaise. Your weakened psychic constitution then becomes susceptible to the contagion of world-weariness and cynicism. We hear this cynicism in expressions like: "You just can't win;" or "Six of one, half a dozen of another;" or "Same shit, different day." We suspect that Baudelaire was correct when he wrote, "Life is a hospital, in which all of the patients are continually trying to change beds." For "beds" we can substitute jobs, homes, husbands, etcetera. Mark Twain summed it up when he said, "Life is one damn thing after another." But while many wind up skeptics, if not cynics, they have not gone on to ask why "life is one damn thing after another."

Rounding Up the Usual Suspect Answers

For many people it isn't really a question. Bad things happen and there's no explanation. But they do have sort of an explanation. They presume that something external comes about to ruin one's happiness. In the Biblical tale, Job asks why. But even that profound story begins with the sense that Job was doing quite nicely until tragedy struck. People today are less inclined to blame their gods for their present woes than they are to blame their childhood experiences, parents, past lives, political leaders, society, and so on. In all cases, the implication is that the negative came and eclipsed what is normally a sunny state of affairs.

Others assume that they suffer because of something that needs to happen that has not happened, and may never happen. "I haven't met the right person yet," or, "I haven't hit it big." Many people view being a wage earner as equivalent to being a slave on a galley ship. Every week it is decided, by means of the state lottery, who will become a multi-millionaire and leave the ship to live like a king or a queen. The rest of us must go back to our oars, until the next drawing.

Is unhappiness fundamentally due to something in particular--that has or has not happened? If someone were asked why he was unhappy and he answered, "Because I lost my farm," or "Because my dog died," his response would be quite reasonable. If he then declared, "It didn't have to happen!" he would still be right. But he would also be naive, because his focus would only be on his suffering's immediate cause. He would have failed to consider its ultimate cause.

The immediate cause is always something in particular, and the fact that it happened may be purely accidental. But the fact that we suffer at all--apart from the particular form that our suffering may take--is not accidental. If it's not a lost farm, or a dead dog, it must, out of necessity, be other things, equally negative, that plague us. What is this dark necessity? To discover the ultimate cause of human suffering, we need to perceive--behind the myriad shapes of suffering--the shape-shifter himself.

Good and Bad: Separated at Birth

There must be something intrinsic to life's pleasures, joys and satisfactions that makes them evanescent, thus bringing us back to the state of dissatisfaction. Their evanescent quality is not due to the fact that things fade and then vanish, like flowers with the coming of the winter frost. Time is not the real culprit, because even when life is in full bloom, life disappoints us--especially then. What is it about happiness that makes it evanescent?

Examine the relation between the good things in your life and the bad things. You will discover, not that the bad destroys the good, but that, on the contrary, the good entirely depends upon the bad! The pleasure of eating depends upon the preceding hunger pangs. The pleasure of friendship depends upon the experience of loneliness. Those who most truly appreciate wealth are those who have known poverty. The father in the biblical story showed greater love for his returning prodigal son than for his obedient son who never strayed. Those who have been to death's door can most appreciate life. As Schopenhauer noted, "good" is nothing more than a synonym for, "the removal of the bad."

As the bad departs, with the satisfied desire or the solved problem, so does the good! When our hunger vanishes, the pleasure of eating fades. The pleasure of a warm house vanishes as we forget what it was like to be shivering outside. Forgetting our loneliness, we begin to take our friend for granted. Our newfound joy in being alive diminishes as our near-death encounter begins to fade from memory. Positive and negative are inextricably joined. For as the bad departs, the good must also take leave of us. And as the fleeting moment of satisfaction departs, our ever-present sense of lack returns.

What makes happiness evanescent, therefore, is that it is always dependent upon the awareness of a concomitant dissatisfaction. Consequently, the very achievement of happiness, which ends the particular dissatisfaction, paradoxically ends our happiness.

We shall briefly explore some of the startling implications of the correlative nature of good and bad. Then we shall face the ultimate question, "What lies behind our unremitting sense of dissatisfaction; what do we really want?"

Critique of Pure Sunshine

Insights can be unsettling, sobering, and wondrous--all three at once. That is what it feels like to perceive deeply that the good has no reality apart from the bad, that the two are joined at the hip. The perception is unsettling because it undermines our hope for a happy life, free of hardships and woes.

A person who concludes that a happy life isn't possible, because the conditions are not right, will either feel anxious, if he still has hope, or depressed, if he has lost hope. But to realize that even under the best of circumstances, happiness isn't attainable, because the problem is intrinsic to the nature of happiness itself, is deeply unsettling and disorienting. That's because one's guiding star, the pursuit of happiness, no longer shines so brightly.

A person might still seek to be happier, but "happier" pales before one's original inner image of an everlasting and unalloyed state of perfect happiness, the happiness suggested in the 1930's song, *Blue Skies*. When there is "nothing but blue skies," suffering soon returns in the form of a restless boredom. Shakespeare's Prince Hal observes: "Nothing is more unendurable than a succession of sunny days." But this is the very thing that most people earnestly, and naively, seek.

The Monster Returns!

One of the salient features of modern life is the effort to deny the inseparability of these polar opposites, the good and the bad. This is seen in the attempt to have sex without the responsibilities that result from procreation, to have money without work, to create without having to clean up the consequent mess that is intrinsic to creation; in other words, to divide the part of life that we want from the part that we do not want.

For example, since the negative dimension of acquiring things is paying for them, a person may seek to separate the good (buying) from the bad (paying) by means of a credit card, or in the case of the government, by means of deficit spending. When the bad returns, it usually returns with a wallop. It's as if the bad were lonely, and comes rushing back to join its missing half, the good.

Much of modern life involves efforts to keep the good while transferring the bad to someone else. It is as if we were involved with a giant game of "hot potato," or "tag, you're it." The gods on Mount Olympus daily witness the comical spectacle of humans scurrying around, trying to reap life's benefits, while sneaking the bill into the other fellow's pocket.

The advance of technology is, to a large extent, driven by this effort to enjoy the goods of life without experiencing a concomitant bad. We can have heat and hot water, for example, without having to chop wood and fetch water. But not chopping wood means we become flabby, we do not appreciate the warmth of our house nearly as much, and of course there is the fuel bill.

Technology has caused the negative to transform in a more frightening way, creating problems of a global magnitude. These include: air and water pollution, as well as the threat of nuclear and chemical warfare--to say nothing of traffic jams, minds weakened from excessive television watching and an alienating loss of contact with life's fundamental realities. This isn't a Luddite argument against technology; our concern here is to explore how the effort to be free of the bad causes the bad to return in new and monstrous forms.

Another example of the effort to separate the good from the bad is "positive thinking." Motivational speakers are the evangelists of positive thinking, but everyone from life coaches to business leaders also espouse the gospel. Here is a religion in which negative thoughts are anathematized. Negative thoughts are the product of self-doubt. And self-doubt is the voice of the devil.

Authentic self-doubt springs from genuine insight about the nature of egocentricity, selfhood, and the meaning of life. What we see about ourselves at such moments is often difficult to face. But evolution to higher levels of consciousness is not possible without self-doubt. To flee from self-doubt by means of that self-lobotomy called positive thinking is a sure sign of desperation, both for a person and for a nation.

Good and bad, positive and negative, happiness and sadness, are correlative. They are no more separable than up and down, right and left or heads and tails. The effort to have the good without the bad merely causes the bad to shift its shape and suffering to be conserved.

Giving Two Impostors the Bum's Rush

> *"If you can meet with Triumph and Disaster*
> *And treat those two impostors just the same"*
>
> *-- Kipling*

It is quite sobering to realize that good and bad are interdependent, making it impossible to attain "nothing but blue skies." Paradoxically, this realization, rather than being heavy, is liberating. It makes you feel lighter and happier. That is because, at the moment when false expectations depart, so does the anxiety that you might miss your chance for happiness and the depression over having missed it. This is a great relief! Indeed, if you will daily contemplate the true relation of good and bad, you will begin to feel a rare peace of mind, owing to your un-attachment from ceaseless striving, contending, worry, and strife.

To achieve psychological maturity, we must accept our status as limited, finite, mortal creatures enmeshed in a life of trade-offs, realizing that we can't have it all, accepting that the bad comes with the good. On the other hand, if that is the extent of our aspirations as a human being, then we have shrunk, or settled. Shrinking involves a degeneration of spirit. The longing for being, fulfillment, happiness, the infinite, can never really be abandoned. But we can change the level in which we seek fulfillment. To get to a new level, requires that we clarify our desires. It's vital, then, to answer Epicurus' question, and discover what is really lacking, for only then can we end our ever-present hunger. Let us, then, continue on this detective adventure, hot on the trail of the elusive shape-shifter of human suffering.

The Void Within

We've seen that when the bad departs, the good follows suit. What happens then? The sense of lack returns, but in a new form. As the satisfaction of entering a warm house diminishes, we may search for something to eat, even if we are not really hungry. As the pleasure of eating palls, we are restless for distraction. This perception led Schopenhauer to propose that lack is what is most fundamental to human existence.

Schopenhauer suggests that each person has within him something akin to a void, a void that must be filled with suffering. We solve a major problem, and the void is immediately refilled, since nature abhors a vacuum. The void might be filled with a number of smaller problems, but filled it must. Schopenhauer's metaphor of an inner void is useful, since it calls our attention to a fundamental reality of human existence. But his metaphor still leaves unanswered the question: "What are we lacking?"

From Cosmic Hunger to Concrete Desires

We are involved here in an unusual enterprise: a self-conscious inquiry into "what is lacking." It is important that we distinguish this self-conscious search from the usual unreflective type of search continually undertaken by the mind. We are all involved in an unreflective search, whether or not we realize it. Nor do we have any choice but to carry on this search. Our unremitting hunger for something--we know not what--drives us on. Our search for what is lacking might be envisioned as a hamburger, the ideal mate, a new career, or perhaps a new world order. Then, enraptured by this image, off we go in pursuit of the hitherto obscure object of desire.

Consider an analogy. Freud stated that anxiety is formless or "free floating." Anxiety presents a threat to your existence, one you are unable to fend off in a practical fashion. If you are anxious over the inevitability of death, or the threat of meaninglessness, what can you do? An unlisted telephone number or health insurance will not save you from meaninglessness. Freud said that we transform such anxieties into fear. Fear is a threat to our existence with a particular shape. Therefore, fear is manageable. If you fear snakes on your property, you can build a fence around it. If you fear flying in a plane, you can take the bus.

The negativity we are discussing is more fundamental than anxiety, which is a threat to our "being." This original negativity has the character not of a threat, but of an ever-present hunger. Like anxiety, the primordial negativity or lack is formless, shapeless and inchoate. If this underlying negativity remains indeterminate, it is ungraspable. You are probably familiar with those moments when you find yourself restless, but haven't any idea what you wish to do. You are bored, but not bored with anything in particular. You are longing for something, but have no idea what it is. You long to be in desire, for desire is always directed towards an object.

How does the mind respond to this painful cosmic hunger? Just as the mind seeks to transform anxiety into fear, it seeks to transform the primordial and indeterminate sense of lack into concrete desires. It seeks to determine what is missing, in the hope that this painful hunger may be satisfied. Consequently, the primordial lack is transformed into any of a thousand and one images. Each is a picture, or representation, of what we perceive to be fundamentally lacking.

Thus is born the great variety of human desires. We then have an object for our hunger.

Desire, in turn, is the parent of the legion of cravings, fears, quandaries, griefs, frustrations, and terrors--all the forms of misery that plague us. Consider the human condition. We lust after what we don't have, fearful that we might not be able to acquire it, or disappointed that we failed to acquire it, or jealous of someone else who obtained it. We worry that we will lose what we already have, or are grieved that we actually did lose it or are disappointed that what we wanted turned out to be empty. The Buddha said that everything, the entire world, is on fire! It's burning from the heat of desire.

And what is the source of all our suffering? What we think is lacking is not what is truly lacking. Consequently, we are driven in dizzying circles by the whirlwind of endless desires, never finding and satisfying the source of all desire, our fundamental hunger. So we are back to our question: "What are we lacking?"

I've Been Expecting You, Mr. Bond

Our search for the ground of the negative requires the collection of clues and the identification of a culprit, as in any other detective or spy story. We, like James Bond, are on a mission to find "Mr. Big." At first we only encounter Mr. Big's soldiers or henchmen. These are the legion of particular negativities that we encounter in life. If we spend our time, as most people do, battling with life's particular problems, we never win, for Mr. Big has endless numbers of soldiers at his command.

If we are unable to cut through appearances, to perceive the true nature of this protean monster, a hopeless war of attrition ensues, and we die of exhaustion. This is the usual pathetic scenario for human existence. The heroic alternative is to find the elusive Mr. Big, and discover his true identity. If we are to be free of suffering, we must look beyond suffering's myriad expressions, and see the essential negativity.

But how can we know the ultimate lack if it is formless and characterless? It is possible for us to "read" our delusive images. By reading these images, we mean penetrating the depths of our various desires and difficulties to see what it is that we really want. This is comparable to finding and confronting Mr. Big's higher-ups, our more fundamental formulations of life's negatives.

What is a more fundamental formulation? It is to see, for example, that your romantic difficulties result, not from the flaws or faults of your partner, but from the way you relate to the opposite sex, no matter who he or she may be. Deeper still is to see that the problem lies in the nature of erotic union in general. Each formulation or, to continue our analogy, each higher-ranking officer, seems to be more dangerous than the last. You realize, in other words, that the problem runs more deeply than you expected.

It is one thing to perceive that your difficulties are due to the war between the sexes. It is quite another to perceive that your difficulties stem from the very requirements of selfhood being contradictory. In the first case, you might attempt to work out new arrangements of male and female union. But if you see that erotic problems are a species of a fundamental negativity--one cutting to the core of human existence-- you realize that you are faced with a far more difficult question.

If you manage to survive each successively more powerful opponent, you enter into the most dangerous region, a place where no ordinary mortal dares set foot. You enter the inner sanctum of Mr. Big, or to use a more classical analogy, into the center of the maze, where you encounter the Minotaur. If you survive this encounter, you will finally come to know the answer to Epicurus' question. And, you will have overcome your suffering.

Mission: Impossible

How are we to begin our search for Mr. Big? If we become self-conscious of our desires, we see that the exchange of troubles at the core of our being--to use Schopenhauer's analogy--is not arbitrary. There is logic to the sequence of shapes that the negative assumes. To read this logic would be comparable to deciphering the code that determines the shape of human suffering.

Examining our life, we perceive that our solutions to previous problems are often the very source of our present difficulties! How startling, indeed how downright sublime, to catch the Proteus of human suffering in the midst of his transformations! Psychoanalysis, for example, in freeing us from feelings of guilt, has saddled us with the problem of meaninglessness; having becoming a responsible person we now no longer feel carefree; having managed to escape the kinds of conflicts that our parents experience in their relationship, we have become saddled with problems endemic to a new kind of marriage. It takes some time to recognize the haunting connection between our present problems and those we have solved.

Suspecting that solving one problem simply causes another one to appear doesn't mean we give up on finding a solution. Economists know, for example, that raising the tax rate initially brings in more revenue, but, in fact, it may ultimately shrink revenue when marginal businesses become insolvent. Still they hope to finesse the delicate balances in the economy.

Puzzles and games can symbolically picture to the mind our effort to "get it together." There are certain puzzles in which, if we get one piece in order, we may cause another piece to be out of place. Such puzzles dramatize this dilemma: if we are not careful in our solution, the negative will reappear somewhere else in our life. There is a sense that although a solution is difficult to effectuate, it is possible.

The Rubik's Cube puzzle accords with our a priori sense that life starts out "whole," and that somehow it all gets disarranged. The primordial unity is symbolized by each of the colors being in place. The blues are on one side, the reds on another, greens on a third and so on. The jumbling of the cubes has a mythic significance. It symbolizes life hopelessly mixed up in a multiplicity, a chaos, or just a mess.

It's akin to Anaximander's cosmogony. There's an original unity called, "The Boundless," out of which emerges the four elements: earth, air, fire and water. The elements then fight with each other, creating strife and chaos. Humpty Dumpty tells the same story. The One, the cosmic egg, falls, splinters and splatters into a mess. Whether the truth is told cosmologically, mythically, in a puzzle, or in a children's nursery rhyme, it's the same story. We start out whole; life becomes a mess. Somehow it must come together again if we are to inhabit a universe, and not a chaos of conflicting opposites.

What is the driving force of your life? Is it not the assumption that you can "get it together?" If you run into difficulties, you think that you must work harder or that you need to be cleverer. You are confident that you have a solution, but then you realize that your new solution has caused--continuing our Rubik's Cube analogy--one of the colors to be misplaced. You realize that you do not have it together. You succeeded in getting your mother-in-law to vacate your premises, but now you have no one to baby-sit. The result is that your suffering is conserved. But "hope springs eternal;" you remain confident, and try again.

Over time, the dark thought may come to you that pertinacious efforts to make life work are to no avail. This is because in life, unlike in Rubik's Cube, it is not simply a matter of difficulty in getting it together, in bringing the conflicting opposites into a unity. You suspect that it cannot be unified at all, that what you are attempting to accomplish in life is simply contradictory.

Human life is riddled with contradiction. For example, men require women to be feminine, unreflective and immediate. But women are then criticized if they aren't self-directed, reflective and responsible. And they are urged to be both ways, not alternately, but simultaneously. Likewise, men are often urged to be strong and directive, but they also are asked to show feelings and to be both ways simultaneously. The task that men and women demand of each other is no more possible than making a left turn and a right turn at the same time. The contradictions that appear in relationships are but a species of an ultimate contradiction, which we have yet to uncover.

Could it be that the game that we have been handed to play, at birth, is a contradiction? Will there always be Rubik's cubes out of order? Must all attempts at a solution merely alter the form that suffering takes? Is man's effort to find self-fulfillment really a "mission impossible?" For existentialists, such as Jean Paul-Sartre, the answer to these questions is a dreadful "yes." What if Sartre was correct in his dark assessment of the human condition? Where, then, lies the road beyond existentialism?

The Road Paved with Paradoxes

The boon of self-knowledge turns out to be quite different than what you may initially had hoped it to be. It doesn't give you "an answer." On the contrary, it questions the answer that you are already living and which is not proving satisfactory. An "answer" is an inner image of what you hope would bring you fulfillment. It is an image that guides everything you do. It is the hidden blueprint of your life.

Examining this blueprint allows you to know if your answer can succeed. Perceiving that your answer is contradictory allows you to abandon it. Nothing is more liberating than abandoning a "mission impossible." Here, then, is a great paradox: The perception that what you're trying to accomplish is impossible--because it's predicated on a contradiction--elevates your awareness to a level beyond the contradiction and therefore beyond despair. The silver that can be found lining every cloud is liberating self-knowledge.

Afterthought

We have suggested that there exists a level of consciousness beyond the force-field of the conservation of suffering. It's been called, "the still point of a turning world." The Japanese philosopher Nishita described it when he wrote, "My joy and my sorrow do not touch my peace." The way to get there is not by proceeding directly to that which we desire--freedom, immortality, bliss, peace of mind and higher consciousness. Rather, the secret is to proceed in the opposite direction, into the depths. Dante learned from Virgil that the exit out of Hell is to be found at its very center. Likewise, the descent into our interior "heart of darkness," which we enter with penetrating questions, results in illuminating insights that convert suffering into Self-knowledge.

Epicurus' question, "Why is there always something missing?"--which is an intimation of The Conservation of Suffering Principle--delivers us from complacency, renewing our spirit by propelling us on a detective adventure. In a typical detective story, the sleuth knows what is missing, but lacks knowledge of its whereabouts, who has stolen it, and so on. Here, on the other hand, something was first reported missing 2,500 years ago in Greece, and we still don't know what it is! Yet it's vital that we find it or else resign ourselves to, "a life of quiet desperation." All other mysteries pale before this most perplexing of life's mysteries, the enigma of human suffering.

Questions for the reader to ponder

You've already been asked about the conservation of suffering, so there's no need to ask you again. Well maybe just one small question: At this moment, what are you really lacking?

Living in the Moment for a Moment

"Sufficient unto the day is the evil thereof."

-- Mathew 6:34

"There's a special rung in hell reserved for people who waste good scotch."

-- The film *"Inglorious Bastards"*

From an early age, our energies become channeled and directed towards a series of goals. As each goal is completed a new one immediately appears. If we do not have a project to complete, we become restless. Such is our Faustian nature. Thus it's the future where we locate our happiness and fulfillment. As Alexander Pope expressed it, "Man never is, but always to be blest."

What makes us future-oriented? We wouldn't be so, were it not that the present always appears lacking, incomplete and insufficient. What's really lacking about the present? That is a profound mystery. Indeed, a famous Zen master used to ask his students: "At this moment, what is lacking?"

The fact that human being are perpetually discontent is the spur to technological advancement, as well as continual changes made on a personal level. But we may begin to suspect, after having lived a certain amount of time, that our plans and projects will not lead to the imagined state of fulfillment. On the contrary, they are bound to lead to more insufficient moments. We might then decide to no longer be deluded by images of future happiness. That would mean living fully in the present moment. Alas, I've never met anyone who can live in the moment, for more than a brief moment, now and then.

The Present Moment Comes as a Surprise

That said, there are moments--and they are relatively rare--when we do find ourselves living fully in the moment. They usually surprise us. It would appear such moments cannot be willed. They are, some would say, a gift of grace. (It's been said that the present is, indeed, a "present," i.e., a gift.) Sometimes, the perception of intense beauty can grab us and then we are in the present moment. But we can chase beautiful sunsets for all our days and still not be graced by such moments.

There are catalysts, besides beauty, that sometimes invite such moments. One is the taste of food, but the context must be right. No spice quite brings out the flavor of food, as does danger and doom. There is an ancient story, from the East, that illustrates my point. It is about a man hanging over a cliff, by a vine. On the top of the cliff lies a tiger and down below is another tiger. To make matters hopeless, there is a mouse gnawing at the vine. The man realizes that he is clearly doomed.

But, just at that moment, the man notices a strawberry growing from the side of the cliff. He plucks the strawberry and bites into it, commenting on how delicious it is. This tale is often used in Zen Buddhism to illustrate our existential fate and we may transcend it through an embrace of the moment. In his *Confessions*, Leo Tolstoy discusses the story, but the story doesn't seem to do much for him. Perhaps, the problem was that he was only reading about such a moment, rather than actually experiencing it.

The recent Quentin Tarantino film, Inglorious Bastards (2009) [Warning: plot spoiler ahead] has that sort of "strawberry moment," except in this case it is not a strawberry but a glass of scotch that tastes so good. And instead of tigers, there are Nazis. The heroic protagonist of this encounter is British Lt. Archie Hicox, who is disguised, with his comrades as Nazi officers. He is seated at a table, in a bar, across from Nazi Major Dieter Hellstrom. Here is how the dialogue proceeds:

Living in the Moment for a Moment

> ***Major Dieter Hellstrom:*** *That was the sound of my Walther pointed right at your testicles.*
>
> ***Lt. Archie Hicox:*** *Why do you have a Luger pointed at my testicles?*
>
> ***Major Dieter Hellstrom:*** *Because you've just given yourself away, Captain. You're no more German than that scotch. Lt.*
>
> ***Archie Hicox:*** *Well, Major...*
>
> ***Bridget von Hammersmark:*** *Major...*
>
> ***Major Dieter Hellstrom:*** *Shut up, slut. You were saying?*
>
> ***Lt. Archie Hicox:*** *I was saying that that makes two of us. I've had a gun pointed at your balls since you sat down.*
>
> ***Stg. Hugo Stiglitz:*** *That makes three of us. [Stiglitz takes Hellstrom by the shoulder and aggressively forces a gun against his crotch] And at this range, I'm a real Frederick Zoller.*
>
> ***Major Dieter Hellstrom:*** *Looks like we have a bit of a sticky situation here.*

The situation, which is a prelude to a Mexican standoff, is desperate and doomed. And so here come the strawberry moment:

> ***Lt. Archie Hicox:*** *Well, if this is it, old boy, I hope you don't mind if I go out speaking the King's?*
>
> ***Major Dieter Hellstrom:*** *By all means, Captain.*
>
> ***Lt. Archie Hicox:*** *[picks up his glass of scotch] There's a special rung in hell reserved for people who waste good scotch. Seeing as I might be rapping on the door momentarily... [drinks it] I must say, damn good stuff, Sir. [sets his glass down and smokes his cigarette]*

There are those who would argue that Lt. Hicox is an aesthete, up to the very last moment. He was, after all, a film critic. But aesthetes do not walk fearlessly into the Valley of the Shadow of Death without

269

crapping out. There is, no doubt, something deeper going on here. Lt. Hicox has had a moment of grace, a moment of perfect appreciation of the goodness of life and, if one is religious, the goodness of God. He knows, at that moment, what King David tells us in Psalm 34:8, "Oh, taste and see that the LORD is good!" Yes, the psalmist recommends that we taste it, whether it be as a strawberry, a glass of scotch, a hamburger or simply the air that we breathe.

Readiness for Grace

> *"...for I love thee, O Eternity!"*
> --Nietzsche

Mystics have spoken of the eternal moment. How paradoxical that one can experience eternity, for example, on Tuesday, at 3:00PM, Eastern Standard Time! And yet, odd though it may sound, it is confirmed by anyone who has experienced it. At the eternal moment, past and present collapse into the present and there is nothing lacking, for at such a moment we attain that which we truly desire, eternity.

The paradox of grace is that we cannot will it, but are commanded to live so as to be capable of receiving it. Elsewhere, I wrote about readiness as Hamlet meant it--"Readiness is all." And as the Boy scouts meant it--"Be prepared." To be ready is too live in the light of truth. Then whatever circumstances dictate--and hopefully we won't be hanging from a vine or have a gun pointed at our groin, but one never knows--we shall be open to the moment of grace, the blessed moment of eternity in time.

Questions for the reader to ponder

1. Have you ever had a "strawberry moment," one in which your awareness of your mortality caused you to live fully in the present? What occasioned it? How long did it last? Were there other occasions when you were fully in the present, such as when experiencing beauty or sublimity?

2. Dostoevsky had a strawberry moment when facing a firing squad. He was set free at the last minute. If I recall, he wrote that the moment lasted for a number of weeks. Read his novel, *The Idiot*, for Dostoevsky's description of it, and his chagrin over it fading away. What do you think it is that drives us out of the present moment? Might it be that the restless hunger returns, the inner search for the obscure object of desire, which we mistake for anything from a donut to a stock option?

3. A brush with death isn't the only event that can occasion a strawberry moment. When I was in my late twenties and living in New York City, I met some friends, one dreary, rainy Sunday evening, for dinner in Chinatown. I neither enjoyed the meal nor the dinner conversation. Furthermore, I was feeling miserable about everything, from my dead-end job to a failed relationship. After the meal, I got on a long line, with my friends, to pay the bill. I then heard a loud crying. I turned around to see a baby boy, of about two years old. His parents tried everything to make him happy--food, toys, hugs--but the angry baby just kept screaming. Ah, it was my fate to be standing in line right next to the shrieking baby. Then the oddest thing happened: My mood suddenly shifted from misery to joyous elation! I started laughing and told my friends how wonderful it was to be alive. They thought that I had gone nuts.

   That moment now makes sense. In a flash of insight, I had seen myself, and all of humanity, as that petulant baby-- forever miserable, despite life's continual efforts to please us. I've always felt sympathy for those suffering, but how puerile, I thought, to be sour about our wondrous earthly existence! My elation lasted for about twenty minutes, but faded as I entered Chinatown's Canal Street subway station. A number of questions have since emerged, including: What had happened when I entered the subway station? Perhaps, more puzzling than the arrival of joy is the return of our discontent. How does our awareness shift downward, in this way?

4. A friend of mine, a Protestant minister, likes the term "Sabbath moment," for he sees the Sabbath as the day of the week when--due to God having rested--we're capable of enjoying the restful bliss of eternity. Imagine having a Sabbath moment on a Wednesday morning, on our rush-hour commute to work! Most of us badly need respite from our temporal anxieties. What can we do to cultivate Sabbath moments?

Nuts Are for Anarchists, Organic Foods for Fascists

When is a hamburger not a hamburger? When the activity of eating is influenced by a host of complex concerns, from emotional needs to philosophical worldviews. For example, if we are religious, we might say grace before a meal, obey kosher laws, or fast. Aesthetic values also influence what and how we eat, which is why there is an art of cooking. But what interests us here are not the obvious social and cultural aspects of food, but the hidden meanings behind our choice of any particular food. For it is these hidden meanings that we are really seeking to consume.

Some "Ruminations" on the Secret Meaning of Food

The key to the psychology of eating lies in the equation "you are what you eat." For example, if we feel frustrated, we might wish to consume crunchy foods, such as nuts or potato chips. Crunchy foods are symbolic of the hard, rigid, limiting and confining structures of society. Our destruction of the nuts is, therefore, a symbolic victory over these confining social and political structures.

Of course, very few people who eat potato chips are aware of their anarchistic longings, at least on a symbolic level. They might claim, "Well, potato chips just taste good." Such denials of deeper meanings derive from: 1. Lack of introspection. 2. The false claim that one's actions--including one's food choices--are made solely on rational grounds. 3. Fear of life's depths. We trust the reader does not suffer from these intellectual maladies or else what follows may be a bit hard to digest.

The desire for psychological wholeness is another fundamental need. That would explain the desire for wholegrain foods. Thus, if you want wholeness in your life, you must eat whole foods. Indeed, there a major food chain called "Whole Foods" that caters to this unconscious demand. It is absurd, though, to think that eating whole foods will make us whole people. But, in lieu of any other answer to the question of how to be a whole person, we turn to symbolic solutions.

The quantity of food is also symbolically important. It has been said that the reason why gluttony is one of the seven deadly sins is that it is essentially an effort to be God, by symbolically consuming the entire world. But, no matter how much we shovel into our stomach, the inner void still remains. Being filled full cannot be a successful surrogate for being fulfilled.

By contrast, the anorexic seeks to avoid the fault involved with eating by refusing to eat. The vegetarian, not quite as extreme, does eat, but only vegetables. The fault, of which we speak, involves the fact that eating involves a killing of some sort. Even if we were not the one's who hunted or slaughtered the animals, the act of killing is still there psychologically. Vegetarianism, on the face of it, is motivated by compassion. And there are certainly vegetarians for whom compassion is the only motivation. But most vegetarians are driven by a certain quasi-moral perfectionism and hubris. After all, the Judeo-Christian god gives his blessing to man, to eat animals. Even those who have not read the Bible or who are declared atheists still share in what Jung called the "Collective Unconscious." A vegetarian is, therefore, claiming to be morally superior to God.

The Mystique of the Organic and Fascism

What are we to make of the interest that many people have, in organic foods? It is an expression of something much larger. The interest in the organic, the holistic, and the natural expresses a certain vision of life, along with a concomitant critique of the modern world. This criticism is that those living today have become separated, or alienated, from nature and its primal rhythms. An allied criticism is that the world has become too mechanized. What comes to mind, in such criticisms, is that period in cultural history, occurring in the Nineteenth Century, known as Romanticism.

But there was another movement, that emerged in the early part of the Twentieth Century, that also glorified the organic the holistic and the natural. That movement, which was founded by the Italian dictator Benita Mussolini, was Fascism. Fascists are critical of traditional Western liberalism and individualism, for they contend that it alienates us from nature, society, the state and the nation, which fascists contend are more real than the individual. Fascism is, therefore, a form of totalitarianism. What is key here is that the totalitarians, of all stripes, seek to appeal to our need for unity, even at the price of negating our individuality and freedom. Unity is to be found by joining together with others, in various social projects, created by the state.

Like Romanticism, Fascism is thoroughly anti-intellectual. It regards a life of feelings as more authentic and better than a life of thought. Fascists view the modern world as fallen, or decadent. They see it as a fall from a state of purity, wholeness, and goodness that supposedly once existed in the world. But whereas Romantics mostly yearn for Paradise lost, fascists often have a political program for national revival.

Are those captivated by the mystique of the organic, wholeness and the holistic fascists? Indeed, the appeal of such foods is certainly not just about health, but about losing the burdensome sense of being a separate individual, alienated from both nature and from other people. Organic broccoli and carrots, for example, are therefore not just broccoli and carrots. In consuming them, a person is symbolically consuming unity with the world and, as such, becoming a whole person. If only it was so easy, but it isn't, for after the meal we remain just as alienated.

Slimy Foods

We can also gain valuable insights into who we are, based on the foods that we dislike. For example, many people have an aversion to that which is sticky, or viscous. We speak of a sticky situation, a sticky wicket, or say a person has a slimy handshake. The philosopher Jean Paul Sartre explained that when we try to do things in the world, to create things, to make the world into our own image, or objectify ourselves, the world has a curious habit of grabbing us in the process and limiting our freedom. When we seize the world, it sticks to us.

Psychologically, we fear that the world threatens to suck us back into itself. That is why many products advertise, "No muss, no fuss," "No wax buildup," "Melts in your mouth, not in your hand," appealing to the desire for the clean and stick-free.

But here we come to a paradox, for creation itself is a slimy affair. Consider the egg. What could be more sticky and slimy? There's the expression about getting egg on our face--not a good thing. But although eggs' stickiness threatens to limit our freedom, they are also a powerful symbol of creation. Vance Packard, in his classic, *The Hidden Persuaders* (1957), tells how in the 1950s Betty Crocker created an instant cake mix to appeal to the practical concerns of busy women. But sales of the cake mix were disappointing. What went wrong? Women who used the product had the unfulfilling sense that they had not created anything. Betty Crocker caught on to what the real problem was and changed their cake mix, requiring housewives to crack an egg into the mix. Why an egg and not flour, sugar, or baking soda? Here, again, eggs are the very symbol of creation itself and gave the housewife the sense that she was creating the cake. And so it is that we might have an ambivalent relation to that messy thing called life and it shows up with our relation to eggs and other sticky foods.

A Fellow with His Own Kosher Law

Sometimes what is disliked is not a particular food, but having certain foods contact each other. Very often, we seem to have our own set own of kosher laws, in that respect. For example, a client of mine recently told me that for breakfast he has eggs and sausage, along with French toast and maple syrup, both on the same plate. He stated that he will first eat the eggs and sausage and then the French toast. But if the maple syrup should touch the eggs and sausage, he will feel a sense of horror, as though he had been defiled.

How can we explain his sense of defilement? I think that my client has a traditional sense of morality, which means first the work, then the desert. To have the desert prior to the work would, therefore, seem immoral. In this case, the French toast, with the sweet maple syrup seemed like a desert. The work was the eggs and sausage. The sausage, in particular, comes from a dead animal. Thus the eggs and sausage symbolized, to my client, the masculine world of hunting, of laboring for one's food. To have the desert prior to the work seemed immoral. Hence he had a sense of defilement--which is really the physical expression of the sting of immorality--over the syrup touching the eggs and sausage.

The Zen of Eating

It is truly amazing that eating--an activity that in animals is simply biological--can be influenced by sophisticated worldviews. Thus, as humans, we do not just eat foods. We consume meanings. There is a Buddhist story of a student asking a Zen master how he should practice Zen. The master replied, "Rest when you're tired, and eat when you're hungry." That's a difficult thing to do! After all, we often eat when we're feeling bored, anxious, unfulfilled, working out inner conflicts, and seeking meaning.

Were we to illuminate the meaning of food in our life, food would become just food, rather than a repository for our hopes, dreams, anxieties and conflicts.

Questions for the Reader to Ponder

1. Is your eating imbued with symbolic meanings? What is your favorite food? Can you discern why it's your favorite?

2. What food do you abhor? Can you discern the symbolic reason why you abhor it?

3. Have you ever had a period in your life, when you suddenly craved a particular food? (Being pregnant doesn't count.)

4. Similarly, have you ever lost interest in a food you loved? Might your change in food preferences be associated with an inner change on your part?

Pepsi Flavored Coke

You can tell a lot about yourself from the jokes that make you laugh. And you can tell a lot from those jokes that don't go down so well, in your system. So, it is that jokes are a Rorschach test, as valid as any inkblot for revealing who we are--which leads to my story...

Some time back, I attended a talk given at a local bookstore. The speaker was a joke writer for a national humor magazine, as well as a former stand-up comic. He told the audience that his friends often sent him jokes that they wrote, but that they were rarely funny. Ironically, the joke that he offered as an example of an unfunny joke, written by his friend, was the joke that made me laugh the hardest that evening.

The joke goes like this: "Did you hear that Coke, in an effort to attract Pepsi drinkers, just came out with Pepsi flavored Coke?" The joke has to do with the contradiction between character and worldly success. In order to succeed in the world, we must, to varying degrees, be who we are not. At one extreme, there are celebrities whose public persona is quite different from their true self. At the other extreme is the person whose persona corresponds to his or her true self. Most of us fall somewhere in the middle.

Thus, Coke can create Pepsi-flavored Coke to lure Pepsi drinkers. But, in seeking to be successful, to get more customers, it would lose its very identity. After all, if Coke were Pepsi-flavored, it would no longer be Coke. In point of fact, Coke tried that some years back. It came out with New Coke, but when its marketing strategy backfired, it came out with Coke Classic. Behind all of this are people anxious unconscious questions about self-identity and success: What price success, if I am no longer who I am? Or as the Bible asks, "What profiteth a man if he gain the world but lose his soul?" Everyone is faced with this same dilemma: To succeed we must appeal to public tastes, but if in doing so we are no longer ourselves, then have we really succeeded? Or have we merely become Pepsi-flavored Coke?

I don't think that a person who laughs at this joke consciously realizes all this. But I do think he or she unconsciously does. The laugh relieves us from the anxiety and heaviness of suffering a contradiction. In the moment of laughter, we are beyond the contradiction.

Questions for the Reader to Ponder

1. We had earlier discussed this conradiction, in relation to Ricky's conflict between wishing to be succesful and wishing to be true to himself as a musician. I.E., if he sells out, he will feel that he has lost his identity and will become "Pepsi Flavored Coke." How has this conflict, which is founded on a contradiciton, affected you in your life?

2. Examine a joke that you like to see if it similarly involves a contradiction, one that you may be suffering. (Read the essay, contained here, on the Dr. Epstein joke, for another example.)

The Psychological Appeal of Angry Whoppers

I once gave a seminar, at a local college, on the psychology of food. The class explored the psychological notion that we are what we eat. Selfhood is on the proverbial table, when we sit down for a meal. For example, oysters and other slimy foods repulse many people, for they feel that they will become slimy if they consume what is slimy. (See Jean-Paul Sartre's analysis of the slimy in *Being and Nothingness*, 1943)

On the other hand, if we feel alienated, we can eat whole-grain and organic foods and feel like we have gained wholeness, as we've discussed previously. This sort of thing doesn't make rational sense, but we are certainly not rational creatures at the dinner table. On the contrary, our awareness is often on what can be called a "symbolic level consciousness," where not only are we the food that we eat, but we are the clothes we wear, the car we drive, etc.

A woman, in the class, asked: "What's the appeal of Burger King's 'Angry Whopper?'" (For those who never tried one, it consists of a regular Whopper that has ingredients added, such as Jalapeño peppers that make it hot and spicy.) She was perplexed by the fact that we usually think of anger as a negative emotion. It would, indeed, seem counterintuitive that someone would wish to eat an Angry Whopper and thus--through the symbolism that you are what you eat--to become angry.

Before we could proceed with an analysis, another student in the class objected that *Burger King's* commercials for the *Angry Whooper* are humorous, which they are. They are really poking fun at the notion of a burger being so hot with peppers and spices as to be angry, and that by eating one, a person would become angry. They may even be mocking the emotion of anger itself, in a way that professional wrestling, for example, does or Moe from "The Three Stooges" used to do. Along these same lines, *Burger King* created an "Angry Gram" website, where you can create an angry/humorous letter and send it to somebody.

But, as it's been said, "Many a true word is said in jest." Both Kierkegaard and Schopenhauer distinguish irony from humor. When a person is ironic, he is outwardly serious, but concealing the fact that he is really kidding (laughing up his sleeve). Humor, by contrast, appears to be a jest, but conceals a deeper seriousness. The Angry Whopper ads for Burger King are, in that sense humorous. Let us, then, examine what deeper meaning lies concealed between the buns.

Instant Thumos

What, then, could be the psychological appeal of eating an *Angry Whopper*? To answer that question, we must analyze the psychological appeal of anger. Consider the fact that many people feel tired, complaisant and bored with their "ho hum," quotidian lives. (That's why there's always a market for motivational speakers, who promise to reenergize them.) Sometimes they need a long vacation, or perhaps a more interesting and challenging job, or a new career. But oftentimes they may be suffering from a lack of meaning, purpose and direction in their lives. Anger is often employed as a surrogate for meaning, purpose and direction. It can get our adrenalin flowing and provide an object for our frustrations. It serves to direct our energies, as does meaning.

Anger can also serve to remove inhibitions. Apropos of the motivating power of anger, I am reminded of a fellow I knew, when I worked, quite some years back, as a stock and commodities broker on Wall Street. He was one of the top brokers in our office. By that I mean that he was a topnotch salesman, for a stockbroker is essentially a salesman. He once confessed to me one of the secrets of his sales ability. During his lunch break, he would take the elevator down from our office at the World Trade Center and stroll over to the American Stock Exchange. As he walked along, he would smoke a joint, while listening, on his SONY Walkman, to a recording of Tchaikovsky's *1812 Overture*. (That piece is charged with anger, for Tchaikovsky, like his fellow Russians, was enraged by Napoleon's invasion of Russia. The music expresses the Russian's battle and victory against Napoleon's forces.)

My friend would then return to the office and be a sales dynamo on the telephone. The marijuana combined with the anger-charged patriotic music had the effect of drowning out all of his moral inhibitions. Those inhibitions were, to a large extent, founded on the fact that the product everyone in the office was selling--options on gold futures--although perfectly legal, was far from being a sound investment. (The problem was that that the high price of the options made their break-even point way too steep.)

I mention this because I think that the energy this fellow gained by listening to *The 1812 Overture,* while stoned, is akin to the type of energy that people seek by eating an Angry Whopper. After consuming one, we become like Popeye after having eaten a can of spinach. What the ancient Greeks called *thumos*, the spirited part of the human soul, energizes us. We would then have the courage to go out and do what needs to be done--anything from asking our boss for a raise to selling commodity options, from proposing marriage to our sweetheart to demanding that a store refund our money on a shoddy piece of merchandise. Thus do the ads for the Angry Whopper promise far more than a burger with all the trimmings. They promise that we shall, after consuming one, have the courage to "take arms against a sea of troubles and by opposing end them." That certainly is "a consummation devoutly to be wished"!

Questions for the Reader to Ponder

1. We explored how anger can act as a surrogate for the meaning that we really need to energize us. It's possible, though, to elevate one's anger to a higher level. Getting angry at our faults, foibles, weaknesses, habits, and inner demons can help us to overcome them. For example, one time I was taking a turbulent flight. Rather than becoming fearful, as I had done on all previous occasions, odd though it may sound, I got angry at my fear, at the plane, the wind that was causing the turbulence and at all else. Of course, I had already analyzed the deeper reasons for my fear, but getting angry gave me the push that I needed, and I was never fearful about

flying or by turbulence since then. Can you think of how you might put your anger to productive use in your efforts at self-overcoming?

2. Could it be that if we direct our anger to it's appropriate object, namely our weaknesses, that we will be less prone to become angry with other people?

3. If it's true that we are what we eat, what have you been eating lately and what does it say about you?

4. We mentioned the "Angry Gram." What other examples of humor, in contradistinction to irony, can you find?

Tattoos and the Quest for Identity

It would sense that tattoos are popular in prisons. After all, if you wear a uniform, you can't express yourself through your clothing. But if we, who aren't incarcerated, are free to express our identity through clothing why, then, the need to make our very bodies into vehicles for self-expression? Furthermore, why have tattoos become so popular in recent years? Apparently, tattoos promise to accomplish something, psychologically, that clothing cannot. What might it be?

The ease with which we can divest ourselves of our sense of our identity and put on a new identity, through a simple change of clothing, has its appeal. It is the appeal of freedom from the limits of a fixed identity. Of course, whom we decide to become is influenced by the vicissitudes of fashion. But the very fluid identity that clothing allows can also seem unreal and empty. Like water, an identity predicated on appearances never becomes anything solid. The contemporary interest in becoming tattooed is indicative of a craving for a permanent and abiding identity.

The present zeitgeist is one in which people suffer a lack of identity. Apropos is Natan Sharansky's book *Defending Identity: Its Indispensable Role in Defending Democracy*. (Public Affairs, 2008) The book is a defense of national and cultural differences, in the face of globalization, the United Nations, the European Union, and most generally, the rise of internationalism.

Previous generations of Americans had a strong identification with being American. They also identified with their particular region of the country. They identified with their family, profession, their interests, and all else. But ours is an abstract age, in which the notion of having a strong sense of identity is judged to be naïve. Or else, it is viewed as dangerous, for such identifications are divisive and can lead to conflict and to war. Not everyone has negative feelings about identity. Certainly, those who are politically liberal tend to have much stronger anti-identity proclivities, but the animus against identity has affected our culture at large.

Without a sense of identity, people feel lost, disconnected from life, like Camus' stranger. It would appear, then, that the present faddish interest in tattoos is indicative of a craving for identity. But, there seems to be something desperately superficial about expressing one's identity with a tattoo. Leviticus 19:28, states: "And you must not make cuts in your flesh for a deceased soul, and you must not put tattoo marking upon yourselves. I am Jehovah." Why the biblical prohibition against tattoos? It's because if one's identity is to be legitimate, it must come from God.

Rather than being on the mere surface, our true identity must reach the depths of our soul. It is expressed in all that we do, in our entire way of life, from morning till night. An identity bereft of inwardness, i.e., a identity that is merely on the surface i.e., on one skin, is mere idol worship. Hence, there exists a biblical prohibition. Although relatively permanent, it is as superficial as declaring one's identity by wearing a tee shirt that has on it the insignia of a company, a clothing designer, a certain city, etc.

Now we come to a related mystery: the present popularity of tattoos among women. It is curious that tattoos have now become popular with young women. A woman with a tattoo is saying to men, "You can't give me your identity, for I already have an identity." They are saying this, for they feel that to take on their husband's identity, to be Mrs. Fred Jones, would feel limiting. Thus, the popularity of tattoos among many women speaks volumes about marriage today.

The Quest for Significance

Related to the quest for identity is the desire to be significant, as a person, i.e., to stand out from the crowd as someone special. The true means to do so is by working hard to work hard to accomplish a worthwhile goal, to make something of one's life, by excelling in a field of endeavor. Ah, but not everyone wishes to work to become someone significant. Young people are often impatient. Their sense of insignificance, invisibility and nothingness is galling to them. They wish to be regarded as special right now, rather than after years of hard work. That is where not just tattoos, but all sorts of outré clothing, skin piercings, and other adornments enter the scene. Why spend years struggling in a profession, to become somebody? It's so much easier to say to the world, "Look at my odd-looking tattoos and look at my hair, which I've dyed purple! I may look like a freak, but at least I'm someone significant!"

The paradox of fashion, though, is that one imagines oneself as a nonconformist, rebel and an anti-establishment pirate, despite the fact that everyone else is doing the very same thing. I.E., millions of other people are also having their body tattooed, thus denying the claim that one is a nonconformist rebel. It's all rather pitiful.

This desperate quest for significance finds expression in a related phenomenon: There are those who will do anything, no mater, how trivial, so as to get themselves in the *Guinness Book of Records*. One can then hold one's head high, as one enters the room, knowing that one has the record for eating the most hotdogs in a single meal.

Questions for the Reader to Ponder

1. Why do most people need to have other people perceive their identity, whether through clothing, tattoos, or material objects? Earlier, in the dialogues, we discussed Berkeley's notion, "to be is to be seen." Is that what's going on?

2. We discussed, as an alternative to tattoos and other whacky adornments, actually becoming somebody significant, through accomplishments. Beyond that is the possibility of transcending the very need for recognition, at least on the level of ego. After all, if you think about it, fame is a rather transient affair. As Shakespeare's Prince Hamlet sagely observes, during the gravediggers scene:

   "Alexander died, Alexander was buried, Alexander returneth to dust, the dust is earth, of earth we make loam--and why of that loam, whereto he was converted, might they not stop a beer barrel?

> *Imperious Caesar, dead and turned to clay,*
> *Might stop a hole to keep the wind away.*
> *Oh, that that earth, which kept the world in awe,*
> *Should patch a wall t' expel the winter's flaw!"*

Dear reader, what thinketh thou of the transiency of fame and the hollowness of the quest for significance?

3. Read Herman Melville's excellent short story, "The Fiddler." Melville wrote it when he was in despair, over his lack of fame as a writer. Also contemplate what Hemingway wrote early in his career, when he thought that he would remain unknown, for the rest of his life, "Who the hell wants fame on a Saturday morning. I just want to write well." Relate this to your own quest for significance.

4. There are many people who, having resigned themselves to the fact that they will not become significant, invest in the hope that their children will become someone. Of course, all this reeks of desperation. You're not one of these people, are you?

5. The Buddhists speak of an empty mirror reflecting into an empty mirror. Here we find recognition at its highest level: two awakened beings gazing into each other's eyes, such that the Self recognizes Itself. Could it be that this is the ultimate source of the yearning for identity and recognition, even in its most unilluminated manifestations? If so, at the root of something as low level as tattoos is the quest for Self-realization, even if we don't realize that that is what's going on.

The Deeper Meaning of Zombies

Have you noticed all the books, films and articles about zombies? (If not, you might be a zombie yourself!) There are bestsellers, such as *Pride, Prejudice, and Zombies*--a fictional retelling of Jane Austen's classic novel--by Seth Grahame-Smith. There are also pseudo-nonfiction works, such as *The Zombie Survival Guide* by Max Brooks. There are websites devoted to zombies, an increasing number of films about zombie invasions, and scholarly conferences devoted to zombies. Is this obsession with zombies the obsession of a relatively few weird individuals or does it reflect something important about the zeitgeist? I shall argue for the latter.

It's true that the fascination with zombies is nothing new. In regard to American culture and society, the key date is 1956. That's when the cult classic, *Invasion of the Body Snatchers,* was released. Another seminal film was *Night of the Living Dead,* which appeared in 1968. Of course, much of today's zombie literature is tongue and cheek. But, it's rightly been said, "Many a true word is said in jest." Could it be that the recent spate of humorous zombie books and films is a defense mechanism against an underlying anxiety?

Zombies threaten to possess one's body and one's mind. In regard to the latter, they threaten to eat one's flesh, at least according to popular films about zombies. Other zombies can make one a zombie oneself, one of the walking dead! (In that sense, they are akin to vampires, for a bite by a vampire can transform one into a vampire.) The anxiety in question is of a paranoiac quality, for paranoia is, essentially, a fear of being possessed and thus losing one's autonomy. A related paranoid anxiety is that one's borders will be violated, for if they are, one will lose the integrity of self, thus losing one's autonomy.

There exists, in all human societies, many types of borders. One of the most fundamental is the border between the living and the dead. When that border is transgressed--whether it be by visitations from the spirit world or simply by memories of the deceased--we feel haunted. Thus religious rites and rituals are created to ensure that the dead do not intrude upon the realm of the living. In zombie books and films, that is exactly what happens. Paranoid narratives often take the form of conspiracy theories and apocalyptic fantasies. The zombie apocalypse involves the emergence of the dead, thus "the night of the living dead."

If the fear of zombies is prevalent today, it's because this is an age in which borders are being transgressed, on many fronts. Sometimes, borders are being literally transgressed, as is the Mexico/US border. They're also being transgressed socially. Marriage, if it's not to be just an empty abstraction, must have certain parameters. A marriage cannot, for example, consist of three people, nor consist in a union of a man and an animal. The advocates of homosexual marriages wish to violate traditional limits. An example, in the economic realm, is socialism and communism. They seek to dissolve, by fiat, economic distinctions. Finally, such movements as diversity, multiculturalism and globalization are threatening to dissolve the identity of various nations.

Most relevant here is how the borders between the human and the inhuman are being transgressed. There are animal rights activities that claim that humans are guilty of "speciesism," which consists of placing a higher value on human beings than other beings, whether they be animals, plants, or bacteria. Philosophers, like Peter Sanger, view speciesism as morally equivalent to racism. Then there are the computer theorists who claim that humans are essentially no different than computers. They like to point to "Big Blue," the IBM computer that defeated the chess Grand Master Gary Kasparov.

Thinking isn't essentially what distinguishes us from both animals and computers. What distinguishes us from everything else is self-consciousness. We have the amazing ability to reflect upon ourselves. The existence of consciousness is being denied, by computer theorists and by philosophers like Daniel Dennett and Richard Dawkins. In so doing, the border between the human and the nonhuman is being dissolved.

It's been said, "Sometimes paranoids are right." There, indeed, exists a nefarious effort to dissolve the fundamental distinctions that limit and define the human realm, the realm of culture and civilization, and make selfhood possible. Nightmarish tales of zombies stem from our fear of an atavism to the pre-human realm. When essential borders are dissolved and true selfhood is destroyed, we transform into mindless beings, bereft of humanity, roaming the streets, seeking to feed on those who are still vibrant and alive. There lies the danger and that is the source of our anxiety about zombies.

Questions for the Reader to Ponder

1. Are the walking dead, i.e., zombies, envious of those who are alive? Do they envy their innocence, immediacy, faith in life, belief in God and solid core of ethical values? For example, while the football quarterback, Tim Tebow, is much admired, some resent it that he doesn't hide his religious faith. Are those who hate Mr. Tebow zombies? See Soren Kierkegaard's *The Present Age* (1846), Max Scheler's *Resentment* (1912) and T.S. Eliot's poem *The Hollow Men* (1925).

2. Human values and life itself can't exist without form, limits and borders (the identity factor). Might the real zombie apocalypse consist in the reduction of everything to a uniform, valueless mush? This apocalypse, which is in the name of equality, is motivated by envy towards those who are alive. Analyze news articles for examples of this death wish, this longing for the zombie apocalypse. Read Guenon's *The Reign of Quantity* (1945), for his discussion of the Kali Yuga. If the Hindus are correct, this apocalypse, this dissolution of form, has been underway for a very long time.

The Deeper Meaning of Dr. Epstein's Gas

It's been said that when truth comes down from the mountain and enters the marketplace, it often wears a mask. Some contend that it's out of modesty, but it's really to protect people from its delusion-destroying power. After all, no one can gaze directly at the truth and survive. The truth often wears the antic mask of a clown, trickster, or joke-telling comedian. It's an ingenious disguise, for few suspect that even the silliest of jokes can plumb the depths of human existence and offer precious gems of insight.

When we laugh, it's because we intuit such profundities, but cannot consciously articulate what we perceive. It's just as well, for if we really saw to the depths of the cosmic belly laugh, such powerful insights would cause us to *plotz*. Actually, we sometimes do explode from laughter, but we invariably manage to reconstitute ourselves, like a science fiction super-villain whose pieces strangely reunite, after he has been blown to smithereens.

The joke that follows is a case in point of wisdom arising, like a divine afflatus, from the deepest bowels of human existence. So as not to have this preface become too "long winded," we shall proceed directly to the joke:

The Dr. Epstein Joke

Dr. Epstein was a renowned physician who earned his undergraduate, graduate, and medical degrees in his hometown and then left for Manhattan, where he quickly rose to the top of his field. Soon he was invited to deliver a significant paper, at a conference, coincidentally held in his hometown. He walked on stage and placed his papers on the lectern, but they slid off onto the floor. As he bent over to retrieve them, at precisely the wrong instant, he inadvertently farted.

The microphone amplified his mistake resoundingly through the room and reverberated it down the hall! He was quite embarrassed but somehow regained his composure just enough to deliver his paper. He ignored the resounding applause and raced out the stage door, never to be seen in his hometown again.

Decades later, when his elderly mother was ill, he returned to visit her. He reserved a hotel room under the name of Levy and arrived under cover of darkness. The desk clerk asked him, "Is this your first visit to our city, Mr. Levy?"

Dr. Epstein replied, "Well, young man, no, it isn't. I grew up here and received my education here, but then I moved away."

Why haven't you visited?" asked the desk clerk.

Actually, I did visit once, many years ago, but an embarrassing thing happened and since then I've been too ashamed to return."

The clerk consoled him. "Sir, while I don't have your life experience, one thing I have learned is that often what seems embarrassing to me isn't even remembered by others. I bet that's true of your incident too."

Dr. Epstein replied, "I doubt that's the case with my incident."

"Was it a long time ago?"

"Yes, son, many years."

The clerk asked, "Was it before or after the Epstein Fart?"

(A friend of mine e-mailed me the joke. I'd like to attribute it to somebody, but cannot determine the identity of its author. That is often the case with jokes.)

Life's Incongruities

What can we make of the Dr. Epstein's fart? It's been observed that humor derives from the perception of incongruity. For example, comedy teams often have motley pairs of clowns, such as Laurel and Hardy, Lucy and Desi, Felix and Oscar (the Odd Couple), and the cast of Seinfeld. We intuit, from such incongruous couplings, that any attempt to bring the world together into a harmonious unity is utterly hopeless. Rather than leading to despair, the perception of hopelessness comes as a great relief.

Comic incongruity takes many other forms. For example, Henny Youngman said, "I miss my wives cooking... as frequently as possible." That line is funny because Youngman has shifted from feeling of tender affection to the often dyspeptic realities of marriage. The two sides of marriage create an incongruous picture. Another example is a short essay, by Woody Allen, called "If the Impressionists Had Been Dentists." The image of the painters Van Gogh and Gauguin drilling teeth is quite incongruous. The perception that life contains elements, as disparate as impressionists and dentists, foils our efforts to bring the world together into any sort of intelligible unity. When we realize this, we let go and laugh. In any case, there is not a single joke or comic situation that is not founded on an incongruity.

Anatomy of a Joke

The Dr. Epstein joke points to a fundamental incongruity lying at the core of the human condition. On the one hand, we are beings who can reason, create great works of literature, art, music and philosophy. We are capable of selfless acts of heroism and can dedicate our lives to serving a high ideal. We are capable of communing with the divine, of ascending to great spiritual heights.

On the other hand, we are fleshly beings. We eat, sleep and defecate. Furthermore, even the best of us has his faults and foibles. One of the profoundest sources of our limits is in the area of knowledge. For even the the most intelligent people are involved in game of blind-man's bluff we call life. Indeed, our finitude manifests itself in 1001 ways, not least of which is our mortality. If all that wasn't sufficient to instill in us a modicum of humility, the Dr. Epstein joke reminds us that we might--at the most inauspicious moment--break wind. As Blaise Pascal felicitously stated:

> "What a chimera man really is! What an extraordinary monster, what a chaos, what a contradictory thing, what a marvelous oddity! Judge of all things.

> Helpless earth-worm; protector of truth, cesspool of ignorance and error: glory and scum of the universe. Who will untangle this knot?" (Pensees. 1999. New York: Oxford University Press.)

The unfortunate Dr. Epstein embodies this incongruity. We learn from the joke that he is not just any physician. He is a renowned physician. In that sense, he is a person of importance, one whom people respect and admire. No doubt, he has valiantly devoted his life to fighting disease and coming to the aid of the infirm. Ah, but to the mind of the comedian, that is only half the picture. Something essential has been left out. Our gaze must descend to this renowned individual's feet of clay. Dr. Epstein might have slipped on a banana peel, got a pie in the face or suffered some other indignity, as is the custom in comedy. Instead, it was an accidental fart that reminds us of the other dimension of his being.

Whether we realize it or not, in laughing at Dr. Epstein, we are really laughing at ourselves. The joke resonates with an essential truth: each of us is, like Dr. Epstein, an incongruous being, for to be human is to be incongruous. We are neither god nor animal, but an mélange of both! That is, as Pascal pointed out, the odd thing about us. Suffering from inner-conflict, we spend our days seeking to reconcile disparate interests. For example, secular ambitions and spiritual longings might be competing for our attention. Or we struggle to reconcile our desire for security with our lust for adventure. We might feel lonely and seek the company of other people, but also seek to free of them. We seek balances of all sorts, but such balances are fragile, for they are founded upon irresolvable contradictions. The moment that precedes laughter is when we perceive the hopelessness of resolving the many incongruities that constitute our life. Rather than despairing, we feel liberated, for there is a great relief in realizing that a puzzle cannot be solved and thus abandoning a futile effort.

The Fruits of Youthful Dreams

The Dr. Epstein joke reveals yet another incongruity. Kierkegaard, writing ironically about how adulthood realizes the dreams of youth, pointed out that in Jonathan Swift's youth he idealistically dreamed of building an asylum to care for the insane. He got to have it built. But, going mad himself Swift became an inhabitant of that very asylum. The Epstein joke reveals another dark irony involving aspirations. We can imagine Dr. Epstein as a young man, setting off for college, hoping one day to become his hometown's favorite son. Instead, he has become eternally memorialized, not for his medical achievements, but for his fart.

Dr. Epstein's fate symbolizes the contradiction at the heart of all human striving: we seek the world's acclaim, but, as the poem by John Burns states, "the best laid plans, of mice and men, often go astray." The joke also suggests that idiots, indifferent to true achievement, inhabit the world. Indeed, the world is resentful of excellence and seeks to embarrass anyone accomplishing anything of merit. Dr. Epstein's fate expresses a galling incongruity between youthful dreams and adult realities.

We laugh because we, too, wish to become a success and are anxious about whether or not our efforts will bear fruit. Worldly success is predicated, though, on the opinions of other people. Alas, their opinions are often foolish and always fickle. We laugh at the hapless Dr. Epstein for we intuit the ultimate hollowness of fame. We are really laughing at ourselves, in that regard. At such moments of lucidity, we are liberated from the tiring effort to have people think well of us.

Why, Then, Do We Laugh?

The despairing existentialist, Jean-Paul Sartre, said that to be a human being is to be involved with a futile project. We are, after all, finite beings longing to be infinite, mortal being longing to be gods. Contradictions of this sort are not resolvable. It would seem, then, that we are doomed to a life of frustrated aspirations and misery. It all seems rather tragic. How is it, then, that we are able to laugh our plight?

The moment that precedes laughter is a moment of clarity. We realize that what we are fundamentally attempting to do in life is contradictory and, therefore, impossible to achieve. When we perceive that impossibility--and we attain the necessary emotional distance, that is a *sine qua non* for the emergence of laughter--rather than despairing, we are suddenly released from our incessant efforts to "get it together," to make our life work. It is for this reason that the German philosopher of laughter, Helmuth Plessner, said that the formula for comedy should be "Situation hopeless, but not serious." (*Laughing and Crying*. Northwestern, 1970.) The moment of release from the exhausting effort to get it together expresses itself as laughter.

A Farewell to Seriousness

It's often been said that laughter is healing. But is it really? After all, consider the phrases that are used to describe the effects of getting the joke. We say that a person exploded with laughter, or split his sides, or we say to the comedian "stop, you're killing me!" All this sounds rather destructive. But laughter is healing not in the restorative sense, but in the transformative sense. The insight that precipitates the joke explodes our efforts at synthesizing the disparate elements of our life. Thus, instead of getting it together, we become released from the exhausting demand to get it together. I.E., we become released from the oppressive burden of life's seriousness. In that sense, laugher is an intimation of mystical release. And so, in conclusion, Viva Dr. Epstein! May all who hear the sound of his divine afflatus attain joyous enlightenment!

Questions for the Reader to Ponder

1. Do you ever feel like Dr. Epstein? In other words, do you ever look at your life and have a sense of cosmic absurdity?

2. Are you able to perceive life's incongruities and laugh, not just bitterly, but joyously? Witnessing such incongruities in a situation comedy, we laugh. Can you witness your own encounter, with such incongruities, with a certain aesthetic distance?

3. A far more difficult exercise involves balancing feeling the pain involved with experiencing such incongruities with an aesthetic distance. I.E., can you balance the grown of existence with the laughter of existence? If you find yourself falling on one side, you've lost the balance.

4. There's a tragic aspect to the Dr. Epstein story, but there also exists a road beyond tragedy. It lies in Nietzsche's notion of loving one's fate and then transforming it into one's destiny. Write a story in which Dr. Epstein retires, settles in his hometown, tries to remain anonymous, but his real identity is discovered. He is then nominated for mayor. His political opponent accuses Dr. Epstein of being full of hot air, but Dr. Epstein is elected, becomes a wise statesman, has a medical school named after him, and earns the respect and admiration of all.

   In any case, the question here is about transforming tragic fate into destiny. Helen Keller is an example of overcoming tragedy, so as to become a truly remarkable person. Lou Gehrig also emerged heroic is the face of tragedy. What is your fate? How can you transform it into your destiny?

The Deeper Meaning of Green Kryptonite

As fans of comic book superheroes know, the one thing that can weaken Superman and eventually kill him is a substance called green kryptonite. Why green kryptonite of all things? A valuable clue to this mystery can be found in Greek mythology, more specifically in the life and death of the legendary superhero, Achilles. No, Achilles didn't die from kryptonite, but there are certain intriguing similarities between Achilles and Superman, in regard to their weak points, where they were vulnerable to attack.

As Homer tells it, when Achilles--the hero of the Trojan War--was born his mother had dipped him in the magical river Styx, to make him immortal. Alas, she held the baby by the heel, with her thumb and forefinger. Consequently, the heel was the one place that the elixir of immortality didn't touch, making that it his one vulnerable spot.

Achilles died when a poison arrow, shot by the archer Paris, struck his heel. That is why a person's weakness is sometimes metaphorically referred to as his Achilles Heel.

Yes, everyone has his weaknesses--from alcoholic beverages to gambling, from argumentativeness to poor judgment of other people, from a proclivity for get-rich-quick schemes to indolence, from excess sentimentality to moroseness. In one episode of the Simpsons, Homer states that beer is his Achilles Heel. There are thousands of possible weaknesses. No doubt there is one such weakness, which, for each person, constitutes his fatal flaw.

But the stories of Achilles and Superman do not really seem to be about tragic character weaknesses. Achilles was prone to an anger that could become madness, but that is not what killed him. Nor does green kryptonite have anything to do with a fatal character flaw on Superman's part. It would appear, then, that both Achilles' vulnerable heel and Superman's vulnerability to green kryptonite have a deeper symbolic meaning.

Why the Heel?

In myths, as in dreams, there are no arbitrary elements. On the contrary, every detail exists out of an artistic necessity. So we may ask, why was Achilles' weak spot his heel? Why not his arm or some other part of his body? There exists a symbolic connection between the soles of the feet and the soul in the metaphysical and spiritual sense. That's where our bodies touch the earth. Even with the advent of shoes, the symbolic significance of feet is still evident. The feet connect and root us to the earth, belying whatever claims we make to being self-sufficient individuals.

What then is the meaning of the earth, upon which we trod? It symbolizes our home, the place where we began. That's why, archetypally speaking, it's called "Mother Earth." The earth appeals to us as an image of a primordial unity and oneness that existed, before we emerged as separate individuals. It's interesting, in that regard, that Achilles' mother was, by her actions when he was a baby, both the source of his superhuman strength, but also accidentally of his downfall.

Consequently, that most vulnerable part of the feet, the soul, is that dimension of the self that seeks to transcend its separateness. That is why the soul is associated with our feelings, longings, and aspirations. It is the locus both of our humanity and of our longing to transcend our humanity. For Plato, the soul is a kind of daemon, connecting our finite, mortal being to the eternal. In the case of Achilles, it is the heel that is key, but the heel is contiguous to the sole and can be considered an extension of it.

The Unbearable Greenness of Kryptonite

In the case of Superman, it is not some truly alien element that threatens him. On the contrary, it is a substance that comes from his native planet, Krypton! So, here too, archetypal connections exist between home, one's native soil and one's mortality.

As we learn from the comic books, kryptonite comes in a variety of colors, each color having a different untoward effect on superman.

Why, then, should the deadly type of kryptonite be green? Green is the color of life, which, by its very nature, has within it the seeds of death. As Dylan Thomas states: "The force that through the green fuse drives the flower is my destroyer."

Thus Superman--that flying man who symbolically is associated with the transcendent heavens--is weakened or destroyed when in contact with kryptonite, which is a certain type of debris from his home planet, Krypton. We might add that many people have fled toxic families, marriages, neighborhoods, organizations, and nations. But memories of the past can still haunt them. Freud called it "the return of the repressed." Thus they find themselves weakened by the kryptonite of the memories that follow them to their new abode, like kryptonite followed Superman to Planet Earth.

We find nightmarish examples of the return of memory in dramas, such as Arthur Miller's *Death of a Salesman* (1949), and Tennessee Williams *A Streetcar Named Desire* (1947). Haunting memories are the green kryptonite that helps to destroy both Willie Loman and Blanche Dubois. Memory and all that is associated with home can, of course, be a source of great strength. But we are, for purposes of analysis, focusing on its dark side. Maybe we'll consider its salutary effects in another essay.

The Refusal of Immortality

How dull would be the stories of Achilles and of Superman if they were immortal! The fact that they are mortal men is what makes them heroic and interesting to us. In Homer's tale, it was prophesized that Achilles would die in battle at an early age. Achilles knew of the prophecy, which means that he could have forsaken the life of a warrior. The fact that he continued to do battle was what made him heroic.

There was no such prophecy in the story of Superman. All the same, Superman knew that there were evil men, like Lex Luther, out to kill him. He refused to settle down to the life of a news reporter, disguised as Clark Kent, and to a marriage to Louis Lane. He refused because of his commitment to "truth, justice and the American way."

It is interesting, in this regard, that Soren Kierkegaard, in his diaries, describes his decision to break his engagement to his beloved, Regina Olsen, as analogous to Achilles' decision to refuse the temptation of a comfortable life, so that he could pursue the destiny that the gods had created for him. Kierkegaard's destiny, of course, was to be one of the great philosophers.

And so, anyone who aspires to the glories of a heroic life must in essence declare: "Green kryptonite be damned! I shall follow my destiny, though it lead me to my doom!"

Questions for the Reader to Ponder

1. Do you have an "Achilles's Heel," a certain weakness, or personality flaw, that can endanger you? In point of fact, it's common to have not one, but a number of such chronic weaknesses. Try to view this weakness an answer, albeit a poor one, to the question of how to be a real self in a real world. Try to get to the root of this weakness, so as to overcome it.

2. Do you have any memories that act like green kryptonite, weakening your energy, will and spirit? Certain emotional attachments can also act as green kryptonite. Castaneda's teacher, Don Juan Matus, spoke of "severing the bonds of affection." This doesn't mean that one becomes a cold fish, for there are aspects of times past that can inspire us with courage, faith, hope and charity, and there's something to be said in praise of *Auld Laing Syne*. It takes discernment, then, to know what to sever.

3. Sometimes the bonds that need to be severed are not to people, but to our familiar habits and routines. Can you think of some examples from you own life? (See related essay, "How Not to Bring Yourself with You, When You Move.")

4. Read the following quotation from Sir Kenneth Clarke's book "Civilization:

"Seen by itself the David's body might be some unusually taut and vivid work of antiquity; it is only when we come to the head that we are aware of a spiritual force that the ancient world never knew. I suppose that this quality, which I may call heroic, is not a part of most people's idea of civilisation. It involves a contempt for convenience and a sacrifice of all those pleasures that contribute to what we call civilised life. It is the enemy of happiness. And yet we recognise that to despise material obstacles, and even to defy the blind forces of fate, is man's supreme achievement; and since, in the end, civilisation depends on man extending his powers of mind and spirit to the utmost, we must reckon the emergence of Michelangelo as one of the great events in the history of western man." (BBC Books, 1969)

a. What does Clarke mean by "spiritual force" and what does it have to do with the heroic? Why does Clarke believe it to be a modern phenomenon, rather than an ancient?

b. Let's assume that Clarke is correct, that the heroic is the enemy of happiness. Do you wish to lead a happy life or a heroic life? If you've chosen to lead a heroic life, are you willing to accept the consequences of your decision, without looking back, without bemoaning your fate, without hedging your bet? Is the longing for happiness, pleasure and convenience actually effeminate? Might that longing be the deadliest variety of green kryptonite, when it comes to leading the heroic life?

A Multiple Choice Exam Called Your Life

In his *Confessions*, the great Russian novelist Leo Tolstoy describes how, in latter life, he was ambushed by the specter of meaninglessness. It was his mortality that seemed most troubling to him, for if everything we do eventually vanishes into oblivion, what significance can life have? Staring into the void, Tolstoy was perplexed enough to consider suicide.

This led him to observe the lives of his fellow men. What is it, Tolstoy wondered, that gets them through the day? At first glance, other people seem to be getting on pretty well. At least they weren't in despair. Tolstoy concludes that there are four basic answers to the ultimate question of how life should be lived. (Readers might consider this a multiple-choice test. Choose only one.)

1. **Ignorance**: "It consists in not knowing, not understanding that life is an evil and an absurdity. People of this sort--chiefly women, or very young or very dull people--have not yet understood that question of life which presented itself to Schopenhauer, Solomon, and Buddha." (Leo Tolstoy, *A Confession*. Translated by Aylmer Maude. 1921)

2. **Epicureanism**: "It consists, while knowing the hopelessness of life, in making use meanwhile of the advantages one has... The dullness of these people's imagination enables them to forget the things that gave Buddha no peace--the inevitability of sickness, old age and death, which today or tomorrow will destroy all these pleasures."

3. **Strength and Energy**: "It consists in destroying life, when one has understood it to be an evil and an absurdity." Tolstoy is suggesting that suicide is an act of strength.

4. **Weakness**: "It consists of seeing the truth of the situation and yet clinging to life, knowing in advance that nothing can come of it." (Ibid. Tolstoy)

5. **God**: Tolstoy finally chooses a fifth answer, the belief in God, which involves for him an enormous inner struggle. After all, for an intellectual, an answer based on reason is easy, but one based on faith does not go down easy. It should be noted, though, that in turning to God Tolstoy still rejects organized religion.

OK, which answer did you choose? Be honest, now, for your deliverance from despair depends on it. It may be, though, that the correct answer for you is, quite honesty, "none of the above." For there are certain answers that Tolstoy didn't consider, at least in his *Confessions*.

Idolatry: 21st Century Style

The question of whether or not God exists--and, if not, how then to live in the face of meaninglessness--not only concerned Tolstoy, but also Schopenhauer, Nietzsche and the existentialists of the 1930s and 1940s. Indeed, it continued to be a major concern of many thoughtful people, though the late 1960s. After that, there is a significantly diminished interest in the question of how to live in the face of meaninglessness.

Were people, from then on, no longer waiting for Godot? Did they find a replacement for God? Nietzsche thought that once people no longer believe in God that they would run to the sea, like lemmings, to drown. Apparently, he was wrong. What, then, happened? Nietzsche didn't envision is the emergence or reemergence of various forms of secular idolatry, which consists in making a god out of that which is intrinsically finite. An example would be worshipping a politician, as if he were the savior. Of course, that sort of idolatry usually ends not long after a politician is elected, just as romance ends shortly after marriage. There are many other forms of idolatry. We shall consider only two of them...

6. **Humanism**: The humanistic worldview proposes that human beings do not need God or religion, but are able to find happiness and fulfillment solely in the secular domain. In truth, no one can live without the absolute, so something must be regarded as such. Science and progress end up being worshipped. In the case of Marxism, a utopian vision of a perfect world--one in which there will no longer be any inequality--is viewed as the millennium.

7. **Pantheism**: This is the belief that God is not transcendent, but that the earth, or life itself, is divine. Thus nature is worshipped along with everything natural and primitive. Mythically speaking, it consists in worshiping the Great Mother. These ideals are embodied in film, *Avatar* (2009). It valorizes a fictional primitive society and make American society appear to be evil. This worship of nature is folly, for nature is the realm of destruction and death. That is why traditional religions reject it as our salvation.

Conclusion

There are many other possible "answers" to the question of life's meaning. Some of them are shallow and some of them profound. A satisfactory answer must connect us to the absolute. Where, then, lies your absolute, your meaning?

Friendship's Darker Dynamic

"God protect me from my friends."

--Voltaire

We had previously analyzed the episode of Seinfeld, in which George Costanza--realizing that every decision that he has made in life has turned out to be a bad one--decides that, from now on he will do the exact opposite of what his usual instincts tell him to do. As a result, George's situation in life undergoes a dramatic improvement. He gets an attractive girlfriend; he moves out of his parent's house; and he gets a dream job with the New York Yankees. What interests us here, though, is how George's transformation affects his friendships.

The person whom it specifically affects is Elaine. After George's transformation, everything begins to go wrong for her. Elaine gets thrown out of her apartment. And carelessness, on Elaine's part, causes her publishing house to lose a major contract. Sitting at their familiar restaurant table Elaine, Jerry, and Kramer discuss the matter:

> **Elaine:** Do you know what's going on here? Can't you see what's happened? I've become George.
>
> **Jerry:** Don't say that.
>
> **Elaine:** It's true. I'm George! I'm George!

Elaine realizes, in horror, that she has inherited George's bad fortune. But, is this really possible? It is, according to the school of psychology known as "family systems theory." The theory contends that there are certain roles available to family members. If, for example, one family member is the serious scholar, that role is now taken and a younger member of the family needs to adopt a different role. It might, for example, be that of underdog, rebel, clown, or athlete. This same claiming of roles also occurs in relationships. For example if one person takes the role of being careless with money, the other partner will have to become the responsible one.

How do these family systems dynamics apply to friendships? Since George--after his "do the opposite" transformation--is no longer the schlemiel, or hapless loser, someone else, out of a curious psychological necessity, must assume that role. That person could have been Jerry or Kramer, but the curse falls on Elaine. Jerry attempts to offer Elaine some philosophical solace: *"Elaine, don't get too down. Everything'll even out, see, I have two friends, you were up, he was down. Now he's up, you're down. You see how it all evens out for me?"*

People intuitively realize that this dynamic exists. That's why if someone they know starts to do better, they might try to trip him or her up. Usually, this dynamic occurs unconsciously. It can, though, be quite conscious and demonic, as illustrated in the film *The Razor's Edge* (1946). Sophie is a recovering alcoholic. Larry, her new husband, has helped her to go straight. Isabel, out of jealousy over Sophie's marriage to Larry, tempts Sophie to return to her drinking. Usually, other people's efforts to bring us back to our old self isn't so egregious. But it can be all the more insidious, in its subtlety.

The Sense of Betrayal

Often, those who knew the transformed person as a suffering sad sack will feel betrayed. They will feel betrayed out of an inner sense that these roles had been agreed upon, and now these roles have been changed or even reversed. Sometimes, it's simply the case that a friendship is predicated on the roles that two people had been playing. When one of the pair changes, the other person will often feel that he has lost a friend, simply by virtue of the person no longer being the person he had been.

Indeed, friendship may simply no longer be possible. Consider, for example, Shakespeare's *King Henry IV, (Part Two)*. When Prince

Hal becomes king, he rises to the occasion, putting aside riotous living. He becomes a serious and responsible person, as befits his new role in life. When Hal, now Henry the Fifth, is greeted by Sir John Falstaff, his former drinking and carousing buddy, he coldly replies: "I know ye not old man." Falstaff is crushed by Hal's words.

Sometimes, the feeling of betrayal may also have another sense to it. Most people have a sense that they need to change their life around. When they see that a friend has done precisely that, they feel threatened by a kind of inner accusation: "See, your friend Mary has changed. Why can't you?" It's true that misery loves company, so if we renounce our formerly miserable state, we are no longer good company to those who are still miserable.

Dread of the Uncanny

Apart from these family systems dynamics, a real change can be frightening for other people. Indeed, it evokes the uncanny, of which Freud rightly observed, there is nothing more terrifying. After all, our sense of reality--and our sanity too--is predicated on objects being what they are and people being who they are. We may enjoy the transformations effectuated by a stage magician, for we know, full well, that it involves trickery, but, if we witnessed a thing or person actually transforming into something or someone else, we would likely get sick to our stomach or faint, for we would become unhinged from our fundamental orientation to the world. In point of fact, people do, on rare occasion, undergo a major transformation, which unhinges his friends and family. It's unsettling to realize, as have the existentialists, that the self is not a fixed thing, or an object, but is what Kierkegaard called "a freedom," that it's fluid and can become anything. Consequently, for the sake of their own psychological survival, people may try to bring the transformed person back to his or her prior state of being.

Needless to say, not all friends and family members are nefarious, in this way. Some are genuinely delighted by the person's transformation and experience a beneficent joy that he who had been lost is now found. That felicity is dramatized by Dickens' story *The Christmas Carol*, when Scrooge undergoes something akin to a spiritual rebirth. Such as change can be a relief to everyone. For example, the irresponsible fool, who had been a financial drain to the family, need no longer burden them. Or perhaps she, who had always been somber and serious, is now lighthearted.

That said, there is still often a psychological investment, on the part of friends and family, to bring us back to being the man we had been, for they dread the uncanny. The subtext of what they say is, "Please, for the sake of my sanity, be the person familiar to me!" Thus a serious obstacle for those wishing to change their life, are other people's expectations. And that is why it's often necessary, when we have undergone a change, to leave town. Of course, that isn't always feasible. Sometimes, after a break with the past, former friendships can be renewed, but only if reformed on a much different basis.

Questions for the Reader to Ponder

1. Have you and a friend ever parted company, after either of you had undergone a significant change? Were you latter able to renew the friendship on a new level?

2. Hal had to break free of Falstaff, when he became king. But can we ever really free ourselves of our "inner Falstaff," i.e., what Jung calls, "the trickster archetype?" Or does he return, to borrow the title of Conrad's novelette, as, "The Secret Sharer," i.e., as that which has been repressed when we became serious and consolidated our identity? It's significant, in this respect, that kings have always had their court clowns, for the clown symbolizes what's missing--chaos and completeness.

Socialism's Incestuous Relation to the Mother

A nation with a socialized economy is aptly called a "nanny state." Like an overly protective mother, it stifles self-reliance, individual initiative, and ultimately liberty itself. The Leviathan that socialism creates invariably infantilizes us. We are to forsake our status as citizens to become subjects, under the aegis of various ministers, or czars, who administer to our needs. As our dependency on government increases, we become, in effect, wards of the state. Yes, governmental "smother love" is a pernicious thing, which leads one to wonder: why would anyone crave the degraded, ignominious form of existence wrought by socialism? Here lies a mystery!

Socialism Versus Capitalism

Consider, by way of contrast, capitalism. It financially rewards hard work, ingenuity, risk taking and individual achievement. The downside is that we must pay the price for our errors. Accepting responsibility for our actions is intrinsic to being a mature adult. Socialism, by contrast, promises to protect us from the consequences of our actions. For example, if we fail to save for a rainy day and disaster strikes, the state come to the rescue. It does so by robbing, i.e., taxing, Peter to pay Paul. In that sense, the lure of socialism is a regressive wish to forsake the burdens of adulthood.

Socialism also appeals to the longing for equality. Socialists contend that any distribution of goods, based on achievement, is intrinsically unfair. The implication is that life is a zero-sum game, and that one person's gain is another person's loss. As a solution, Karl Marx advocated the philosophy and the call to action, "From each according to his abilities to each according to his needs." Implicit here is a view of the state as a large family, with only so much food to go around. If some of the family members have large portions, then everyone else will have less. Of course, this metaphor is absurd, for the world is not a large family, even if many Utopian socialists believe it to be so. (Nor is it a village, as Hillary Clinton implied in her book *It Takes a Village* (1996).

We have mentioned two of socialism's appeals, the wish not to have to take responsibility for one's errors and the craving for equality. There's a third appeal, one that is never stated, because it initially seems counterintuitive. It's to create a world where one doesn't need to be charitable. This may sound rather surprising, since those on the political left pride themselves on their compassion. Alas, their compassion really consists in forcing those with some money to give to those who have less. Apropos is Aristotle's reason for rejecting socialism. He contended that charity is good for the soul and under socialism there's no need to be charitable, for the state gives us what we need. Socialists, then, seek to create a world where no one need ever be charitable. Why, seek to create such a world? It's because the socialist knows that to give to others contradicts the desire that is at the heart of socialism, the wish to be given and not have to give, i.e., the wish to stay as a child. In that world, the soul withers and dies, in its puerility.

Pa is to Blame for Everything

Consider socialism and capitalism, in terms of Jungian archetypes. The mother does not require that her children accomplish anything to receive a piece of the pie. They all receive equal portions. This matriarchal mode of distribution is socialism's ideal. Now consider the father, in his many archetypal forms--including one's personal father, God, one's pastor and one's teachers. Unlike the mother who, out of unconditional love, makes no demands, the father divvies up the pie based on individual merit.

Socialists rail against the father's manner of distribution, accusing him of favoritism and bias, of lacking compassion, of being altogether unfair. Their accusations towards the father cloak their true animus: socialists hate and resent the father for requiring that they become responsible adults. They similarly hate that the father's love is conditional, in that respect. In the language of Freud, they hate the father for forcing them to renounce the pleasure principle and to accept the reality principle. For in truth, socialism, like all Utopian creeds, is a flight from reality.

Certainly there are injustices in the world, but most often the accusation of unfairness is a childish protest against the demands of adulthood, one often darkened by a baleful dose of envy of those who have more. They claim that if it wasn't for the father, everyone could have an equal piece of the pie. The revolution that socialists wish to foment is one that would kill the father and put the "mother" in charge of the world.

This patricide can take many forms, from contempt for culture and tradition to anti-Americanism, from atheism to antisemitism. In regard to the latter, the Jewish people have always embodied the morality of God, the father. Even if particular Jews embrace socialism, and even if particular Jews renounce morality, the Jewish people are forever branded as the people who have chosen God, the father.

Socialism and the Oedipus Complex

All cultures have an incest taboo. They know that a violation can have grave results, for the individual and for society. Freud referred to the dynamic, by which the child's incestuous longings are punished, as the "Oedipus Complex." As we've been suggesting, socialism is really a longing for the mother. In other words, socialism is the creation of those who--despite the guilt engendered by the Oedipus Complex--have refused to renounce their longings for the mother. (The consequence of ignoring one's Oedipal guilt is a diminished sense of self, but that is another story for another essay.)

The original version of the film, *The Manchurian Candidate* (1962) evokes this noxious connection between communism, i.e., socialism taken to its logical conclusion, and the mother. In that nightmarish story, a POW named Raymond Shaw is brainwashed and turned into a political assassin, by the Chinese communists, during the Korean War. The film suggests that Raymond has an incestuous relation with his domineering mother. (The book, by the same title, went further down that road.) A casual remark by the film's protagonist, Major

Marko, parallels Raymond's relation to his mother and difficulties that Orestes had with his mother, Clytemnestra.

Raymond's mother, although apparently a virulent anti-communist, is really in league with the communists, who've brainwashed her son. What triggers hypnotized Raymond to obey commands is the site of the queen of hearts. That playing card represents his mother. This film evokes the connection between communism (socialism in its final form) and an unresolved Oedipus complex. Marx wrote: "A specter is haunting Europe, the specter of communism." Were Marx psychologically astute, he would have realized that the real specter haunting Europe, the US, and the rest of the world, is the mother archetype, or what Erich Neumann called "the Great Mother."

The Swinging of the Pendulum

As Hegel's dialectic reveals, when the pendulum of history swings to one extreme, it invariably swings to the opposite extreme. What, then, lies on the opposite extreme of socialism? The other end of the pendulum's arc is Islamism. It's concomitantly a fanatical faith in the father (Allah) and a violent rejection of the mother. Islamists perceive that both the socialistic and the capitalistic nations that exist today are under the sway of the feminine. Western leaders promise the blessing of liberty, to the peoples of the world. But, to the Islamist, what good is liberty if it brings, in its train, mother worship, in its myriad forms, from fashion shows to pornography to feminism?

If liberal Western democracies are to defeat Islamic fanaticism--not just militarily, but also ideologically--if they are to win hearts and minds, they must offer men, in developing nations, a viable alternative to Islamic fanaticism. Socialism isn't a viable alternative, for it erodes our belief in culture, values and ideals, thus weakening our will to fight. And although socialism and communism might appeal to rebellious adolescents--as represented by the perverse adoration of the murderous Che Guevara--its protest against the father, naturally, fails to fulfill the need that young men have for true manhood, which means becoming, psychologically speaking, a father oneself.

A viable alternative to both socialism and Islamic fanaticism requires reconciling liberty with masculine values. It also requires honoring the feminine, without deifying her. It's quite feasible. After all, in America, we reconciled patriarchy, individual liberty and respect for the feminine, for almost 200 years. It would require another essay to analyze why that synthesis decayed, causing the drift into debauchery and decadence. Is it still possible to renew the synthesis, on some higher level? That's anyone's guess.

Questions for the Reader to Ponder

1. Why do leftists--and other types of totalitarians--tend to be far more unhappy, mentally unbalanced, intolerant and dissolute than the average person? Read Eric Hoffer's *The True Believer* (1951). Do you agree with Hoffer's analysis?

2. It's been argued that the communists, in Weimer Germany, set the stage for the advent of National Socialism (the Nazis). Read historians--such as Ian Kershaw & Walter Laqueur--and consider if it's true. Do contemporary parallels exist? I.E., are leftists facilitating Islamic hegemony by undermining the West's self-confidence?

3. True inner freedom requires abandoning not just socialism, as a worldview, but all utopian longings. Indeed it requires rejecting all false idols. Read Nicolai Berdyaev's *Slavery and Freedom* (1939). He explores the many types of inner-slavery that exist under both communism and capitalism. Among those Berdyaev discusses are the slavery to money, God, civilization, sexuality and even to art and beauty! Determine if you've enslaved yourself, in some way, and then labor diligently to free yourself.

The Deeper Meaning of Adultery

If you haven't seen the hit TV drama *Mad Men*, it's about a New York advertising agency, in the year 1960. Its protagonist is a philandering advertising executive, named Don Draper. The other members of the firm are also philandering, but since this is a short essay, we'll focus on Don Draper.

Don loves his attractive wife, but he cheats on her. Why? Obviously, for sexual satisfaction, but for other reasons as well. These include personal vanity; being a lothario is important to his self-image. Then there is the egotistical thrill of being naughty without consequence, as well as the excitement of evading detection. His overactive libido is also a product of the stress of his job, coupled with boredom, depression, emptiness and a need to distract himself from the deeper questions about life that are pursuing him.

There's yet another reason for his unfaithfulness, and it's the one that particularly interests us here. Although, on one level, Don is a loving husband and good father, he would appear to be running away from his wife. Even when he is physically with her, he eludes the emotional intimacy that she desires from him. His affairs with other women is really the flipside of his flight from his wife. It could be argued, though, that Don is a bit of a cold fish in general. For example, he heartlessly distances himself from his long lost brother, Adam, who had eagerly wished to reestablish relations with him. But our focus here will be on Don's relation to women. What is he really seeking and what is he really running away from?

A Clue to the Whole Affair

Language can often offer clues to life's mysteries. Consider the word "cheating," a word most frequently used in the context of sports and games. How curious that it is also a synonym for adultery. It suggests that a marriage is a competition of some sort and that one can seek to gain an unfair advantage. The interaction between the sexes has, indeed, often been called a game, as well as a "battle," when that interaction becomes more contentious. Sometimes it's been thought of as a dance. A dance--especially the Tango--often mimics a competition between man and the woman. In any case, the game-like dimension of male/female relationships suggests that there can be a winner and a loser.

What, though, does it mean to win? Feminine and masculine are two poles of reality. They are viewed mythically as Mother Earth and Father Sky. Or they can be viewed metaphysically as matter and form. Each one needs its polar opposite in order to be complete. But each wants to be the supreme principle. Is there any surprise, then, that there would be a battle of the sexes?

An aspect of this erotic battle involves the wife seeking to have her husband invest their marriage with ultimate importance. The husband, fearing the loss of freedom and masculine potency --that comes with domestication--wishes to regard his marriage as a significant dimension of his life, but not as ultimate. His wife can seek to draw him closer through a variety of means. Her cooking can, for example, addict him to life's comforts. Furthermore, by agreeing with his opinions she can be for him an emotional refuge, from the cares and conflicts that fill his workday. He, on the other hand, can use his work and other interests to stay distant and so maintain his individuality. Among those other interests can be other women.

In a certain respect, Don Draper is fearful of his wife. What he actually fears is the care that he has for her. He dreads that care could cause him to lose his emotional distance. Were that to happen, he would no longer be able to maintain himself as an independent, self-sufficient being, apart from his wife and family. Gone would be the sense that he has of himself as a freewheeling playboy.

This is where cheating comes in. To cheat is to obtain an unfair advantage--in the masculine/feminine game that one has with one's partner--by secretly bringing in another person. In so doing, Don Draper diminishes the significance that his wife has for him, for now she is no longer the only embodiment of the feminine principle in his life. Furthermore, having a secret--especially a big secret, like marital infidelity--in itself, creates a distance between two people, thus destroying intimacy.

In that sense, Don Draper is not really married, for a marriage is not just a relationship. A relationship can exist between two independent beings. A marriage, on the other hand, requires a transformation in which the two become one. In seeking to have a "marriage," without losing his sense of self-sufficiency, he is really seeking to get something for nothing. Furthermore, the fact that Don Draper needs to cheat suggests that he is not strong enough to win fair and square.

Falling Down to Earth

Our fate in life is there from the beginning. At the beginning of each segment of *Mad Men*, as the credits start to roll by, we see smoke rising up, as if from a lit cigarette. The show's director is making good use of symbolism, for Don Draper's whole life is really like a cigarette, one that is smoked after sex, so as to diminish the significance of the self-transcending intimacy of the love-making. This is because cigarette smoking is a competing form of transcendence, as is drinking. (In another essay, I had discussed Sartre's notion that, psychologically speaking, cigarette smoking is a symbolic way to be free of the world by sucking it in, and thus destroying the world. Thus, the aim of cigarette smoking is freedom.)

Then, right after the smoke, we see animated sequence of a man falling down to Earth, from a tall building. As he falls, he passes images of women. But, unlike Icarus, Don Draper lands safely in a comfortable chair, suggesting that the story of Don Draper need not end tragically. The sequence makes sense, for that is really what's happening to Don Draper: He is falling down to Earth, from a dizzying dream of wealth, success and glamour. Psychologically understood, he is falling down to Earth from his love affair with himself. Hopefully, as a result, he will have a deeper relation to other people, including his wife.

[There is, of course, much more to be said about the subject of adultery. And we haven't even discussed why women cheat. But tomorrow is another day.]

Questions for the Reader to Ponder

1. Do you know anyone who is an adulterer? Does our analysis of Don Draper apply to him or is there anything that we have left out?

2. We haven't discussed women who cheat, but what do you think motivates an adulteress? Read Flaubert's *Madame Bovary* (1856) for clues.

3. Socrates contended that the good person is the happy person. Does the adulterer disagree with Socrates? Does he or she, in effect, say, "Nice guys finish last." Or is it that adulterers actually believe that they are good people? In other words, are they bundles of rationalizations and lies? In other words, do they stink excuse?

The Secret of Uncanny Valley

Japanese scientists have been making rapid strides creating automatons that look and act like human beings. But, in recent years, they've encountered a disturbing phenomenon. Mori Masahiro, the roboticist, named it "uncanny valley."

Here is what happens: Up to a point, the more lifelike a robot appears, the more favorable will be our emotional response to it. Were we to represent this on a graph, we would see an upward pointing diagonal line, representing the positive correlation between a robot's lifelikeness and emotionally warm feelings on our part. But, at a certain point--when the robot's looks and actions become almost indistinguishable from that of a human being--the robot will elicit in us feelings of revulsion. Indeed, it will elicit in us that horrifying sense of dread associated with the uncanny. By the uncanny, we mean the supernatural, strange, eerie, or weird. The encounter with the uncanny can be the most terrifying of all experiences.

To represent this shift--when the correlation between lifelikeness and affection becomes negative--the line on the graph precipitously descends, creating a dip, or valley, known as "uncanny valley." (For more information on this, see the article in Wikipedia: http://en.wikipedia.org/wiki/Uncanny_valley)

A number of "scientific" explanations for uncanny valley--from the fear of death to poor mate selection--have been proposed, all of which derive from theoretically ungrounded abstractions. It's not surprising that scientists--tending to be out of touch with their emotions, fearful of the irrational and disdainful of metaphysics--would formulate such farfetched theories. What, then, is really involved here? The revulsion to hyper-realistic robots is but a species of the uncanny. Exploring some of its other varieties may offer us clues to this intriguing mystery. As we're about to discover, the dip, or valley--that these robotic engineers have stumbled upon--leads down the metaphysical rabbit hole, through a kind of wormhole, to the edge of the intelligible world.

When Home Sweet Home Becomes Dreadfully Unfamiliar

In his intriguing essay on the uncanny, Sigmund Freud offers a valuable clue to its meaning:

> "The German word 'unheimlich' is obviously the opposite of 'heimlich' ['homely'], 'heimisch' ['native'] the opposite of what is familiar; and we are tempted to conclude that what is 'uncanny' is frightening precisely because it is not known and familiar. Naturally not everything that is new and unfamiliar is frightening, however; the relation is not capable of inversion." (Essay on the Uncanny, by Sigmund Freud, 1919)

Freud then proceeds to analyze what he considers to be the factors that, under certain circumstances, make the unfamiliar frightening. We wont explore Freud's psychoanalytic theory of repression and the uncanny. Suffice it to say that like other theorists of the uncanny, Freud's theory fails to discern the key to the phenomenon. It's neither the unknown nor the revelation of that which had been hidden (or repressed) that is most terrifying, but rather the loss of the familiar! Another way of saying this is that it it's leaving home that invites the uncanny. What is most frightening is when home begins to look disturbingly strange. Let us consider several instances of this phenomenon, before finally returning to the subject of robotics.

An example from my own life comes to mind. It is akin to the Uncanny Valley in so far as it involves a disturbingly close resemblance between the real and the unreal. As a child, I remember getting lost several times and, just for a moment, being relieved to find my apartment building. Ah, but then a moment latter I realized that it was not my apartment building, but one that looked just like it. That was an easy mistake to make, because the apartment house in which I grew up, as a boy in Brooklyn, New York, was identical to about thirty other apartments in the same building complex.

The feeling of being lost is very unpleasant, and can be a dreadful one for a child. But the feeling of mistakenly taking the wrong house to be one's own evokes the horror of the uncanny. The same sort of horror is evoked when as a child I became lost and would, for an instance, think that I recognized one of my parents, only to realize that it was a stranger who resembled either of them.

Alfred Hitchcock has an instance like that in his classic film *The Lady Vanishes* (1938). There is a moment when the protagonist believes that he has found the missing Ms. Froy, sitting on the train. But when the women turns around, he realizes that it is someone else, who vaguely resembles her. The viewer of the film experiences that queasiness associated with the uncanny.

The Uncanniness that Emerges from Self-Reflection

A particularly powerful experience of the uncanny can occur at a moment of self-reflection. Indeed, imagine looking into a mirror and feeling like one is viewing a stranger. The sociologists Peter L. Berger and Thomas Luckmann suggest that that experience is not uncommon. But human beings have ways of fleeing from the import of such metaphysical terrors. The authors offer an example of how a morning, train ride to work is used by many people to exorcise such uncanny perceptions.

> *"The individual may not know anyone on the train and may speak to no one. All the same, the crowd of fellow-commuters reaffirms the basic structure of everyday life. By their overall conduct the fellow-commuters extract the individual from the tenuous reality of early-morning grogginess and proclaim to him in no uncertain terms that the world consists of earnest men going to work, of responsibility and schedules, of the New Haven Railroad and the New York Times. The last, of course, reaffirms the widest coordinates of the individual's reality. From the weather reports to the help-wanted ads it assures him that he is, indeed, in the most real world possible. Concomitantly, it affirms the less-than-real status of the sinister ecstasies experienced before breakfast--the alien shape of allegedly familiar objects upon waking from a disturbing dream, the shock of non-recognition of one's own face*

> in the bathroom mirror, the unmistakable suspicion a
> little latter that one's wife and children are mysterious
> strangers." ("The Social Construction of Reality." An-
> chor Books: 1967, pp. 149-150)

And, as Berger and Luckmann point out, one can have the perception that one's spouse and children are complete strangers. In a very real sense, it may be true. It's just that one never realized it before. There was a film very aptly named *Lovers and Other Strangers* (1970). In any case, these are powerful perceptions of the uncanny.

A Schlemiel Experiences the Uncanny

Let us consider one last example of this phenomenon, as it finds expression in a short story by Isaac Bashevis Singer entitled *When Schlemiel Went to Warsaw* (1979). It is about a foolish fellow, a schlemiel, who decides to take a trip from his hometown to Warsaw Poland. As far as I can recall, about half way to Warsaw, he takes his boots off, and points them in the direction of Warsaw. Then he goes off to sleep.

If I'm not mistaken, an elf of some sort reverses the direction of Schlemiel's boots. Consequently, when Schlemiel awakens the next morning--not realizing that his boots have been turned around--he unwittingly proceeds back to his hometown imagining that he has arrived in Warsaw. How strange, Schlemiel foolishly thinks, that everything in Warsaw is exactly like it is in his hometown. There is even a house like his house, with a woman who claims to be his wife!

Singer's story about Schlemiel is invariably mistaken for a humorous children's story, but beneath the surface of this amusing tale lie the terrors of the uncanny. Singer's story resonates with his readers, for there are frightening moments when we awaken to realize that everything appears to be the same but is not at all! What, then, is the difference? It's rather hard to get a hold of. In truth, the place is the same, but something has happened to the person, thus making the place look different to him or her.

Singer's story illustrates what happens when we begin to awaken, not just literally as happened to Schlemiel, but in the deeper sense of the word. The world then appears to be unfamiliar; it appears as an unfathomable mystery. Furthermore, we neither recognize ourselves, nor the people we've known for many years. (There are certain resemblances, in regard to a journey back home, to Carlos Castaneda's *Journey to Ixtlan*. 1972) It's not that the world has become mysterious for the first time. It always was mysterious. Here, again, it's just that we never realized it, until now. Why, then, is this so horrifying? Plato may offer us a clue.

Leaving the Cave

Plato's Allegory of the Cave, from "The Republic," invokes the uncanny. The basic narrative is that we are, metaphorically speaking, prisoners viewing shadows on the wall of a cave, imagining that these shadows are the real thing. What is disturbing is not that Plato takes us to strange lands, but that what we ordinarily take to be true reality is seen to be unreal, or at best half-real. Films, like *The Matrix* (1999), have had plot lines based on one or more characters realizing that their world is no more than an illusion.

In Plato's Allegory, one prisoner is released from his bonds and allowed to leave the cave of illusion. But he doesn't want to, so two guards have to drag him out of the cave and to the light while he is kicking and screaming! You can't really blame him, for it means the end of his world, as well as the end of who he takes himself to be. But isn't it liberating? Indeed, it is, but due to what the Buddhists call "attachment," we stubbornly cling to ourselves. Without that clinging, there wouldn't be the uncanny. Why, then, the need to cling? That is a mystery we shall need to explore on another occasion.

Return to the Robot

What light can our previous examples throw on the uncanny and its relation to the Japanese robots? Certain qualities that we normally attribute to people--freedom and autonomy--are lacking. We don't mean that everybody is literally a robot or a mechanical assemblage of parts. Rather, the uncanny valley evokes, in a symbolic, way, a fundamental truth: people really are mechanical, or robotic, in the metaphysical sense.

To be mechanical is to lack volition, as well as self-awareness. As P.D. Ouspensky expressed it: "Divide in yourself the mechanical from the conscious, see how little there is of the conscious, how seldom it works, and how strong is the mechanical--mechanical attitudes, mechanical intentions, mechanical thoughts, mechanical desires."

Most people are mechanical because they are born with certain attitudes that are not challenged in college or else are instilled with politically correct beliefs, which are no more than shadows on the wall of Plato's cave. Inner freedom, on the other hand, is a serious accomplishment, for it requires self-knowledge, which is a rare thing.

Witnessing a lifelike robot unconsciously invites the dangerous perception that robots inhabit this planet. So do films in which characters--believed to be human beings--are discovered to really be robots. *The Stepford Wives* (1975) and *Aliens* (1986) would be examples. It's a dangerous perception because, on a deeper level, it is a true perception.

Here, again, I do not mean robots in the literal sense, but rather robots in the sense of people living mechanically, as Ouspensky meant it. As in all cases of the uncanny, the world that one had been familiar with and comfortable with threatens to disappear, to be replaced by the world as it really is.

To summarize, the uncanny fear that people are really robots is based on a true perception about life. But 99% of the people who have such uncanny fears --whether all the time or just when viewing horror films or seeing robots, like the one pictured above--have no idea what it is that they really fear. They fear the truth about life.

An Antidote to the Terrors of the Uncanny

Awakenings happen, whether or not we seek them. For life is essentially about awakening, despite the fact that we arrange our lives so that we may continue to sleepwalk. Any awakening, to any degree, will evoke the terrors of the uncanny. A life devoted to self-knowledge--assuming that it is genuine and not yet another hideout from the truth of human existence--will evoke it all the more.

The remedy to life's terrors involves balance. In one of Carlos Castaneda's books, Don Juan Matus, recommends balancing the terrors of life with the sense of wonder. There are other transcendent emotions, in addition to wonder, including: amazement, awe and, for want of a better term, cosmic laughter. This balancing act is, in its own way, as artful as anything that the tightrope walker, Philippe Petit, has attempted. If we are to survive the rigors of the journey to self-knowledge and inner freedom, we must walk the tightrope that hangs over that abyss--known as the Uncanny Valley--at every moment of every day.

Questions for the Reader to Ponder

1. Have you ever experienced the uncanny?

2. What precipitated the experience?

3. How were you able to reconnect to your world and end the terror?

4. What insights did you gain from the encounter?

The Mystery of Bobby Fisher's Madness

The chess champion Gary Kasparov wrote an interesting book entitled *How Life Imitates Chess* (2007). Yes, life does imitate chess, but chess' real appeal lies in how very different it is from life. To understand that difference is to understand Bobby Fisher. Edward Rothstein, of the NY Times, provides us with a clue in that regard: "But there is still something about Mr. Fischer's craziness that is closely connected with the essential nature of chess...The world itself, with its more messy human interactions, its complicated histories, its emotional conflicts, can be put aside, and attention focused on an intricate bounded cosmos." The real world is, indeed, messy; chess, by contrast, has a logical purity, clarity and lucidity.

There exists a connection between Mr. Fisher's longing for logical clarity and paranoia. Paranoia is essentially a desperate effort to make sense of what is unintelligible. It's an attempt to find meaning and coherence in a world in which, in the language of Yeats, "things fall apart; the center cannot hold." Consider conspiracy theories, which are the stock and trade of the paranoid. It is, for example, absurd to think that a lone gunman, a worthless loser, can have a major effect on the course of history. It's absurd, because it defies logic that a small cause can produce a gigantic effect. But that is precisely what happened when Lee Harvey Oswald assassinated President Kennedy. The paranoid cannot accept the absurdity and so conceives a conspiracy theory of gigantic proportions to give meaning to an event, where meaning is lacking. When Fisher's world was confined to chess tournaments, it was the Russians who he accused of cheating at chess and thus conspiring to defeat him. When Fisher's world extended beyond the chessboard, he accused the Jews. He remained a conspiracy theorist throughout.

How very different, then, chess is from life. Generals, who fight real battles, are acquainted with "the fog of war," for one is surrounded by uncertainties and surprises. Often, the victor is the one making the least blunders. In the game of chess, by contrast, everything is clearly laid out on the chessboard. Life really imitates poker far more than chess, for in poker you do not know what cards your opponents are holding. Nor do you know what cards you'll draw. But chance, luck, and contingency are absent from the game of chess. That has been chess' universal appeal, and it certainly was that for Bobby Fisher who, in flight from this messy affair called life, became addicted to chess.

Brian M. Carney, in an article in the "Wall Street Journal," noted that Fisher, from early on, nurtured a sense of grievance. Indeed, the essential feeling of paranoids is that they have a just grievance, which is accompanied by feelings of self-pity, anger and bitterness. No narrative is more baleful to the development of character and morality. (It is, by the way, the predominant mood of many people today, including Islamics, feminists, socialists, and students indoctrinated at politically correct universities.) The sense of grievance was the poison that increasingly polluted Fisher's soul.

As to whether Bobby Fisher was clinically paranoid is anyone's guess. It is clear, though, that his way of seeing the world was indicative of what historian Richard Hofstadter called the "paranoid style." That was the source of Fisher's power as well as his downfall. When he saw his enemy to be the Soviet Union, he became supercharged for battle, for a Manichean worldview is key to the paranoid style. After all, life is most often full of messy moral ambiguities. It's a relief to the paranoid to see the world in black and white, like the pieces on the chessboard. (Of course, the Russians have always acted politically to lend credence to the saying "Sometimes paranoids are right.")

For Fisher to have to defend his chess title wasn't congruent with his paranoid narrative. After all, the other side of paranoia is delusions of grandeur. When a person knows he is the greatest--and with justification, for Fisher was an incredible chess player--he has nothing to gain and everything to lose. So Fisher refused to defend his title against Anatoly Karpov and lost it by default. That was the beginning of the end. Fisher's paranoia had been contained by the closed world of chess, but when he abandoned the game, and his paranoia seeped through the bounds of that closed world, his sanity was soon gone, although he continued to live for many years more.

In his latter years, Fisher, whose parents were Jewish, became a rabid antisemite. The Jews have always been the favorite target of paranoid conspiracy theorists. It is not, as some have claimed, because of their money or power. It is due to the fact that the Jewish religion embodies a concern for fairness, justice and morality, coupled with a strong sympathy for other people. It's particularly the quality of sympathy that is antithetical to the paranoid view of the world. What Fisher found to be threatening was, therefore, not by the Jews, but by what they represented to him. He feared that he might become a *mensch*, a moral and decent person. Then he would be checkmated. Nurturing a grievance is an attempt at self-vindication and, as such, is a very poor surrogate for morality. As such, it is a flight from morality. Madness is the ultimate flight.

Questions for the Reader to Ponder

Write a dialogue in which you're a philosophical counselor and Bobby Fisher is your client. You start to share with Mr. Fisher some of the insights that you gained from this essay, upon which Mr. Fisher accuses you of working for the CIA and Dr. Dillof of being a Russian spy. Hmm, you need a new approach. What can you do to help Mr. Fisher? Here's a clue from Robert Greene: "When dealing with people who are lost in the reflections of fantasy worlds (including the host of people who do not live in mental hospitals), never try to push them into reality by shattering their mirrors. Instead, enter their world and operate inside it, under their rules, gently guiding them out of the hall of mirrors they have entered." --R. Greene. *The 48 Laws of Power*, Viking Press, p. 387.

The Law of Attraction as Flight From Reality

"If Wishes were Horses, Beggars would ride."

--J. Kelly Scottish, Proverbs

In the "new-age" section of any large bookstore, there is a subsection of volumes about the "Law of Attraction." There you'll find the grandfather of the genre Think and Grow Rich, by Napoleon Hill, as well as the recent bestseller The Secret by Rhonda Byrne, and hundreds of other titles. If you surf the web, you'll find a whole slew of sites devoted to the subject. This is not a fad, but a kind of belief system, with an ever-growing number of adherents. In its various forms, it's been around at least from the early 19th Century. It's worth examining for what it reveals about the present zeitgeist.

The Law of Attraction is the belief that by shifting your mindset in a positive way, you'll attain worldly success. The idea is that if you have a negative attitude, you'll attract negative things, but if you have a positive attitude, you'll attract positive things. Does there actually exist a law called "The Law of Attraction?" It has never been established--by physicists, mathematicians, psychologists, or by anybody--that such a law exists, but its adherents call it a law to give it the cachet of science. It's really just a wooly blend of pseudo-science and new-age pseudo-religion.

To a certain extent, it's true that a positive outlook on life can favorably influence other people, which can sometimes increase the odds that our endeavors will be successful. But the advocates of The Law of Attraction go so far in that direction that they neglect to consider the real prerequisites of success, such as hard work, a willingness to sacrifice for one's goals, determination, endurance over the long haul, a winnable business strategy, adequate start-up capital, connections, sufficient self-knowledge to avoid shooting oneself in the foot, too often, and a good measure of luck.

Furthermore, the road to success usually involves a good deal of failing, along the way. It's full of hardships, bitter disappointments, frustrations, heartbreak, calamity, and disillusionment. I.E., it's no different than life itself. (If one needs an example of this, read a biography of Lincoln.) Those who become successful persevere in the face of adversity. Even then, it's possible to achieve greatness and fail by worldly standards. Consider Vincent Van Gogh. During his entire lifetime, he sold only one painting. How different real life is from the easy path to success promised by The Law of Attraction. It's popular because it promises success without the hardships!

The Least Significant Factor in Worldly Success

A positive attitude towards life is probably the least significant factor in worldly success, for there have probably been at least as many grouchy pessimists who enjoy material success as there are cheerful optimists. Consider a few examples: Was George Steinbrenner, owner of the NY Yankees, known for his likable personality and positive attitude? Is Rupert Murdoch, the newspaper magnate? How about Donald Trump? They are known for hard work, risk-taking, shrewdness, and ruthlessness. On those occasions when they do seem positive and cheerful, it's probably because they just ate a competitor for lunch. They certainly have little interest in being well-liked.

It's true that a billionaire will often, in later life, wish to be well-liked and so become a philanthropist. Names like Andrew Carnegie, John D. Rockefeller, and Bill Gates come to mind. Their generosity is certainly commendable and it is inspiring to see a Scrooge become a likable fellow. But being well-liked isn't how they made their billions.

This notion that positive thinking and popularity is the very key to success is an American myth, one as old as Horatio Alger. It was given a boost in such bestsellers as Norman Vincent Peale's *The Power of Positive Thinking* (1952) When you perpetrate a falsehood or a half-truth, it's bound to have negative consequences. One such consequence is that there are millions of people going through life with a frozen smile, forcing themselves to be positive all of the time. It's not too good for one's mental health to be a smiling zombie. Nor can it do wonders for their social life. After all, too much positivity can be rather warring on friends and family.

Chronic positive thinking can even have tragic consequences. Apropos is Arthur Miller's play, *Death of a Salesman* (1949), which is about a true believer in the myth of positive thinking. The protagonist of the play, Willy Loman, believed that "a smile and a shoeshine" was the key to success. Like any tragic hero, he lacked self-knowledge. He didn't know himself enough to realize that he simply wasn't cut out to be a successful salesman, but would have likely been far more successful in some other profession.

The world is full of Willy Lomans, trying to sell everything from *Amway* to investments. Each year, they attend brainwashing sessions--i.e., motivational seminars--where they meet with thousands of other smiling zombies. When they return home, they try to reinvoke the hypnagogic state by means of motivational tapes. It's unsettling to see those who are in desperate flight from reality, for behind their layers of repression lies the dawning realization that they've been deluding themselves.

Positive Thinking as Puerile Thinking

What, then, is the real psychological appeal of The Law of Attraction? This brings us to Freud. He distinguished between two modes of psychological functioning: primary and secondary processes. Primary process--at the service of the "pleasure principle"--involves imagining or wishing for something. Secondary process--at the service of the "reality principle--is where you go out and get it. It's all the difference between dreaming of a hamburger and actually driving to a restaurant and ordering one. Freud realized that we need both wishes and action to function.

The appeal of the Law of Attraction lies in a delusion: if you dream hard enough of the hamburger, it will come to you. This is the pleasure principle to the exclusion of the reality principle. I.E., the

Law of Attraction involves an exclusive reliance on primary process, or magical thinking. That is what makes it childish. It's appeal is that positive thinking will, by virtue of The Law of Attraction, act like Aladdin's magic lamp. It will magically supply you with money, love, everything you could wish for. It's really a wish to get something for nothing. To top it off, it's all under the guise of pseudo-spirituality.

The whole notion of ridding oneself of negative thoughts is a dubious psychological strategy. Take, for example, self doubts. It's true that unreasonable doubts and fears can block us from succeeding. But, quite often, there's a reason for our doubts and it's foolish not to address it. As Kierkegaard contends, in *The Concept of Dread*, anxiety is a teacher that guides us where we need to go. The same is true of our doubts.

Life is neither all clouds nor all sunshine. It is a combination of both. The Yin Yang symbol represents the interrelationship between opposites. To seek to have all positive without negative, is as foolish as seeking to have all sun with no clouds. What is needed, then, isn't positive thinking but a kind of dialectical thinking, in which one recognizes the necessary interplay of positive and negative.

Questions for the Reader to Ponder

1. Positive thinking? Ha! Ha! The negative is the catalyst for self-transformation. Who would you be today if you hadn't suffered in that crucible?

2. Does the belief that certain herbs and vitamins are panaceas involve magical thinking? Does romance involve magical thinking? Come to think of it, might Frank's gambling really be a form of magical thinking? What are other examples?

What Makes for a Free Spirit?

In the film, *Yes Man* (2008), Jim Carey plays the part of Carl, a conventional, introverted, cautious fellow who works as a bank loan officer. We gather that Carl has never really recovered from his divorce and has, since then, socially withdrawn. Carl's friends try to draw him out of his shell, but to little avail. Finally something does happen that transforms Carl's life. He is convinced--after attending a meeting led by Terrence, a motivational speaker and guru--to say, "yes" to everything that comes his way.

As evidence of his transformation, we see Carl engaging in unconventional, somewhat risky behavior. Here, then, is an intriguing example of someone employing a variant of the George Costanza strategy of "doing the opposite" of what he is accustomed to do. In this case, it involved rejecting life's possibilities to a new openness to them. The film is also reminiscent, in that respect, to *Groundhog Day* (1993).

Naturally, almost every Hollywood film must have its romantic interest. So it that Carl encounters a young woman named Alison, who offers him a ride on her motorcycle. To reinforce that Alison is a free spirit, we see her singing in a punk rock band, doing photography, driving her motorcycle, in a carefree and reckless fashion, and being altogether spontaneous and bohemian. In time, Carl and Alison fall in love.

Their relationship proceeds swimmingly, until Allison asks Carl to move in with her. Carl thinks for a moment before agreeing. Allison takes umbrage over Carl's moment of hesitation, so she immediately breaks up with him. Carl then seeks to win her back. He finally convinces her of his love and they live happily ever after.

This leads us to an interesting question: what constitutes a free spirit? Does riding a motorcycle, warring tattoos, and playing in a rock band mean that one's spirit is free? The fact that Alison was so hurt and angered by Carl's moment of hesitation indicates that she is subject to the type of longings all too familiar in male/female relationships. More specifically, Alison's view of romance involves being loved unconditionally, with no qualifications whatsoever. The fact that Carl hesitated before agreeing to move in with her means that his love is conditional. This wounded Alison's vanity, for it implies that she is not everything to him, that she is not a goddess.

Alison is a child of the times, the age of Carl Rogers, with his foolish notion that true love, between everybody--including man and wife--must be unconditional. Yes, love between a parent and a young child is unconditional, but all other forms of love must be conditional, if they are to endure. This is certainly true of the love of between a husband a wife, for both partners are required to fulfill duties and obligations to each other, if they are to remain worthy of each other's love and respect. Indeed, in the scene where they reconcile, Carl explains to Alison that moving in together is a serious thing and requires a certain amount of sober-minded reflection. Carl, in other words, reveals himself to be a responsible person, one who is capable of a more mature and lasting love.

Have Alison's dark feelings been inwardly illuminated by Carl's explanation? One would like to think so. It's more likely, though, that their first fight and breakup has set the tone for their future marriage. I.E., Alison will wish to be loved unconditionally, Carl shall err, and he shall be doing a lot of apologizing, explaining, begging, and groveling to win her back. Needless to say, this is not a very happy prognosis for either of them. We see, then, that Alison is subject to the same sort of puerile longings that anyone, whose heart is uneducated about love and by life, would have. In that sense, she is awfully conventional and is anything but a free spirit. (For more on relationships, read *Awakening with the Enemy: The Origin and End of Male/Female Conflict.* 2000)

This leads us back to the question: what constitutes a free spirit? Those who are truly free have liberated themselves from the plethora of beliefs, assumptions, and ideas, endemic to the present age. This is not simply an intellectual accomplishment, for all of the dark corners of one's personal life must also be illuminated, if one is to be free. We offered Carl and Alison's relationship as an example, but male/female relationships are only one of a number of areas in need of clarification. This is not something one accomplishes overnight. It requires years of concerted effort.

Furthermore, to become truly free, one must liberate oneself not only from the present zeitgeist, but from all of the residual thought-forms that we have unwittingly inherited from earlier centuries. It means illuminating, on a personal level, the last 2500 years of Western culture and ideas.

Hollywood films reflect prevailing notions of freedom, happiness and fulfillment. All in all, the idea of freedom hasn't matured much since Marlon Brando came roaring into town in *The Wild One* (1953). It's still all about riding a motorcycle, being unconventional, defying authority, and acting wild and crazy. It's all encapsulated in the Michael Jackson song, where he brags about being "bad." These images of freedom represent the adolescence of the spirit. Becoming a truly free spirit, on the other hand, is a great accomplishment and something very rare.

Even were Hollywood able to grasp elevated notions of freedom, such notions are not the driving energy of motion pictures, for inner freedom is difficult to render dramatically. That is because inner freedom is, in its essence, constituted not by drama but by a lack of drama, i.e., by inner peace.

Questions for the Reader to Ponder

1. Are you a free spirit? If not, are you willing to do all that's required to attain inner-liberation? What steps are you taking? What would be true hipness?

2. Do you think you're hip because you wear a tattoo, stare at an I-Pad at *Starbucks*, recycle, worship Gaia and blather politically correct nostrums about social justice? Aristotle wrote, "The gods too are fond of a joke." Do you ever suspect that they're laughing at you?

344

The Anxiety Underlying Global Warming Hysteria

Why are the overwhelming majority of people who fear "global warming" politically left of center? The obvious answer is that the left is critical of business and industry, which they regard as the major producers of "greenhouse gases." But the left has had an animus towards big business long before they became preoccupied with environmental fears. We won't explore, here, the origins of their anti-business bias. Suffice it to say that this animus is only part of the reason anyway. There is something deeper going on that is the real source of their environmental fears.

Leftwing thought is really a certain species of the humanistic worldview. Humanism has its origins in the Renaissance, when the shift from religious to secular interests and concerns first began. A humanist believes that the future is not in God's hands, but in our own. Thus it is solely up to us to make and shape our world and our future. Since God plays a vastly diminished role in the humanistic worldview, humanists easily slide from theism to deism and then finally into atheism.

This worldview has produced remarkable achievements in culture and civilization. It has freed the mind of dogma and granted us the independence to think for ourselves. Kant encapsulated this enlightenment of the mind, when he wrote: *Sapere aude!* (Dare to be wise!) Alas, every worldview has its limits and those limits register in us as certain types of anxiety. As we shall see, the fear of global warming reflects the type of anxieties endemic to secular humanism.

To understand these anxieties, we must remember that those who no longer believe in God always find other objects of worship, for everyone craves the absolute and the eternal. Instead of seeking Heaven, as religious people do, humanists seek to create a heaven on Earth. Thus do they make an idol of the nation-state, believing that it can become transformed into something wonderful and glorious. Their

Utopia invariably reflects the puerile longing that everyone be equal economically. When humanism takes on a utopian political agenda it easily transforms into fascism, socialism and communism, for these are utopian creeds with a plan of action. We shall now consider what this worldview has to do with environmental fears.

Humanism: A Burdened and Anxious Way of Being

There's no denying that human beings can damage the planet and that we should seek, as much as possible, to conserve its beauty and to ensure that it remains a salutary and livable place. It's quite another thing, though, to dread the cycles of hot and cold that naturally occur, but rather to insist that they are solely the fault of man, despite ample scientific evidence to the contrary.

These fears derive from the anxiety of inhabiting a godless universe, thus having the fate of the world solely depend upon us. Consequently, we fear that if something is not done immediately to gain control over the environment, we are doomed. What a burdened and anxious thing it is to be a humanist, believing that it is up us human beings, in all our fallibility--this "crooked timbre of humanity," as Kant called us--to be the caretakers of the planet. It also creates a mood ripe for demagogues. Thus do we so often hear, from the saviors of the political left: "We, from big government, can save you! We shall punish those evil polluting corporations!"

Paradoxically, through a curious dialectic, contemporary humanism often transforms into a kind of anti-humanism, which agues that human beings are the one thing on the planet that is unnatural and, therefore, a plague upon the innocence of nature. This anti-humanistic naturalism makes a fetish of the natural, viewing human beings as violators of pristine nature. Their solution, then, is to curtail the actions on human beings, in so far as they impact the natural world. This leads to a terrible dread that nemesis is on the way, for man's Promethean hubris in seeking to master nature. (It is also paradoxical that those who claim to be free of religion still retain this carryover of religious consciousness.) When people are driven by apocalyptic anxieties, they lose all sense of balance and proportion. In other words, they become extremists--in this case environmental extremists.

Anxiety also leads to paranoia and then to cult thinking, with its us/them view of the world and its demonization of one's opponents. It also leads to massive propaganda efforts to convert people to one's cause. Thus we find that the true believers in global warming have mounted an insidious campaign to indoctrinate grade school children with their belief system. The main tool at their disposal is fear. Children now are as anxious about the future of the planet as are the fanatics. They have robbed childhood of the joyful insouciance that it once possessed.

Faith in God, Nature and the Universe

The opposite attitude to the humanist's anxious insecurity about the future of the world is at attitude of faith, a belief that there are larger forces that are the ground of our existence. Whatever we call it--God, Nature or the Universe--we are kept alive by its grace. In a brilliant passage, two Zen Buddhists express this faith:

> *"If we abandon the feeling that we are separate, fragile egos in unreliable bodies and a dangerous, alien universe, we will naturally take on the feeling that we ourselves are the nondual combination, the organism-environment complex. Many dangers undeniably exist, but if the combination were not primarily favorable to survival, we wouldn't be here. The odds are in our favor. To struggle for an underlying security and to think that we have achieved it may well alter the odds against us. We are better off accepting the fact that the world gives no annuity guaranteeing us life, health, and happiness. The Fates, said the Romans, find a path for the willing and betray the unwilling."* (Holmes, Stewart W. and Chimyo Horioka. Zen Art for Meditation. Charles E. Tuttle Company. Rutland Vermont: 1990. p. 80.)

This doesn't mean that we adopt a fatalistic attitude towards the planet. Nor does it mean that we lead a careless life, unnecessarily exposing ourselves to dangers. We must, as Holmes and Horioka contend, still seek, as much as it is in our power, to keep our powder dry. It behooves us, though, to recognize and come to terms with who we are and to accept--even better to appreciate--life's uncertainty and precariousness. When we accept the human condition and come to realize that we are sustained by something greater than ourselves, we become liberated from the Chicken Little panic over nature's vicissitudes. What a relief it is to let go of anxiety about the morrow!

Questions for the Reader to Ponder

1. Do you intend to go through life like Chicken Little (bock, bock, bock, bock, bock, begowwwwk) or do you intend to let go and embrace the void?

2. In Walt Kelly's comic strip, *Pogo,* Albert the Alligator has been falsely accused of having eaten a puppy and is standing trial before a very large set of gallows, just built with him in mind. Albert faints and is revived with a bucket of water. Porkypine then says to Albert, *"Don't take life so serious, son... It ain't* **NO HOW** *permanent."* Write a 20,000 word philosophical exegesis of Porkypine's comment, comparing it to what the jailor said to the condemned Socrates, when he handed him the cup of hemlock that he was latter to drink, *"Try to bear lightly that which must be."* Have your essay professionally edited and peer reviewed by a committee of at least 200 distinguished scholars, from at least seven continents. Then print up copies and sell it at flea markets, hawk it on the streets of downtown Manhattan (wearing a sandwich board) or give away autographed copies as a holiday gift or a birthday present. Then have a beer.

The Transformative Power of Doing the Opposite

> *"The wise have always said the same things, and fools, who are the majority, have always done just the opposite."*
>
> --Arthur Schopenhauer

> *"If every instinct you have is wrong, then the opposite would have to be right."*
>
> --Jerry Seinfeld

There is a classic episode of *Seinfeld*, in which George Costanza--in despair over the never-ending series of failures that constitutes his existence--tells Jerry and Elaine that since everything he does is invariably the wrong thing to do, that he will do the opposite. Thus, when the waitress arrives at their table, George decides to break with custom. Instead of ordering a tuna salad sandwich with coffee, he orders a chicken salad sandwich with tea.

George then sees an attractive woman sitting alone at the lunch counter. The usual thing he does, owing to a lack of confidence, is nothing. But, with the encouragement of Jerry, George gets up from the table and approaches her. George initiates a conversation with the woman. Here, too, he does the opposite; instead of trying to impress her with his usual blarney, George bluntly tells her the truth: "Hi I'm George. I'm unemployed and I live with my parents." The woman, Victoria, finds George's bold honesty refreshing and appealing. She becomes romantically involved with him, and then arranges an interview for George with her uncle, who works for the Yankees. Her uncle then introduces George Costanza to George Steinbrenner, who owns the Yankees. George then does the opposite of what anyone else would do at an interview: instead of fawning over Steinbrenner or at least being polite, he criticizes him for mismanaging the Yankees. Steinbrenner immediately hires him and George gets his dream job.

Doing the opposite has completely transformed George's life, both inwardly and outwardly. The amazing thing is that it all began by ordering chicken salad and tea instead of tuna salad and coffee. Can a seemingly trivial change really precipitate major changes in a person's life? It often can, if we consider that all of our interests, desires, activities, and conflicts are linked together, in an invisible chain, in ways that we do not realize.

For example, that George eats tuna salad everyday for lunch is not insignificant. On the contrary, it is intrinsic to who he is as a person and to his present struggles and conflicts. (I won't venture into what tuna salad might have meant for George psychologically, since he is a fictional character. But the episode rings true enough to actual life.) In any case, when a person changes one thing in his life, it breaks the chains of habit such that everything else--big things, like social relations and career prospects--can also undergo a transmutation. Here, then, in the words of the *I-Ching,* is the transforming power of the small.

In a prior essay, I soberly explored the binding power of fate, i.e., the fixity of our character, or personality, to determine our life possibilities. Can the leveraging power of a seemingly inconsequential change free us from our fate? The prospect of inner freedom is intoxicating! But, there is a catch: making a slight change can often be immensely difficult. That is because little things often symbolize really big things. For example, giving up a single scoop of chocolate ice cream can symbolize the beginning of a life of self-renunciation. Certainly, a seemingly trivial change can evoke the fear of the unknown. We might, for example, decide to take a walk down a different street, but such as seemingly minor change can symbolize setting out in a new life direction.

Not all minor changes will lead to major life transformations, but most can still have a significant, if less dramatic, effect. A lot depends upon the ripeness of a person, his or her readiness for change. Such ripeness is a function of despair, the realization that one's current mode of existence is hopeless, and cannot bring one happiness and fulfillment. Despair, as Kierkegaard knew so well, is the doorway to a new life. As to whether or not we enter the door is, of course, another story.

A Related Phenomenon

There is another, somewhat related, phenomenon that we should consider. It can sometimes happen that we do change in some significant way, but don't realize it. Then, one day, we are surprised to discover that we no longer wish to do what we had always been doing. We might find, for example, that we suddenly have no interest in drinking a peach brandy, but would rather have a scotch on the rocks. Or, perhaps, we look in the mirror and, for the first time, feel that the hairstyle that we have had for many years no longer seems appropriate. These little things are often indicative of big changes.

Albert Camus wrote, "Great ideas... come into the world as gently as doves." As such, they often enter unnoticed. The same is true of the great changes that can occur in one's character. When a major shift occurs, it often enters "as gently as doves." Of course, what led up to the change was the alchemy of insight. I.E., insight gradually illuminates our life experiences. Then, one day, a tipping-point is reached--we now know too much to be the same person--and the change occurs.

The thing to do, then, is to take an inventory of all one's doings in the world, in all domains, from food preferences to one's manner of dress, from how one sits, stands, and walks to the words or expressions one uses in conversation. After completing this inventory, one should follow George Costanza's example and do the opposite of what one is wont to do. If, for example, one wears knit shirts, one should switch to button-downs, and vice versa. If one avoids striking up conversations with strangers, one should initiate conversations with strangers. If one frequents the ballpark, one should frequent the opera, or vice versa.

After his strategy proves successful, George says to Jerry and Elaine: "And it's all happening because I'm completely ignoring every urge to common sense and good judgment I've ever had. This is no longer some crazy notion. Elaine, Jerry, this is my religion." But we must beware, for here is where resistance can set in. After all, are we truly prepared to jettison our common sense and good judgment? That loss can be quite disorienting. As George explains, up will seem down, and down will seem up. If we are not prepared to lose our touchstone of reasonability, we will find ourselves regressing to our habitual way of being in the world.

Of course, what we had considered to be common sense and good judgment was really life seen through the distorted mirror of our misconceptions, egotism, fears, and all else that grows from the darkness within. And so, like Kierkegaard's knight of faith, the biblical Abraham, we are required to abandon our judgment, common sense, and reason if we are to transform into the type of person who is able to receive God's blessings, his wish that we may be fruitful and multiply.

In any case, if we implement George Costanza's "do the opposite" strategy, we may find that we have the leverage to alter the course of our fate. A change of this sort is nothing short of miraculous.

Questions for the Reader to Ponder

1. Make a list of everything that you do habitually, including little things like always ordering the same kind of sandwich, wearing the same style of clothing, or having the same kind of stride when you walk. Now, seek to do the opposite of everything on your list. Actually, it would probably be better to start with just one thing that you do. Doing the opposite of that one thing might be powerful enough to effectuate some major changes. What was the result, for you, of this practice?

2. Let us suppose that you this practice has led to major changes in your life, just as it did for George Costanza. If there exists a "Conservation of Suffering Principle, as we have contended earlier, then the "new you" isn't really any happier than the

"old you," for the negative has merely taken on a new form. For example, if you had been poor, but now are rich, you are now unsure whether people really like you for who you are or just for your money. Have you, then, detected the conservation of suffering in regard to the new you?

The Psychological Fascination with Batman

How very different are the world's of Superman and Batman. Superman inhabits the heavenly realm of Apollo, as suggested by the iconic image of him flying through the sky. He even comes to Earth, from somewhere in the heavens, the planet Krypton. Superman is really a demigod. He is a mythic expression of the hope that many people have, of a savior who will bring come to the rescue of the weak, in the name of justice.

Batman, on the other hand, doesn't possess superpowers. Thus, unlike Superman, he is not a demigod, but a mortal being. That is what makes him a hero. Batman inhabits a much different world than Superman. His is not the realm of Apollo, but the dark underworld of Pluto. Everything about Batman suggests bats, caves, and the dark depths. The name of the most recent Batman film, *Dark Knight* (2008), suggests that he inhabits that realm.

On those evenings, when he sees the bat signal flash across the sky--indicating that Gotham City needs his help--Batman returns to those subterranean depths to fight crime. He does so not because he has been condemned to be there, like a denizen of Dante's Inferno. On the contrary, he returns there, for it is his mission to battle evil in that hellish realm.

It has rightly been said that clothes make the man. Superman's outfit is an inspiring red, yellow and blue, not far afield from the colors of the American flag. Batman's bat costume is a lot more somber looking and is intended to be frightening to criminals. In so far as what we wear reflects our inner being, Batman's garb suggests that there is something dark about him. This theme is hinted at, but not really explored in the Batman comic books and films. Indeed, Batman never becomes the type of antihero that finds expression in the noir detective novels and films of the 1940s and 1950s. The suggestion, in any case, is that to spend one's life in the underworld, one must become a bit dark oneself.

Interestingly enough, in the recent Batman film *Dark Knight* (2008), the crime-fighting district attorney, Harvey Dent, does become corrupted, terribly so, expressing the truth of Nietzsche's maxim "Battle not with monsters, lest ye become one." Perhaps, then, DA Dent is a foil for Batman, for to not become corrupted one must be not just a man, but a saint.

1939: A Dark Year

It makes sense that Bob Kane created the comic book hero Batman, in 1939. For that was a time when millions of soldiers were leaving America to fight abroad, in the darker climes of Europe and Asia. And they were fighting very dark, deadly foes, the Nazis and the Japanese. Like those soldiers, Batman was there not because he wanted to be--for America could have avoided entering the war, at least for a time--but out of a sense of moral obligation. If Batman is popular, once again, it is because American forces are "over there," once again, only this time in Iraq and Afghanistan. And they may soon be in other nations as well.

Soldiers, in uniform, are, to a large degree, anonymous. Their anonymity reflects the ideal of non-egotism. Similarly, Batman is disguised. Few know his true identity. (He is a lot like the Lone Ranger, in that respect.) By day, he is Bruce Wayne, the billionaire industrialist. Mr. Wayne cannot receive credit for Batman's heroism.

We had stated earlier that Batman is seeking justice, and that is true. But he is also seeking revenge. As a young boy, he witnessed his parents being murdered by criminals. He thus seeks vengeance, but vengeance tempered by justice. His tragic past and his mixed motives makes Batman a more human and a more interesting character than Superman.

Batman as Doppelganger

There are a number of literary characters that represent the doppelganger, or double, theme. Sometimes, the double consists of a person who represents some element of character missing from the protagonist. Examples include Conrad's short story *The Secret Sharer* and Dostoevsky's *The Double.* In the case of Stevenson's *Dr. Jekyll and Mr. Hide,* the protagonist has developed a split personality. The evil Mr. Hyde is the good Dr. Jekyll's dark side.

We see the doppelganger effect in both the Superman and the Batman epics. Superman's disguise is that of the news reporter Clark Kent. Clark, who is described as "mild-mannered," is good-natured, but a bit dull. At least his fellow reporter, Lois Lane, feels that way about him. What is missing from Clark's personality is heroism. In a sense, Clark is everyman who--like Walter Mitty--dreams that his true being is that of a hero.

Batman's disguise is that of billionaire industrialist, Bruce Wayne. Here, again, it is really the other ways around. We might say that Batman represents the "secret sharer," the alter ego, of every person who has become a bit bored by his comfortable lifestyle and who feels an inner calling to pursue a greater cause. In the film *Casablanca* (1942), we see Rick's transformation from comfortable, but cynically jaded, restaurant owner, back to being the hero he once was. Clark Kent and Bruce Wayne need not transform, for their doubles actualize their heroic potential.

Afterword: Superhero or Normal Person? Which is the Real Disguise?

Sherlock Holmes is almost always appears wearing his trademark deerstalker hat, cloaked coat, clutching a magnifying glass, except on those rare occasions when he goes undercover. He has no double life, but Superman and Batman do. We have explored this doubling in regard to the doppelganger archetype. There may, though, be more involved here. When Clark Kent and Bruce Wayne go out in the world to fight crime, they become Superman and Batman. Everyone can tell, by their garb, that they are superheroes. It is often the case, though, that those who have great aspirations must, if they are to succeed in the world, hide their light under a bushel. That means going through the world appearing as a regular person, in a common profession.

Soren Kierkegaard, in one of his diaries, states that if he had not become a philosopher, he would have made a good spy. He meant that he had the ability to talk with men and women, ferreting out their secrets from them. The secrets, to which he was referring, had to do with their philosophy of life. He could also challenge their view, in a gently Socratic fashion. Socrates, after all, came across not as the philosophical superhero, which he was, but as a humble man who was just searching for the truth. He readily acknowledged his ignorance. A latter day version of Socrates is Police Lieutenant Colombo (played by Peter Falk). So it is that he or she, who would do great things, must often conceal the fact that they are superheroes and do their work undercover.

Questions for the Reader to Ponder

1. Who is your favorite superhero? Why?

2. If you could have only one superpower, what would it be? You may recall, that for Dorothy it was the ability to breathe underwater. Write a dialogue or screenplay about a person who has this superpower. (If the film gets produced, please be sure to spell "Dillof" correctly, when you thank me, in the credits.)

3. Then write a critical analysis of your dialogue, in which you seek to see how your mode of being has influenced your choice of superpower and the plot of the story.

The Deeper Mystery of the Faux Brownstone

There's an apartment building in Brooklyn that's not what it seems to be. It's really a subway entrance! Furthermore, there are subway entrances, disguised like this one, throughout New York City. A news item about the faux brownstone recently appeared in a number of papers, captivating quite a few readers. What is it about this fake building that's so fascinating? Why are such appearance/reality mysteries so intriguing?

Classified Secrets of the Manhattan Transit Authority

Before delving into the heart of the real mystery, which is metaphysical, let's try to understand the ostensible mystery. Why did the MTA, the agency that runs the New York City subway system, wish to build a subway entrance at that particular location? One cannot, from the newspaper accounts, discern precisely why. Some suggest that it has something to do with counter-terrorism. But it's unclear as to how these disguised entrances would function in that capacity or as part of any other stealth operation.

Furthermore, the people living in the neighborhood of this particular faux brownstone have long known that it's a secret subway entrance. We also learn, from the newspaper articles that MTA workers will often enter and leave the secret entrance and have their lunch on the steps of the building. So it can't be all that much of a top secret.

Let's say that, for whatever the reason, the MTA needed to have a subway entrance at that particular location. Perhaps, then, they thought that it should be aesthetically pleasing, that it blend in with the surrounding buildings and not be an eyesore. All that is reasonable enough. Yes, the MTA used both security and aesthetics to justify the project. All the same, unless city workers have souls of mud, the clandestine project must have intrigued them, even if they couldn't admit it, for fear of having the taxpayers scrutinize the expenditures for the faux building. Perhaps, they thought to themselves: "Wow! We're building a secret subway entrance. Holy James Bond! This is super cool!" The secret entrance certainly evokes images from spy stories and films of intrigue. One can imagine Harry Lime emerging out of the brownstone, as he did from the secret entrance, from the sewers of Vienna, in the film *The Third Man*. (1949)

Evoking Appearance and Reality

The deeper question here is not about the motives of the MTA. It's really about why secret entrances--and all things disguised--engender a certain thrilling sense of wonderment and perplexity? They seem to tap into the fundamental metaphysical belief that things are not what they seem. Indeed, it evokes the appearance/reality distinction that lies at the heart of philosophy, mysticism and paranoia. The notion that we are sleepwalkers in a dream--one from which, with great effort, we can awaken--is quite ancient. We find it in the ancient Hindu *Upanishads* and in Plato's *Allegory of the Cave*.

If the defining moment of ancient philosophy was Plato's *Allegory*, the seminal moment of modern philosophy was Descartes' metaphysical doubt, which he resolved--perhaps a bit too facilely--by his realization "I think, therefore I am." And we find this same doubt expressed in films like *The Matrix* (1999), and *The Truman Show* (1998).

Odd though it seems, everyone suspects that things aren't what they appear to be. We are born with such metaphysical doubts. Rather then turning to philosophy to uncover the true reality underlying appearances, many people become interested in conspiracy theories. For example, it may appear that a lone gunman assassinated President Kennedy, but the underlying reality is, according to the conspiracy theorists, that some powerful group was really involved. This isn't to deny that actual conspiracies exist. But the interest in them involves a kind of primitive appearance/reality distinction. The fascination with the faux brownstone belongs to that conspiratorial sense.

Buildings and the Uncanny

Let's conclude by turning to two painting that evoke the appearance/reality distinction. De Chirico's "Mystery and Melancholy of a Street" is replete with a haunting sense of mystery. The mystery is simultaneously hidden--for the viewer is not clear about what's happening in the painting--and yet apparent, for everything is infused with by an uncanny sense of an enigma, even if it remains beyond our conceptual grasp.

Now consider Edward Hopper's painting "Early Sunday Morning," with its row of shops and second floor apartments. Here, too, dark emotions find expression, as in De Chirico's paintings--loneliness, an eerie and uncanny silence, a sense of foreboding and a deep longing, perhaps for the divine to shatter that unearthly silence. In a certain sense, Hopper's painting is more unsettling than De Chirico's, because it's able to evoke the omnipresent enigma of everyday life without recourse to surrealism. Thus the viewer can't easily reject it, for it's all too familiar. Thus if it's mystery we crave, we needn't travel to Brooklyn in search of faux brownstones. It's always there, right before us, if we dare turn our head to gaze upon it.

Questions for the Reader to Ponder

1. Read Plato's *Allegory of the Cave*. Close your eyes & imagine you're being led out of the cave. Your're now outside the cave! Write down how you feel and what you see.

2. View De Chirico's & Hopper's paintings. Enter deep into their mystery. Write down what you discern & your feelings. Now turn your attention from the paintings to what's in front of you--your desk, the people in your office, your coffee cup, etc. See if you can evoke this same mystery and feel its presence. Write down your thoughts.

The Deeper Meaning of Michigan J. Frog

The most critically acclaimed cartoon, indeed what is considered to be the "Citizen Kane" of this genre, is "One Froggy Evening." It was created in 1955, with a story by Michael Maltese and directed by Chuck Jones. Its protagonist was latter named Michigan J. Frog. [Before reading any further, please see if you can view it on YouTube.]

Here's a run down of the plot. A building is being destroyed. A construction worker discovers, in its 1892 cornerstone, a box. He open it, whereupon out pops a singing frog. The frog, Michigan J. Frog, wears a top hat, carries a cane and sings popular songs from the turn of the century, like "I'm Just Wild About Harry" and "Hello Ma Baby." The construction worker becomes excited by the possibility of getting rich. He brings the frog to a talent agent, but when the frog is in front of the agent, he wont sing. Back home the frog sings again, so the construction worker rents out a theater. But when the frog is in front of the audience, again he wont sing.

Finally, he puts the frog back in the box and seals him up in the cornerstone of the new building. A hundred years goes by; it is the year 2056. Another construction worker, in a space suit destroys, the new building. He then finds the old 1956 cornerstone with the box in it. The box is opened and out pops Michigan J. Frog. The construction worker with the space suit then has the same plan to exploit the frog's singing. The cartoon thus has an ironical, running gag, Twilight Zone type of ending.

What Does It Mean?

Here is Roger Ebert's take on it:

> *"There are tragedies in conflict here: (a) a frog who is a song and dance star, who has been locked in the dark for*

> *decades but cannot perform in public, and (b) a worker who dreams of wealth and is considered a fool and a liar. The story of "One Froggy Evening" involves an endless loop of frustration."* (Roger Ebert, cf. *Chuck Jones: Three Cartoons, 1953-1957*)

I think that Mr. Ebert is perceptive in his analysis. He contends that the story's form is that of a double tragedy, but I myself would contend that the types of frustrations involved here are more likely to be the province of comedy. It could also be argued that since this tale is dripping with dark irony about human aspirations, that it's really what is known as a dark comedy.

But let us proceed to analyze the symbolic meaning of this cartoon parable. There is beauty, culture, ideas and truths of past ages intended for one's own ears only. We might very much wish to share these things with other people--whether our interests are love or money--but are only able to so, to varying degrees. Indeed, sometimes our appreciation for various ideas or aesthetic experiences is simply incommunicable to a larger audience.

Yes, it's true that the frog's music is not high art, but simply Tin Pan Alley ditties. (Although at one point he sings an aria from Rossini's *The Barber of Seville*.) But still, such music can be wonderfully entertaining. It can lift one's spirits, allowing the sunbeams of joy to breakthrough the clouds of worry and concern. The construction worker might have simply enjoyed the frog's fine singing. He might have regarded it as a divine gift, for him alone or perhaps to be shared with a few friends. But, out of greed, he decides to exploit the frog. He seeks to bring people into the auditorium by appealing to their lower nature, i.e., by offering them free beer.

But when the curtain rises for the performance, the frog becomes mute, which symbolically means that those without developed aesthetic capacities cannot hear things of beauty. It would be like inviting pigs to an opera, i.e., casting one's pearls before swine. (It takes a person who has spent years trying to introduce philosophical ideas to the general public, to fully appreciate the incommunicability of various ideas.)

Why a Frog?

Why did the cartoons creator, Michael Maltese, decide upon a singing frog? Why not some other animal? The frog has a multiplicity of symbolic meanings. Shakespeare thoughts on the potential of hard times, which he compares to the hidden riches of frogs, may offer us a clue: "Sweet are the uses of adversity, Which, like the toad, ugly and venomous, Wears yet a precious jewel in his head..." Thus the frog, or the toad, is a very lowly being with great unseen potential. Indeed, the frog is the animal that--upon getting kissed by the princess--transforms into a prince. For Shakespeare, adversity was the catalyst that could transform what is base into what is sweet. For the princess, in the fairytale, it is love. Here, again, a frog (or a toad) is involved with this alchemy.

I wonder, then, if Michigan J. Frog represents the construction worker's unrealized potential. Such potential is often uncovered amidst the ruins of one's old life, as is symbolized by the building, from 1892, that has been destroyed. Of course, to make a living, we have to exploit our capacities. Alas, the construction worker takes it to the extreme. But his potential refuses to perform for others, for it's really not his to exploit.

So it is that our abilities, and talents are a gift to us that's on loan, with certain stipulations as to their use. If we try to mercilessly exploit them, they will not perform. Did Michael Maltese fear that if he allowed his artistic talents to be exploited by *Warner Brothers* that his talents would go mute? Was that the fear that gave rise to this ironic tale? No doubt the cartoon would not be so popular were it not that there is something in its story that resonates in each of us.

There's a lot more to say about the deeper meaning of frogs, for we see frogs in lawn ornaments, in Zen art, and even in films, such as the Coen Brothers "Oh Brother, Where Art Thou?" But in the words of another Warner Brother's cartoon character "That's all folks!"

Questions for the Reader to Ponder

1. Here we find another example of the same kind of conflict

that was tormenting Ricky. Except that Ricky, unlike the construction worker, in the cartoon, did not wish to exploit his musical gifts. If Ricky sells out, like Frank recommends that he do, will he end up like the construction worker? After all, the muses of poetry and song have their limits; they will not be exploited. On the other hand, Frank is right that we need to make a living.

2. Although this question is quite hypothetical, what do you think would have happened if the construction worker had just introduced the frog to a few close friends, with no interest in exploiting the frog's talents? Would the frog have sung for them?

Shoelace Tying as Revelation of Spiritual Wisdom

"I did not come to the Maggid of Mezritch to learn interpretation of Torah from him, but to watch how he tied his shoelaces."

--Hassidic Rabbi R. Leib Sarahs

"I judge a philosopher by whether he is able to serve as an example...But the example must be given through visible life and not merely through books, that is as the Greek philosophers taught... though one's expressions, attitudes, clothing, food, and way of life rather than through speaking, and least of all through writing... the freedom and independence of the mind is mere illusion if this achieved limitlessness--is not proved anew with every look and step from morning till night."

--Friedrich Nietzsche

If you gain profound insights, but they remain in your head--failing to penetrate your entire being--you will become inwardly divided. We find extreme examples of this inner division at colleges and universities. Academics are often full of lofty beliefs, ideas, and ideals, which fail to find expression in their everyday life. Thus, instead of meeting, for example, a philosopher, we meet a person who merely teaches courses in philosophy and whose personal life is as dark as any denizen of Plato's cave.

Kierkegaard rightly compares such an inwardly divided man to two actors dressed in a single horse outfit. Because the two actors have not rehearsed enough, the audience sometimes sees the head of the horse and the rear of the horse moving in separate directions. The effect is quite comical. That is what it is like when ideas, ideals, and insights remain in a man's head, while his actual lived life proceeds in an entirely different direction.

For an insight to be efficacious it must find expression in all of one's actions, in everything one does, from morning till night. Otherwise, the needed transformation will abort. For example, we learn from Rabbi Sarahs--see the above quotation--that the revered Maggid of Mezritch didn't just teach the Torah; he was the living embodiment of the wisdom of the Torah. Everything he did, including the smallest actions--such as tying his shoelaces--became the living expression of the Torah. That is what made him so remarkable. Thus, his students needed only to witness the Maggid in action to learn the heart of the Torah.

Nietzsche found the same sort of embodied wisdom in the lives of the ancient Greek philosophers. The Zen Buddhist tradition also offers examples of Zen masters whose every action was an expression of the truth. They would, for example, pour tea in as means of revealing profound truth, in the hope of bringing their students to enlightenment.

What a Simple Action May Reveal

We have discussed, elsewhere, how to gain profound insights into life. The question that we shall now consider is how to have these insights transform one's very being--one's desires, thoughts, and emotions, actions and activities. Anyone interested in gaining such-self illumination cannot proceed directly to the light. He must, instead, begin by examining his actual attitudes towards life, as they find expression in ordinary activities. Thus, instead of seeking to tie his shoelaces like the Maggid of Mezritch or like a Zen master, he must discern how, in point of fact, he does tie his shoelaces. Only when presently existing attitudes are dissolved, though, insight, can something new appear.

I shall offer an example from my own life. Some years ago, I was surprised to discover that I would hold my breath when tying each of my shoelaces, in the morning. Why, I wondered, would I hold my breath in this fashion? I could find no practical reason to do so. And then it dawned on me. Tying my shoes was, for me, a moment of transition. It was, symbolically speaking, the moment when I left the realm of sleep and entered into the world. I would hold my breath as if I were about to dive off a peer and into a lake. In other words, tying my shoes in morning felt like I am diving into life.

It occurred to me that holding my breath was a mode of resistance to life. Symbolically speaking, it was akin to holding my nose to avoid the stench of human existence. If this was my way of entering into the world, it was not a good one, for how one enters can determine one's relation to life for the ensuing day. In other words, it sets the tone. From then on, I desisted from holding my breath while tying my shoelaces. Doing so opened the door to other insights into life.

I have offered the example of tying one's shoelaces, but it is necessary to illuminate all of one's actions and activities if one is to illuminate and therefore one's mode of existence. Even something as simple as reaching for an item from a shelf, in a supermarket, embodies one's mode of being in the world. It is certainly obvious that a person's manner of eating, walking, sitting, and driving a car reveal everything about his relation to life.

The thing is to be able to read the secret language of the body. In any case, if something new is to appear, one must be freed from the attitudes that presently exist. We can only be freed of them by discovering what they are. One might begin by choosing any customary activity. Having discerned oneself in that action, one should then seek to perform the action free of one's customary attitude.

Tying One's Shoelaces Impeccably

There is a story that Carlos Castaneda relates --I believe it is from *The Second Ring of Power* (1977)--that reveals a very new mode of acting in the world. Carlos tells how he and his teacher, Don Juan Matus had been hiking through a very steep ravine when a boulder got loose and landed on the floor of the canyon twenty or thirty feet ahead. Don Juan told Carlos that there is a force that controls our destinies. Sometimes it will make us stop, for just a moment, to tie our shoelaces. As a result, we shall be spared from being crushed to death by the boulder.

But, on another occasion, those forces of destiny would have made us stop to tie our shoelaces, just long enough for another boulder to come down and crush us to death. According to Don Juan, since we have no control over the forces of destiny, our only freedom lies in tying our shoelaces impeccably.

What does it mean to tie one's shoelaces impeccably? For that matter, what does it mean to perform any action impeccably? As Don Juan explains it, to live impeccably is to live in the full awareness that life that the particular act, in which one is engaged, could--due to the uncertainty of life--very well be one's last. Knowing this, who would wish to squander the moment engaged in one's usual foolishness? It is far better to use that last moment to let one's spirit shine.

Of course, one doesn't know what will be one's last moment. But living as if it may be one's last moment leads to much happier and fulfilling mode of existence. It is happier because the awareness of death sobers the spirit, freeing us from the usual dark emotions, habits and indulgences--from anger to self-pity to inner confusion-- that can prey upon us.

Conclusions

We have discussed two ways to transform one's mode of being in the world. The first involves illuminating what, in point of fact, it is. We must learn to discern it in even the smallest actions. Secondly, we discussed Castaneda's notion of acting impeccably. I think that it is best to master the first practice before proceeding to the second.

Thus, for example, we discern our mode of being in the world as embodied in the activity of tying our shoelaces. Then, having gained that self-knowledge, we would proceed to perform the action of tying one's shoelaces impeccably. We would, more than likely, discover the recrudescence of outmoded attitudes, when we had not been performing our actions impeccably. Impeccability, like the practice of mindfulness, prevents old attitudes from being embodied. Thus, if you wish to attain a illuminated, awakened and spiritualized mode of existence, it's not sufficient of have profound insights into who you are and what life is all about. It's also necessary for such insights to find expression in your everyday doings.

Questions for the Reader to Ponder

1. Closely examine any of your actions. Can you detect your attitudes to life and way of being in the world in that action? What is it that you are able to discern?

2. See if you can perform that same action differently than you are accustomed to.

3. After you have discerned the meaning of that action, see if you can perform it impeccably. I.E., perform it as if it well might be your last action on Earth. Evoke the spirit of the Maggid of Mezritch, as you go off to spiritual warfare.

4. View *The Man Who Would be King* (1975). Devote special attention to the scene in which Daniel Dravot (played by Sean Connery) is singing on the rickety footbridge. Are you able to carry yourself with the same degree of dignity, nobility and grace--the ancient Roman's called it "dignitas"--as Daniel did, even under the most trying of circumstances, indeed, even as you stand poised over the abyss? Carry yourself, in this manner, for at least a week. Express dignitas in everything you do, in sitting, standing, eating, speaking, working, resting, tying your shoelaces and brushing your teeth--yes, even in your smallest actions--but especially express it in your walking. If you find yourself losing focus and drifting back to your former bearing, regain your mindfulness and inner poise, and sing, "The Minstrel Boy." Dignitas isn't everything, but the guardian of the gates, to the spiritual realm, doesn't admit soulless wimps.

Is a Tightrope Walker a Balanced Person?

A friend recommended the film *Man on Wire* (2008) which explores Philip Petit's tightrope walk from one tower of the World Trade Center to the other, and back and forth a number of times. For a person, like myself, who is not that fond of heights, I was certainly amazed by his courage.

Paul Tillich, in *The Courage to Be* (1952), states that courage takes many forms. There is, for example, physical, moral, intellectual, and spiritual courage. Tillich distinguishes the courage to stand alone--which every artist must have, including performance artists--from the courage to join with others. The film showed that Petit certainly has the courage to be alone. But he lacked the courage to be with other people, for when he was with others, it was really all about him. Towards the end of the film, we see Petit betraying his girlfriend and soul mate, by sleeping with another woman. Thus Petit lacked the courage to be in a committed relationship. Tillich would say that he lacked moral courage. It would seem, then, that one form of courage does not translate into other types of courage.

Nor does physical balance--which Petit obviously possesses to an incredible degree--translate into being a balanced and centered person, for his actual life was unbalanced and toppled over when he suddenly became famous. Similarly, Achilles was a great warrior, but an unbalanced person. Then there are professional athletes. The excellent qualities that they possess on the playing field--courage, endurance and determination--fail to translate to other activities. Many lack moral courage and are un-centered and unbalanced individuals.

Thus, as Philip Petit's life illustrates, neither courage nor balance extends beyond the physical plane to the other domains of human existence. The cultivation of the body is an excellent thing and should be encouraged for its own sake. And Petit's tightrope from one of the Twin Towers to the other was certainly awe-inspiring. It is a testimony to the courage a person can have to do amazing things. We would be disappointed, though, as many have been by physical courage not transferring over to the other realms, just as we would disappointed if we believed that a beautiful woman would, by necessity, be a beautiful person.

Here, then, is a question for those athletic coaches, who are also true educators: Is there a way to teach athletics, such that physical virtues carryover to the moral and spiritual planes? Does there exist physical, moral and spiritual cross-training? A new discipline is needed, one that can connect these disparate realms. It would be akin to Plato's education of love in his dialogue *The Symposium*. Only in this case it would not be carnal love that is elevated to a higher plane, but such qualities as courage, endurance, balance and determination. Therefore, a school for spiritualized athletics is needed. Similarly, a school is needed to train artists and musicians to be as inwardly beautiful as their art, rather than unbalanced narcissists, which is most often what they become.

Questions for the Reader to Ponder

1. In what ways do you feel that you need to be more balanced? What can throw you off balance? Anxiety? Success? The Passions? Other people?

2. Are you able to balance being in the midst of an activity, while being aware of yourself? Can you balance life's seriousness with being lighthearted?

3. Balance is dandy, but not possible when contradictions are involved. Why is this so?

4. What type of courage do you possess? What type do you feel you lack? (Read Tillich's book, *The Courage to Be* (1952), for more on the various types of courage.)

5. What types of courage did each of the characters in the dialogues possess? What type of courage did they lack? What type did they gain?

The Secret of Judaism's Two Triangles and the Mystery of Antisemitism

Dr. Dillof's essay first appeared in The Journal for the Study of Antisemitism. It's reprinted here, with their kind permission. www.jsantisemitism.org/index.html

The key to understanding antisemitism lies in Judaism itself. This is because what Judaism esteems most highly is the very thing that incurs the wrath of antisemites. There is something that they intuitively hate about Judaism, even though they cannot articulate what it is. Nor do Jews seem to know what it is. And judging from the existing research, those who have studied antisemitism are also in the dark.

What, then, is it about Judaism that incites antisemitism? Of the various theories that have sought to answer that question, two are relevant to our investigation. One focuses on morality and the other on envy. Together, they can get us two-thirds to the answer. The final leg of the journey requires venturing into unknown territory. That's where we shall finally unravel the mystery of antisemitism.

The Dread of Morality

The world is full of people fleeing their conscience. Some are tormented by what they've done. Far more feel guilty for sins of omission. They haven't become the person they know they need to be. Nor are they living as they know they should be living. Among this very large class of people, are those who anathematize anyone who reminds them of their moral failings. Some, for example, lash out at their parents or spouse for this reason. Others despise their clergymen or their teachers. But some hate the Jews.

It's not that the Jews seek to remind them of their faults. Those who are antisemitic may never have actually spoken to a Jew. It's just that the Jews, by being who they are, offer an implicit criticism of the guilt-ridden person's manner of living. This is because at the heart of Judaism is a moral vision of life. The path to salvation is straight and narrow, which means that it is possible to stray from the path, to be in sin and to be punished by God. The antisemite projects upon the Jews his inner-accuser and hates them for that reason.

Obviously, not all Jews obey the Ten Commandments, are observant and subscribe to the tenets of their faith. One can get lost in worldliness, become a humanist, a postmodernist, a relativist, a nihilist, an atheist, an apostate, or a convert to another religion and still not escape the sway of the moral law. Nor does it ultimately matter whether or not one acts righteously. A Jew can even become an antisemite (as was Karl Marx), a hypocrite, a malefactor, a thief or a con artist (such as Bernard Madoff). However, for those under the sway of the moral vision of life, there is never any real escape from "the hound of heaven," the inner demand that one's heart be pure and one's actions be scrupulous.

Even in the most secular of Jews, a kind of collective Jewish consciousness exists, the inheritance of thousands of years of history. Needless to say, all human beings--with the exception of those who are puerile, imbecilic, sociopathic or downright iniquitous--are, to varying degrees, under the sway of "the moral law within," as Immanuel Kant called it. However, for no other people is the demand to be righteous so deeply ingrained in their identity, such that they continually judge their actions under moral categories. This problematic sense of self--which elevates us from the animal level of being, where instinct holds sway, to the truly human--owes much of its development to the moral struggles of the Jewish people.

It is shallow to contend that morality is merely a social phenomenon, as had Nietzsche, Marx, Freud, and other influential modern thinkers. Moral awareness is fundamental to what it means to be a human being, even if it comes into its own, in a decisive way, historically, in Judaism. What is relevant, then, is that to be born Jewish is to be so thoroughly imbued with the moral vision, that all of one's actions are judged in terms of their rectitude or lack of it.

Antisemites, although harboring a distorted view of Judaism, intuit that it embodies a disturbing truth, one that they both fear and loathe. It is morality, then, that they despise and hate. They hate those who are concerned about divine judgment, because it reminds them of their own moral failings.

There is, though, something related to morality for which the Jews are also hated. Like Socrates, the Jewish people are forever asking questions--the big questions. After all, the god of the Jewish people not only permits his people to question him, He insists that they do. Thus have the Jews become freethinkers, philosophers and iconoclasts.

The Greeks, therefore, executed Socrates for the same reason that antisemites have murdered Jews: they hoped to remove the source of their self-doubts. Critical thinking is related to morality, for some of the questions that emerge for a person who becomes reflective are: Is my life founded in truth or do I inhabit a world of ephemeral shadows? How, then, should I be living? What is the good life? What is most holy?

Here, again, it is not that the Jews regularly engage people of other faiths in philosophical debate. It is just that antisemites correctly intuit that the Jewish people are thinkers and are, therefore, dangerous. Thus antisemites project their inner-questioner upon the Jews, who are viewed, in a kind of medieval morality play, as devils casting unsettling doubts everywhere. Freud correctly considered projection to be a defense mechanism.

Apropos are the various anti-intellectual movements, which provide a milieu favorable for the virus of antisemitism to pullulate. Fascism, although not intrinsically antisemitic, is the most notorious of such movements. It rejects the intellect in favor of the body, and thinking in favor of feeling. It views the products of the mind--including ideas, culture, morality, and religion--as alienating us both from our "organic" relation to nature and from our animalistic instincts. And it rejects individualism in favor of collectivism.

Those who despise both mind and morality often anathematize the Jews, who highly value mind and morality. This was certainly the case when Fascism emigrated from Italy to Germany, where it transformed into Nazism. Fascism would merely be of historical interest, were it not for the fact that it has reappeared in what writers like Christopher Hitchens have called "Islamofascism."

The Envy Factor

There is another, equally pernicious, factor that comes into play in antisemitism: envy. Of course, the Jewish people were certainly not always materially successful. They were terribly persecuted in Russia and Europe, even when they were poor peasants. It might seem that in past centuries there wasn't much to envy about them. Worldly success is not, though, just a matter of affluence. It also includes such things as becoming a well-balanced individual, achieving a stable and emotionally satisfying family life, seeing to it that one's children become educated, achieving competence in one's profession, and developing oneself both intellectually and culturally. And, as we've discussed, it means becoming a *mench*, a person of integrity and moral worth. In all these respects, the Jewish people have excelled to such a degree that they have survived and thrived, despite terrible persecution, to become the envy of the world.

If it were simply worldly success at issue, the Jews would be envied and hated, but not with such virulence, throughout the centuries. As we'll now see, it's not success in itself that is envied, but divinely sanctioned success. Both the flight from morality and envy play a decisive role, but in a manner different than previous theories conceived.

The Two Triangles

Can a person pursue worldly happiness while living righteously? Every religion provides its own answer to that question. Consider the Star of David, the symbol of the Jewish religion. It is composed of two triangles, one pointing downward and the other upward. Symbolically, one triangle is pointing to Earth and the other to Heaven. The star symbolizes an ideal--the integration of Earth and Heaven, of happiness with spiritual life, of living as a finite human being in accordance with God's law. The goal, then, is to live your daily life within the purview of a divinely commanded morality.

Judaism believes that a synthesis of Heaven and earthly existence is possible, by virtue of a covenant between God and man (although, in *The Book of Job*, the way in which God fulfills his end of the bargain is deemed unintelligible to human reason). What is, most essentially, envied about the Jews is their ability to integrate ethical and religious values with worldly success. It is envied and hated because it is evidence of God fulfilling his covenant with the Jews. Therefore, what antisemites most envy is the Jews' blessedness, the love that they receive from their heavenly Father. Everything that the Jews may have--from affluence to a cohesive loving family to intellectual achievements--are proof that God is upholding his end of the covenant.

The antisemite, feeling bereft of that blessedness, wishes to vilify or murder those who remind him of his unworthiness before God. In that sense, the Cain of the Bible--who, out of envy for his brother Abel, murdered him--was the progenitor of future generations of antisemites. Sometimes the antisemite murders, but most often he slanders. He accuses the Jews of everything from greed to lust to treachery. In other words, he is accusing the Jews of being immoral. These slanders arise out of the belief that if he traduces the Jews--and everyone comes to believe his lies--that the Jews will then no longer threaten his conscience.

We have been arguing that the antisemite envies and resents the Jews, for their worldly success is evidence that they have, by obeying God's commandments, been granted His blessings. It could be objected, though, that antisemites do not make these theological connections. Perhaps, most have never even heard of the biblical notion of a covenant between God and the Jewish people. Furthermore, some antisemites are atheists, with little interest in religion, other than to denounce it. Finally, some antisemites may discern--as we all do, soon enough--that virtuous people often suffer and that rotten people often seem to prosper. It would seem, then, that those who never heard of a divine covenant as well as those who have rejected in as absurd would have little interest in the Jews and their beliefs. They might mock the Jews for being naïve, but they would not envy and hate them. And, yet, they do envy and hate them! What then is going on here?

The notion of God rewarding a person for virtuous action is not arrived at through reasoning, but is a deep-seated way in which we seek to understand our experience. Furthermore, despite cogent reasons to deny that virtue is rewarded, the continued success of the Jews flies in the face of arguments discounting the efficacy of an ethical and religious life. The mere fact that the Jewish people still exist--despite pogroms, holocausts, and all else--and that they prosper makes one pause for thought: Is virtue really rewarded? Does a covenant really exist between God and the Jews? Whether, in point of fact, there is a God and whether a divine covenant actually exists between God and the Jewish people is not our concern here. We are simply observing that the success of the Jews creates hostility among those people who, whether they consciously realize it or not, have troubling doubts about the morality and legitimacy of the life they are leading.

The love of the Father is a powerful affair, even in the modern world. After all, in many godless totalitarian nations, the people make their dear leader into a god, plastering his photo everywhere. No one gets over the Father archetype so easily.

Demanding that the Jews Ascend the Cross

Why does the United Nations pass endless resolutions condemning Israel? After all, there are presently peoples from all over the globe--from Kosovo to Darfur, from Syria to North Korea--who are being cruelly tortured and murdered. Why, then, is Israel's condemned for supposedly persecuting the Palestinians? And why is this same anti-Israeli sentiment rife at colleges and universities?

It is because what is known as "anti-Zionism" is but the disguise for a certain insidious species of antisemitism. It consists in seeking to make the Jews suffer the trials of integrating worldly interests with ethical and religious values. For example, the wall that Israel erected to keep out suicide-bomber murders is judged by the anti-Zionists, at the UN, to be illegal. The essential accusation is that if the Jews are really ethical they will give up all of their land, rollover and die. Since most Jews do not honor the absurd demands of the anti-Zionists--which is essentially that they ascend the cross and die for the sins of the antisemites--they are accused of being mean-spirited.

Antisemites choose the Jews for this sort of villainy for they intuitively know that the Jews are sensitive to questions of morality. The antisemites then think--by virtue of the Israel's refusal of their demands--that they have proven that God's demand to live ethically is impossible to fulfill. Having apparently proven the Jews hypocrites, the anti-Zionists at the UN, who are, ironically, neither Jewish nor Christian, feel that they are exculpated for their human rights abuses and other criminality. And the many anti-Zionists elsewhere feel free of the moral demands in their own life, such as being honest in business and being faithful to their spouse. There's something truly demonic involved here, a perversion of Christian truth. Such antisemites are essentially saying that unless the Jews ascend the cross, that they, the antisemites, are free to go on sinning.

But many Jews--those of the liberal persuasion--are willing to suffer a crucifixion, to the delight of antisemites. Indeed, some Jews go so far in this direction as to become self-loathing masochists, while simultaneously beating their chests in pride over their apparent moral superiority. These Jews hope that their actions will inspire other people to be moral, selfless and goodhearted.

Such hopes are dangerously foolish, for instead of inspiring antisemites to be good people, the Jews' largess of spirit causes them to be envied and resented all the more. After all, hatred tinged with envy is not ordinary hatred. Ordinarily, if we act kindly to those who hate us, their hatred is likely to abate. But if their hatred is tinged with envy, our kindness will only exacerbate their hatred. It will exacerbate it because now they will envy our largess of spirit. Of course, antisemites would never admit to envying the Jew's goodwill; nor do they ever seek to emulate it.

Other Religions and the Two Triangles

There are certainly other religions that have sought to synthesize ethical and religious values with worldly success. Why, then, haven't the practitioners of other religions been vilified as frequently, as have the Jews? Let us, then, compare other the Judaic synthesis to that of other religions, for clues to that question. Only in Judaism does God appear in the guise of a father who takes an active role in the world. Although the Trinity is central to Christianity, the focus is not on the Father, but on the Son, namely Jesus. As such, Christianity does not evoke the type of envy for the love of the Father that Judaism evokes. After all, who envies Jesus nailed to the cross?

Like the Star of David, the cross symbolizes an effort to integrate the horizontal and vertical dimensions of life. The vertical is longer, though, on the cross, indicating Christianity's shift to otherworldliness. Thus, if the Covenant is to be fulfilled, for Christians, it will have to in Heaven, for this world of ours is a place for suffering and repentance, a "veil of tears." Anti-Christian sentiment, throughout the ages, has had a different basis than antisemitism. It is not based on envy. In recent years, those who are have been murdering Christians in the Middle East and Pakistan are simply Muslim fanatics, who wish to murder those they cannot convert.

Despite the focus on the Son, there have been "Christians" envious towards the Jews for the love of their heavenly Father. Theologians sometimes cite the so-called "scandal of particularity"--in other words, the notion of "the chosen people"--as a major cause of Christian antisemitism. That notion has, of course, been misinterpreted. To be chosen is not akin to winning a lottery. On the contrary, it means that one has to be chosen to suffer in the service of a holy life. In that sense, it is comparable to the Christian notion of bearing one's cross. Although Christianity has a long history of antisemitism, in recent years many Christians, at least in America, have displayed brotherly love towards the Jews and have courageously risen to their defense.

The way to integrate religion with the worldly life, has long been a concern for Hindus, as seen, for example in the *Bhagavad-Gita*. Hinduism is often misunderstood to be polytheistic, but as the perceptive Huston Smith points out, the many gods of the Hindu pantheon are actually manifestations of Brahman, the supreme god. Brahman is really a mystical notion and not a father God. That is why there is far less envy, by the peoples of the world, for Hindus, who are both religious and successful. It is similarly why antisemitism among Hindus is virtually non-existent. The same is true for the other Eastern religions. Buddhism, for example, is a religion without a god. Furthermore, Buddhists are not generally known for worldly ambitions. Consequently, Buddhists are neither envied, nor are themselves prone to envy nor are known to be antisemites.

Islam does have a father God, namely Allah. But Allah is distant and remote, and does not intervene in human affairs the way that the Hebrew god does. Furthermore, Islamic theology is founded upon a deterministic metaphysics. A person's fate was decided before he was born. As such, there is less a sense that worldly success is a sign that a person has won God's favor. Consequently, it less likely that religious Muslims, who attain worldly success, will be envied and hated to the degree that the Jews are. Although Muslims do not inspire envy, they are prone to envy. Islam is still, after all, an Abrahamic religion. It therefore inherits, to a certain degree, the Jewish notion of a God who rewards the faithful. As such, Muslims are capable of envy and antisemitism.

What about paganism? Pagans don't worship the father God, but rather the divine mother, often in the form of nature. Apparently, atheists do not worship anything at all. Upon examination, we discover that some actually have a pseudo-religious notion of the Millennium that will be brought about by scientific progress. Other atheists actually worship the state. Dictators, like Joseph Stalin, correctly perceive that religion is in competition with the worship of the state and its leader.

Consequently, any sort of secular totalitarian creed, whether it be communism or fascism, is likely to be hostile to Judeo-Christian values. Even though those on the political left have consciously rejected Judeo-Christian values, they still have a proclivity for antisemitism. That is because, as we have suggested, they have not truly rejected these values. On the contrary, they have simply put old idols in new bottles.

Summary and Sobering Suggestions

Previous studies of the role of Jews in the Christian and Islamic worlds have told us how antisemitism has been able to spread. We discern that it is carried along by a scandalous narrative, such as the libel that Jews drink the blood of Christian children or the fantasy of a Jewish world conspiracy, articulated in *The Protocols of the Elders of Zion (1903)*. Although helping us to understand Christian and Islamic antisemitism, such studies never get to very heart of the mystery, for antisemitism is thousands of years older than those religions. Indeed, antisemitism is as ancient as Judaism itself. To make sense of this hatred, we have sought to grasp its essence, independent of time, place, circumstances and narrative.

Here, then, is the essential hatred that lies behind a thousand slanders: The Jewish people's worldly success appears to be proof that--by following God's commandments--they have had God's blessings conferred upon them. It is envy for the love and approval of the Heavenly Father that is most bitter to the antisemite. Once again, these connections are not consciously made by the antisemite. Having emerged from subterranean depths, they are all the more powerful.

More than likely, antisemitism will always exist, just as will alcoholism, domestic violence, terrorism, criminal activity and other social ills. What is important is the degree of its severity, for antisemitism can range from relatively mild to virulent. It really depends upon the spirit of a nation. The Jews have thrived in America partly because most Americans are far less susceptible to the poison of envy than most other people. Thanks to capitalism, with the opportunities it offers to improve one's lot in life, most Americans are too busy building their own lives to obsess over what other people have. (Of course, during hard times there is a danger that a demagogue will foment class warfare and envy, thus indirectly creating the type of milieu that breeds antisemitism.)

The Jewish people have also thrived in America because there is a fundamental connection between American exceptionalism and the notion of the chosen people. In other words, Americans have traditionally viewed themselves as having a God-given mission to spread liberty and democracy to the peoples of the world. They have seen themselves chosen in that respect. American idealism has made the United States the most generous nation; time after time, Americans have selflessly contributed their goods and at wartime sacrificed their lives to assist the peoples of other nations. And, like the Jews, they have become hated for their goodness. Indeed, they have become the "ugly Americans." In any case, where the spirit of capitalism, democracy and liberty exists, the Jewish people are welcome, but it is unlikely that this spirit will ever prevail worldwide.

Many people believe that education is the antidote to antisemitism. But the German people, one of the most educated in the world, elected Adolph Hitler to be their leader. Furthermore, antisemitism--in the guise of anti-Zionism--presently flourishes at many universities, including Ivy League ones. That's not surprising since universities have been transformed into indoctrination centers for the leftwing variety of antisemitism. When the doctors have become carriers of the disease, there is little hope.

What is really needed are teachers who--blending exorcism with Socratic midwifery--can free students from antisemitism, as well as the many other demons that can possess the soul, including envy. That would require that they themselves become delivered from evil, but such individuals are hard to find. After all, one of the most influential philosophers of the Twentieth Century, Martin Heidegger, admired Hitler. And one of the profoundest psychologists, C.G. Jung, got aboard the National Socialism bandwagon. Consequently, unless teachers can first become truly educated, there is little hope that education on a mass scale can minister to an ailing body politic.

The world being as it is, the Jewish people must integrate spiritual insight with worldly wisdom, if they are to survive. This requires, as the old song says, praising God and passing the ammunition. Due to increasing secularization, the Jewish people have been praising God far less. That isn't a good sign, for the fear of God is the foundation of Judaic ethics, and Judaic ethics lies at the core of Jewish identity. It's foolish, as it says in the New Testament, "to gain the world, but lose one's soul." Only when the two triangles are aligned, can the Jewish people receive the blessings of Heaven.

The survival of the Jews should be the concern of everyone who values life and liberty, if only for the reason that those nations that threaten to annihilate the Jews eventually seek to enslave and destroy everyone else as well. Furthermore, the Jews embody a vital set of ethical values. When the Jews are murdered or are expelled from a nation, those values cease to have concrete embodiment. In such instances, the moral fiber of a nation has, in essence, been eviscerated and its people weakened.

Questions for the Reader to Ponder

1. How do you seek to integrate the vertical and horizontal dimension of existence, in you life? Might crossword puzzles be a symbolic attempt to unite these dimensions?

2. Envy plays a significant and sometimes deadly role in everyday life, especially in the workplace. Are you prone to envy? Do others envy you? How can you make yourself less subject to the wrath of the envious, while still seeking to be successful?

3. Read Dante's *Purgatorio* for his insights on envy. Read Shakespeare's *Othello*, for his depiction of Iago and read his *Julius Caesar*, for his depiction of Cassius, for any insights that Shakespeare can provide.

4. Think of someone you've known who is good person. Perhaps, it was a classmate who chased away school bullies. How did other people feel about this person? Was it love and admiration or hatred and envy? Try to understand the hatred liberals felt toward President Reagan when he referred to the Soviet Union as "the evil empire."

5. Do you believe that a covenant exists, such that goodness will be rewarded? Or do you believe that, "No good deed goes unpunished"? Can both be true? I.E., can realism about human beings be reconciled with belief in the value of an ethical life?

Is Nature Evil?

"When beholding the tranquil beauty and brilliancy of the ocean's skin, one forgets the tiger heart that pants beneath it; and would not willingly remember that this velvet paw but conceals a remorseless fang."

--Herman Melville, "Moby Dick."

Philosophers have traditionally contended that evil comes in two varieties: human and natural. Human evil is the harm we inflict on ourselves, other people and perhaps on the universe. We do so either through our actions or by failing to act when we should. Natural evil, on the other hand, is the destruction to human life and property caused by naturally occurring events, such as tornados, floods, and earthquakes.

In recent years, there's been a shift in the zeitgeist, such that events, which had always been regarded as natural disasters, are blamed on human beings. Consequently, the category of natural evil has shrunk and that of human evil has expanded. This new zeitgeist finds expression in efforts to explain disasters, such as the devastation wrought by Hurricane Katrina. President Bush was blamed for not having acted sooner to provide disaster relief. The motives, of those who blamed, him were political, but their criticisms could not have held any weight had there not been this shift to blaming human beings for natural disasters.

The preoccupation with climate change is also a product of this wish to attribute the cause of naturally occurring changes that occur over the course of centuries to the misdeeds of people. Not surprisingly, some people have blamed the recent earthquake in Haiti on global warming and, therefore, on human evil.

From Tragic to Moral Vision

What is at issue here is a desire to find meaning in disasters. If a disaster is simply due to nature, then we inhabit a tragic universe, one in which the gods seem indifferent to man's plight. Even worse is the possibility that the gods are malevolent. As Shakespeare expresses it, "As flies to wanton boys, are we to the gods, they kill us for their sport." Here we have the theological quandary: if God is omnipotent, as is claimed, then how could he be good? After all, if he was really omnipotent, he would not permit evil. On the other hand, if he is omnipotent and permits evil, then he is not good. Since natural evil--floods, fires, tornadoes and all the rest--does exist, God must either not be omnipotent or not be good. This theological problem can easily lead a person to atheism and to the sense that life is meaningless.

To avoid meaninglessness, people will instead shift from a kind of tragic vision of the universe to a moral vision. They will claim, in other words, that God is innocent. It is, on the contrary, human beings who are responsible for the calamities that befall them. An example from my personal life comes to mind. Whenever anyone in my family would catch a cold or the flu, my father would attribute it to having violated some law of hygiene, such as not having washed our hands. My father may have often been right, but he was loath to believe that we could get sick without being responsible for our illness. He, therefore, denied the unwilled, tragic dimension of human suffering, preferring to attribute a quasi-moral meaning to it. Thus to save God, to render the universe still meaningful, we humans often agree to take the fall. We'd much prefer to feel guilty than to feel meaninglessness.

The Tragedy at SeaWorld

Some years ago, Dawn Brancheau--an animal trainer, at "SeaWorld" aquarium and park, in Orlando Florida--accidentally fell in a pool and was killed by a killer whale. As it turns out, this particular whale had previously killed two other people. One of the reasons why this became a major news story was that it raised some perplexing questions about man, nature and evil. Most readers are unaware of the real source of their fascination with this news story: their unresolved moral issues.

Following online newspaper articles, were posts by reader blaming the aquarium for having kept the whale pent-up, not allowing it to be in its natural habitat, the ocean. Zoos and aquariums are, after all, captivity. Such sentiments arise partly out of genuine compassion for animals, but partly out of the contemporary romanticizing of nurture. Indeed, many people believe that nature is as pure and innocent as Bambi. The premise of the film *Avatar (2009)* gives new life to the tired notion that those living in accord with their natural surroundings are good and that we, industrialized Americans, are evil.

But one sentiment rarely expressed is that the whale is evil, and not merely in the sense in which we speak of floods and tornados, but downright iniquitous. Is that possible since the categories of good and evil only seem to apply to the human world, not the natural world. In an interview, about the tragedy at SeaWorld, Richard Ellis, a marine conservationist with the American Museum of Natural History, brought up the fact that killer whales have been in captivity for a long time and that it is highly unusual for a killer whale to kill a human being. Mr. Ellis contended that the killer whale actually made a deliberate, intentional decision to kill the animal trainer!

Mr. Ellis didn't speculate on the killer whale's motive. Perhaps the whale was angry at being held in captivity and was seeking revenge. Perhaps it acted out of pure malice. Perhaps whales, in captivity, exhibit psychopathology. In any case, if Mr. Ellis is correct, it might suggest that whales--at least those in captivity--aren't just innocent creatures, driven by instinct. There is, at least, one great American writer who, similarly, wasn't wiling to let nature off the hook. Herman Melville raised the question if the infamous white whale, *Moby Dick,* wasn't simply a victim of human beings and wasn't simply acting to defend himself, but was malevolent. Melville's vision seems to invoke the gnostic idea that the world wasn't the creation of a good god, but of an evil demiurge.

From Tragic Vision to Paranoid Vision

Of course, for the whale to be evil requires that he be capable of free choice. That seems unlikely, for a certain degree of self-awareness, if not self-knowledge, is necessary for free choice, which most humans don't even possess. If Walt Disney romanticized animals in a positive way, might it be that Melville has romanticized animals in a dark, Gothic way, by making Moby Dick not just a whale, but a demon? By entertaining the possibility that Moby and nature itself may, indeed, be evil, Melville creates the ambiguity necessary to make Ahab neither a villain nor a victim, but a tragic character.

The tragic vision of life is ambiguous, for in placing the blame partially on us and partially on the gods ennobles human beings. If instead, the fault for the disasters that befall us is placed neither on man nor on the gods, but on President Bush or some other political leader, then instead of either the tragic vision (where man and the universe share the blame) or the moral vision (in which God or the universe is innocent and we are to blame), we have the paranoid vision, in which a single person or a cabal of conspirators are to blame. The paranoid vision is endemic to the morally undeveloped.

Questions for the Reader to Ponder

1. What is your view of nature? Do you regard it as innocent and good? As sacred? As evil? As amoral? Do natural tragedies just happen for no rhyme or reason?

2. Why was Samantha so offended by my comments about nature? How is it that someone could worship nature?

3. See John Houston's film, *The Treasure of Sierra Madra* (1948). It neither idealizes nor condemns nature, but views it, perhaps, as a ruthless teacher, who enjoys a good joke, often at our expense. Do you agree with Houston's vision of nature and of life?

The Metaphysics of Fitted Bed Sheets

The ancient Greek philosopher Heraclitus contended that the universe is maintained by a tension between opposing forces. What sort of opposing forces? For example: summer and winter, joy and sorrow, male and female, work and play, day and night, young and old, wellness and illness, war and peace, seriousness and mirth, love and hate, waking and sleeping, life and death.

Most people prefer one of the pairs of opposites to the other. They might, for example, prefer peace to strife. But Heraclitus warns us: "Homer was wrong in saying: 'Would that strife might perish from among gods and humans!' He did not see that he was praying for the destruction of the universe; for, if his prayer were heard, all things would pass away." If Heraclitus is right, then be careful what you pray for!

Heraclitus' metaphysical truth made sense to me, one evening, when I was struggling, as I often do, with the fitted sheets that I use on my bed. The four elasticized corners pull in opposing directions. By virtue of this tension, the sheet stays on the bed. But, let's just say that--due to insomnia, troubled dreams or visitations by succubi--my sleep is not so sound, that I'm tossing and turning all night. Well, the odds are that one of the corners of the fitted sheet is going to snap loose. I could then arise from my comfortable bed, in the cool of the evening, to reattach the loose end of the fitted sheet to the mattress. Or I could, as I often do, ignore the problem and seek to return to the dreamland of Morpheus.

The problem, though, with ignoring the snapped end of the sheet, is that the other three corners, having lost their tension, will no longer stay in place. Pretty soon, given enough tossing and turning, I'm sleeping on a bare mattress, with the sheet now crumpled, on either side of the bed or it's near where my feet are or it's fallen to the floor. Yes, I could use safety pins to affix each end of the fitted sheet to the mattress, but my daemon admonished me against cheating in this fashion. So it is that ignoring a problem in one area of our life often causes other areas of our life to become undone, for everything in our life is interconnected, more than we would care to acknowledge.

On the other hand, a small change in one corner of our life, can transform the entire fabric of our life for the better, which is what George Costanza discovered when he ordered chicken salad rather than his customary tuna salad, for lunch. But our interest here is in the negative dimension of the fitted sheet phenomenon. As we shall see, the tension between opposites must be maintained--in fitted sheets as in the universe and in one's life...

The Four Elements as a Fitted Sheet

Ancient Greek medicine consisted in seeking to balance, in a person's soul, the four elements--earth, air, fire and water. They worked with the four elements and I struggle with the four corners of my fitted sheet. In truth, everyone struggles with the daily effort to integrate opposing life concerns. We might, for example, seek to balance our career, family life, hobbies, and spiritual life--those four. To be a balanced person is to integrate, to varying degrees of success, these opposing interests. Alas, how precarious any balance is!

Soren Kierkegaard even believed it necessary, if we are to attain selfhood--and thus self-fulfillment, happiness, and salvation-- to integrate time and eternity, as well as the finite and the infinite. It is difficult, indeed, to have one's mind on God while at work, or shopping or visiting one's stockbroker. There is always a tendency to lose one side of the equation and so to lose one's balance. Kierkegaard contended that to gain the finite, but to lose the infinite, or vice versa, is to be in despair. He also contended that most people, unaware of how imbalanced their life is, are in despair without even realizing it. Could we see the inner person, we would discern that he or she walks through life, unbalanced, like a drunken fool.

Often, we may actually seek to lose one of the opposing sides. Why? Because we tire of the continual effort required to maintain the tension between opposite concerns in our life. We might, then, seek to get drunk, to get distracted with busyness, or to lose self-awareness in a great variety of ways. Thus do we seek to take "moral holidays," as William James called it. Take, for example, the opposition between work and play. Needless to say, most people, if they had their choice, would dissolve the balance, in favor of playing all day. They long to retire, in the hope of dissolving the work/play opposition. The quest to make a lot of money is often fueled by that dissolute longing.

If, upon retirement, a person loses the work/play tension, his life is in danger of dissolution. Schopenhauer spoke of life as a pendulum between anxiety and boredom. When the anxious life of the workplace is gone, only boredom remains. Like a fitted sheet that has become undone, they too have become undone without even realizing it. (Of course, those who retire need not become dissolute. The art of retirement consists in establishing a new balance among opposing forces.)

What Heraclitus said of the universe is, therefore, true of each person's inner universe. It's maintained by balancing opposing forces. Heraclitus called the law that governs this tension of opposites the "Logos." Like a fitted bed sheet, each realm of one's existence must pull in opposite directions and yet we must be balanced by virtue of this opposition. To lose that inner tension is to lose contact wish the Logos and so to suffer moral dissolution. It is to become inwardly flabby and perhaps outwardly too.

A well-balanced life is all the more difficult since we're not static beings, for just as the universe is evolving, so are we, through new life experiences coupled with insight. As new factors emerge, we must readjust our balance, so as to again be in tune with the Logos. What balance we need to walk life's tightrope over the abyss, so that we may proceed, to use Nietzsche's language, beyond ourselves!

Questions for the Reader to Ponder

1. Have you noticed how neglecting one aspect of a balanced life--exercise, diet, family, friends, the spiritual, the financial, etc.--can impact all of the other aspects of your life? Are you able to maintain the Heraclitean tension between opposites,

such that your inner fitted bed sheet stays in place?

2. It's been said that the mission of human beings is to integrate opposites, such as the four elements, the temporal and the eternal, the finite and the infinite, and the actual and the possible. According to Sir Thomas Browne, we're able to do so because we're amphibious beings, possessing the unique ability to dwell within two realms --that of the animals and that of the gods. It's quite a challenging task, but also ennobling, for man is the only being in the universe capable of living at the intersection of time and eternity, as well as the other polar opposites. When you awaken each morning, do you feel a combination of joy and nobility, at having been born to this high estate, that of a human being, despite whatever hardships the day may bring?

3. Have you taken a "moral holiday," letting down the tension holding up life's fitted bed sheet? More than likely, it's the eternal that is being neglected. Read Kierkegaard's book, with the delightful title, "The Sickness Unto Death," where he discusses how failing to effectuate certain syntheses leads to despair. Also take a look at T.S. Eliot's poem, "The Hollow Men." Eliot says that, "Between the idea and the reality Falls the Shadow." It would seem that the shadow falls because one hasn't sought to transform the idea into reality.

4. Do you kvetch, like Ricky does, over the difficulty of synthesizing values (his musical compositions) with the real world (the recalcitrance of club owners to let his band perform them)? Dorothy, on the other hand, contends with the school system and Detective Mueller has the criminal justice system and the courts, as his cross to bear. They periodically let off steam and sometimes feel that they are being driven cuckoo, but they're more resigned to their jobs than is Ricky. Like "Dirty Harry," they do what they have to do, despite not being fully appreciated. Their feeling of heaviness stems from not

being in tune with eternity, for only the eternal can help us to bear our burden lightly. There's always laugh therapy, but without contact with the eternal, laughter can ring hollow. And so, in relation to your job and other duties, are you like Ricky? Like Dorothy and Detective Mueller? Or like a smiling Buddha? I.E., are you able to maintain a Heraclitean tension between opposites?

5. In his poem, "The Age of Anxiety," W.H. Auden writes,

    "The gods are wringing their great worn hands
    For their watchman is away,
    their world engine Creaking and cracking.
    Conjured no more by his master mind
    to wed Their truths to times,
    the Eternal Objects Drift about in a daze:"

    (Random House. New York, NY 1947).

Is our age, indeed, one in which "the Eternal Objects Drift about in a daze" because no one is seeking to embody them in the material world? If the eternal objects drift about in a daze, do we similarly drift about in despair? Is that why we live in an age of anxiety?

Do You Love Your Fate?

> "A man's character is his fate."
> --Heraclitus

> "Amour fati"
> --Nietzsche

> "A man has to be what he is, Joey.
> You can't break the mold.
> I tried it and it didn't work for me."
> --Shane

That which befalls us, the good things and the bad, is our fate. The fact that we are born at a certain time and place is our fate. That we happened to be in the same college class as our future spouse is also our fate. So is the fact that we're driving to work when a drunken driver rams into our car. The key to fate, as Alfred North Whitehead points out, isn't that bad things happen to us. Rather, it is our lack of freedom. It's just that our inability to prevent bad things from happening highlights our lack of freedom. After all, if only good things happened, we would not notice how the world opposes our desires and our will.

We usually think of fate as that which is external to us. There is, though, another aspect to fate, a deeper one. The ancient Greek philosopher Heraclitus wrote, "A man's character is his fate." Thus fate is not just what happens to us, but who we are. We do not realize this when we are young, for we believe that we are the masters of our destiny. And we are, to a certain extent. But anyone who lives long enough realizes how very difficult it is to change anything about oneself. There is, indeed, a certain tragic dimension to human character.

Friedrich Nietzsche recommended "Amor fati!" One should, in other words, love one's fate. Some have compared Nietzsche's advice to the biblical notion of everything that happens being for the best, and to the Stoical notion of calm acceptance of that which befalls us. As Emerson wrote, "Accept the place the divine providence has found for you, the society of your contemporaries, the connection of events. Great men have always done so, and confided themselves childlike to the genius of their age..." *(Self-Reliance)* But, if Heraclitus is correct that our character is our fate, then to love our fate, as Nietzsche recommends, is to love our character. But, character is intrinsically limited. Can one really love a limit?

Often the flip side of a limit is a virtue. The Zen master D.T. Suzuki said that he had a Satori, or awakening, when he realized that the elbow does not bend outward. I.E., the utility of the elbow is predicated on its mechanical limitations. Might not the same be said for character? Our strengths and our weaknesses are often flip sides of the same coin. Of course, appreciating the virtue of limits is not quite the same as loving limits.

We often wander about for a time, in our salad years, finding out what we're most fit for, in terms of our natural abilities, sills and temperament. We may find, for example, that we're better suited to be an entrepreneur than working for a corporation or vice versa. What, then, does it mean to know oneself? Does it mean to be familiar enough with our character such that we do not act in opposition to it? In *Death of a Salesman*, Willie Loman's son states that Willie never knew who he was. He thought that he was a salesman, but he would have been far happier making things with his hands. Willie's failure to come to terms with his character had tragic consequences. Thus we cannot love our fate unless we first know ourselves and, to a certain degree, accept who we are.

When a person knows who he is, he can then choose to live his character at a higher level. Then, what had been his fate becomes transformed into his destiny. In the cowboy film *Shane* (1953), the protagonist explains that there is no escaping who we are. A man has got to be who he is. In the case of Shane, his character is independent, courageous, noble-hearted and alone. The fact that he has to be alone, and that he has to risk his life to help those in need, is the price he pays for his virtues. Shane follows his destiny, without a moment's hesitation, and harbors no regrets.

Look, then, at your life. Be honest and admit how much of it has been the product, for better or worse, of your character, which is your fate. You have not freely chosen it. So many people curse their fate. Are you one of them? Or can you love your fate? And can you elevate your life such that who you are, your fate, becomes your destiny?

Questions for the Reader to Ponder

1. Woody Allan facetiously stated, *"My one regret in life is that I'm not somebody else."* Do you harbor that regret and bemoan who you are? Or do you love your fate?

2. Read Edwin Arlington Robinson's poem, "Miniver Cheevy." (Google it.) It's about a man who wishes that he lived during an earlier age. What are your thoughts on it?

3. Soren Kierkegaard wrote, *"Boredom is the root of all evil-- the despairing refusal to be oneself."* What did Kierkegaard mean by that? Could it be that evil stems from boredom and that boredom stems from the refusal to be oneself? But why would the refusal to be oneself, to love one's fate, lead to boredom?

4. Kierkegaard also wrote, *"Face the facts of being what you are, for that is what changes what you are."* In what way does facing what you are change what you are?

5. Why does Kierkegaard use the phrase, "what you are," rather than "who you are?"

6. Are you able to elevate who or what you are, your character, such that you transform your fate into your destiny?

The Secret Symbolism of Magic Tricks

Might it be that we enjoy magic for reasons that are far deeper than we realize? Magic tricks are, indeed, symbolic. I shall illustrate by analyzing three of my favorite––the Cut and Restored Rope Trick, the Linking Rings, and the Slydini Knots.

The Cut and Restored Rope Trick

In this effect, the magician cuts a rope. He now has two shorter ropes. But, *mirabile dictu*, he restores the rope. It's like it had never been cut! He then cuts the rope a second time, and once again it has been restored. I stumbled upon the deeper meaning of this trick, when investigating the etymology of the word "decide." What motivated me was that decisions have never come easy for me. Oftentimes, when I've needed to make a decision, I would do nothing at all. Of course, my Hamlet-like indecision never really allowed me off the hook, for as William James argues, not to decide is itself a decision.

If we look at the etymology of the word "decide," we see that it means "to cut." There is our clue to the rope trick. What has been cut has changed irrevocably. It can't return to what it was. The original wholeness--consisting of infinite possibilities--has been lost. And that is why it is so hard for many people to decide anything, for in taking a step in a certain direction, all the other possibilities have been forever negated. If we embark upon a certain career, then we cannot embark upon another. If we marry a certain person, we cannot marry another person (assuming we are not a polygamist). There will always be a "road not taken." That is why, Soren Kierkegaard tells us, important decisions involve a leap of faith, and why such leaps are fraught with anxiety.

If only we could decide and yet not decide. In real life we cannot do this, but in the world of magic we can! And that explains the appeal of the cut and restored rope trick. For the rope is cut, i.e., a "decision" is made. But then, it is restored. I.E., the decision has been annulled, as if it had never been made. No wonder the trick is so appealing, for it symbolically denies the irreversible nature of decision.

On a higher level of consciousness, it is indeed possible to act in the world, to decide, while still maintaining our oneness, but that's another story. It's quite possible, though, that the trick resonates from those depths.

The Linking Rings

This is the classic effect in which large metal rings seem to link and unlink. It's very pleasing to watch impenetrable objects link and unlink. The symbolic meaning of this illusion dawned on me when I was interpreting a client's dream. She dreamed that her ex-husband, who wasn't a magician, was linking and unlinking the rings in front of her. What could it mean?

A common concern of this couple was being able to join together without losing their independence. The dream provided the image of a solution. Like impenetrable rings, they could remain themselves. And yet, when they wished to, they could link-up. And they could, just as easily separate. Thus there was really no real marriage here, if by marriage we mean a union in which two people lose their individuality so as to become of one flesh. Instead, there existed that modern form of union called a relationship. Here the two relata fundamentally retain their individuality. I think that the subconscious appeal of the Linking Rings is that it provides a magical answer to a question that many people have: how can we join with each other, while maintaining our individuality?

The Slydini Knots

Years ago, I took magic lessons with an amazing slight of hand artist, Tony Slydini. One of his tricks came to be called, "the Slydini Knots." Slydini would show two silk handkerchiefs, which he would tie together with a knot. Then he would tie a double knot, and would pull the handkerchiefs so that that the knots were very tight. It would certainly take a long time for anyone to remove these formidable knots. He would even pass the knotted handkerchiefs around to the audience. Then he would have a member of the audience hold one end of the knotted handkerchiefs. To the audience's surprise, the knots dissolved; the two handkerchiefs separated from each other!

If that wasn't astounding enough, Slydini repeated the trick, this time having a volunteer tie the handkerchiefs together in a very tight knot. Slydini would have him tie a second knot and then a third. It would take a long time to untie these knots, but Slydini would, again, magically untie them instantly! Wondering about the trick's deeper meaning, I serendipity stumbled upon "The Surangama Sutra." Here the Buddha uses a handkerchief to illustrate freeing oneself of ego consciousness. He makes six knots in a handkerchief, and states that they represent six levels of ego illusion:

> *"Ananda! Let me ask you another question. This handkerchief has six knots tied in it. If I untie them can they all be untied at once?"*
>
> *"No, my Lord. The knots were originally tied by one in a certain order, so when we come to untie them we must follow the reverse order..."*
>
> *"Again the Lord Buddha was pleased at the reply and said: It is the same with the disentanglements of the conceptions of the six senses. The first knot of false conceptions that must be untied, is the one relating to the false conception of an ego personality, one must first of all attain a realization of its utter unreality..."*

(*The Buddhist Bible,* Edited by Dwight Goddard, Beacon Press, 1970, p. 220.)

The Buddha then proceeds to describe the meaning of removing all six of the knots. Our ego is indeed akin to a knot. If the handkerchief represents the Self, then the ego is nothing more than a knot in the Self. We know this subconsciously, which is why the trick resonates in us. After all, it takes an enormous struggle to be free of that knot called ego. The appeal of the Slydini Knots trick is this: the knots that constitute ego consciousness can just magically dissolve. It's actually true that ego consciousness can suddenly dissolve, but it can take twenty years to reach that magical moment. It's like the comedian who said that it took him twenty years to become an overnight success.

These three tricks we analyzed have a certain commonality. They are about that metaphysical mystery called "the two and the one." In the Cut and Restored Rope Trick, the one becomes two, but remains one. In the Linking Rings, the two become one, and yet retain their individuality. And, in the Slydini Knots, the two are tightly bound together, but can just as easily separate, at the command of the magician.

Questions for the Reader to Ponder

1. Analyze a magic trick that your enjoy. What do you think is its symbolic apppeal?

2. *"But the wonderfullest trick of all was the coffin trick. We nailed him into a coffin and he got out of the coffin without removing one nail... There is a trick that would come in handy for me--get me out of this two-by-four situation!.. You know it don't take much intelligence to get yourself into a nailed-up coffin, Laura. But who in hell ever got himself out of one without removing one nail?"* (Tennessee Williams. *The Glass Managerie* (1944) Why would the coffin escape trick be appealing to someone feeling stuck in an unhappy situation? What is symbolically appealing about the fact tha the nails do not need to be removed for the magican to escape?

3. In my essay on the so called "law of attraction," I condemned magical thinking as childish, but might stage magic be valid, if viewed on a higher level? These magical illusions intimate that there exists a solution to the problem of the two and the one, a solution that exists on a mystical level. What is that mystical solution?

The Mystery of Mountain Climbing

Sir Edmund Hillary, along with his Sherpa, Tenzing Norgay, was the first to make it to the top of Mount Everest. After Hillary's death, there was much encomium, but no analysis of why someone would wish to climb Everest. An earlier and fatal attempt to climb Everest was made, in 1924, by George Mallory. When asked, why he wished to climb to the top of that mountain, Mallory famously said, "Because it is there." Apparently, he had no idea as to his motivation. Neither do other mountain climbers. Some suggest that it's about achieving fame, which makes no sense, for people risk life and limb climbing previously climbed mountain, realizing that it won't gain them fame.

What, then, is the explanation for this mystery? Mircea Eliade suggested that to reach the peak of the mountain is, symbolically speaking, to stand at the connecting point between Heaven and Earth, between the sacred and the profane. A biblical image of this connection is God speaking to Moses, when he is at the top of Mount Sinai. Now here is the interesting thing: standing atop a mountain is a symbolic surrogate for having found meaning in one's life, for meaning is what links our everyday activities to eternal values. Meaning, in other words, is what connects Earth and Heaven.

Questions for the Reader to Ponder

To engage in an activity, oblivious to its symbolic appeal, is to be a sleepwalker. Make a list of your interests, desires, activities, conflicts, and anxieties. Can you ferret out the symbolic meaning of each? This isn't an easy to do––and, like Frank, you may find yourself resistant to illuminating the symbolic dimension of life--but it's the price of awakening, and the doorway to wonderment.

When the Door to the Bus Opens, Get On

"This door was intended for you. Now I am going to shut it."

--Kafka, "Before the Law"

We previously explored Hamlet's notion of readiness in relation to the Boy Scout motto "Be Prepared." We shall now examine certain factors that undermine the ready state of mind. If there is a mystery here, it is how we could be oblivious to good fortune.

At every moment, there exist certain opportunities. As to whether we can discern these opportunities, is another story. Is a lack of intelligence the cause of our benighted condition? Or is the real culprit, paradoxically, intelligence itself?! Consider the conclusion to the film *Dumber and Dumber* (1994). [View it on YouTube] After a series of misadventures, Lloyd and Harry find themselves, once again, down on their luck--no jobs, no money, not even a car. Furthermore, Lloyd has discovered that the woman whom he has been pursuing romantically is married. As they walk along the barren highway together, Lloyd laments to Harry: "When are we ever going to catch a break?"

At that moment, a tour bus bearing the sign "Hawaiian Tropic Bikini Tour" pulls up along side of them. We hear the joyous "Hallelujah Chorus," from Handel's "Messiah." It's apparent that a lucky break has finally arrived for the boys, and that this will be their salvation. The door of the bus opens and out comes three beautiful, bikini-clad women. Here is what ensures:

> **Bikini-Clad Woman:** *"We're going on a national bikini tour and we need two oil boys to grease us up before each competition."*

Mysteries in Broad Daylight

Harry: *"You are in luck. There's a town a few miles that way. I'm sure you'll find a couple of guys there."*

Bikini-Clad Woman *(puzzled and perplexed): OK. Thanks.*

[The bus pulls off.]

Lloyd to Harry: *Do you realize what you've done?!*

[Lloyd runs frantically after the bus. The bus stops, and the door opens.]

Lloyd *(out of breath, to the women): You'll have to excuse my friend. He's a little slow... The Town is back that way. (Lloyd points to where the town is.)*

[The bus pulls off.]

Lloyd: *Wow, a couple of lucky guys are going to be driving around with those girls for the next couple of months.*

Harry: *Don't worry. We'll catch our break too. We just got to keep our eyes open.*

Lloyd: *Yep.*

The idea here is that Lloyd and Harry were too dumb to take advantage of this golden opportunity. But, in truth, they made the kind of cognitive error for which intellectuals have a proclivity. I.E., when the bikini women asked them if they knew of anyone who could work as oil boys, Lloyd and Harry shifted into the mindset of distant observers. They became experts, commenting on where oil boys might be found.

As observers, they forgot that they are also existential beings, i.e., guys looking for a job and for love. That's why the scene would have made more sense if Lloyd and Harry were college professors, for it's a certain abstract intellectuality that can get in the way of discerning and capitalizing on opportunities. Their mode of being contrasts with the other characters in the film, who are ruthless opportunists, incapable of adopting a disinterred, objective attitude. Naturally, in real life, few people are as oblivious to opportunity as Lloyd and Harry. But the scene registers with filmgoers and has made it a cult classic, for it symbolizes the obtuseness that most of us display, from time to time.

There was another, related factor that blinded Lloyd and Harry to the tour bus opportunity. Throughout the film, they display a certain good-natured selflessness, congruent with the conclusion of the film where they, in their concern for the women on the bus, neglect their own self-interest. Thus, if Lloyd and Harry are idiots, they're akin to Prince Myshkin, the protagonist of Dostoevsky's novel *The Idiot*, who was highly intelligent. Myshkin's selflessness blinded him to the machinations of other people. It's that quixotic naïveté and obtuseness that makes Myshkin very admirable as a person, but, in Dostoevsky's estimation, an idiot--thus the title of his novel. To summarize, there were two factors that blinded Lloyd and Harry to the opportunity before them:

1. Their cognitive shift from existing beings to distant observers. Thus they forgot that they too are guys and, therefore, able to work as oil boys. That shift, in itself, isn't a bad thing. Indeed, it is a sign of a morally evolved person. It's just that this shift occurred, for them at precisely the wrong moment. In comedy, as in life, timing is everything.

2. Selflessness--at the wrong moment--also made Lloyd and Harry forget that they are existential beings and capable of being oil boys. Some would say that Lloyd and Harry weren't all there, but more precisely they weren't there at all, since "being there" means that one is an existential being and aware of oneself as such. (Jerzy Kosinski's novel about an idiot, named Chauncey Gardner, is ironically entitled *Being There*.)

The ability to know when to get on the bus doesn't only apply to success in business and love, but to all domains, from the mundane to the spiritual. In regard to the latter, the door that opens may be--as in Kafka's parable, "Before the Law"--the doorway to spiritual salvation. Naturally, we must be sure to board the right bus. Our journey will be very different if we take the one that says "Hawaiian Tropic Bikini Tour" versus the one that's headed for a monastery. That said, it's better to get on some bus, any bus, rather than just standing there like an idiot. On the other hand, sometimes it's best not to get on the bus, but to "walk on," as the Zen masters recommend.

The factors we discussed are certainly not the only ones that prevent us from capitalizing on life's opportunities. Here's another major stumbling block: we may perceive an opportunity, but be too fearful of taking advantage of it. As Shakespeare writes: "Our doubts are traitors and make us lose the good we oft might win by fearing to attempt." Sometimes, indeed, life requires what Kierkegaard called a leap of faith. Such moments are fraught with anxiety. But that is another story, for another time.

Questions for the Reader to Ponder

1. Do you ever feel that you missed the bus? What stopped you from boarding?

2. Ever take, to use Williams' metaphor, "a streetcar named desire"? Did the driver promise to take you to the Elysian Fields, but instead drop you off in Hell? How does that happen? Wrong bus? Or the one you needed to take for your soul's awakening?

3. OK, forget buses and streetcars. Using Kafka's metaphor, how do you know which door is the one intended for you alone? Who really is the guard in Kafka's parable?

4. Are you able to be there, in both senses of the word?

    a. As an existential being, who has self-interest

    b. As a person who is capable of being transcendent to self-interest and who, therefore, is able to adopt an objective, moral standpoint?

5. Is the Bard correct that doubts are traitors? Is it true that

we are more likely to regret what we don't do than what we do? How can you distinguish valid self-doubt from traitorous doubts?

The Case of the Blown Newspaper

There is a force in the universe--whether we call it God, the light of truth, or by some other name--that is continually trying to communicate with us. Whatever it may be, it does not speak English. Rather, it communicates through signs. At least, that is the term that the philosopher Martin Buber used. Buber didn't offer examples, but I would say that a sign could be, for example, a haunting dream, a message on the side of a bus that communicates far more than it was intended to, the look of a child, or a wrong turn down an unfamiliar street. I shall offer here an example of a sign, from my own life.

It was around 1988, on a windy day either in early March that I took my car into a service station to be repaired. It was located on one of Binghamton's oddest looking dead-end streets, inhabited by a newspaper recycling business, a motorcycle shop, a plate glass repair, a Howard Johnson's restaurant, and other such commercial ventures that looked like they hadn't changed the slightest in the last fifty years. Rather than calling a friend or a taxi, I decided to get some exercise and walk home. Perhaps, it was the setting sun over the odd looking landscape, but I was beginning to get a feeling of being alone, unknown and unrecognized. Whatever fame I had sought, over the years, had eluded me, and I felt "in disgrace with fortune and men's eyes."

To return home, I had to cross Route 17. There is a long and narrow pedestrian bridge that crosses over that highway. I got about halfway across when I saw a sheet from an old newspaper. I can't remember whether it was from the Daily News, the Post, or the Herald Tribune, but I do remember that it was from the early 1960s. How did a paper, from that long ago, get there, and why hadn't the elements destroyed it by now? I conjectured that, somehow, it must have blown there from the newspaper recycling plant. Why, though, would it take them about 25 years to recycle a newspaper? Maybe it had accidentally fallen behind one of the recycling machines and hid there.

I picked up the folded sheet of newspaper and started reading it. On the inside was a Broadway gossip column, perhaps by Earl Wilson or some other journalist popular back then. It had a photo of a beautiful Latin singer and dancer. The article said that this rising star would be performing at the *Copacabana* or some similar venue.

As I read through the article about the singer, I was blown over by a sublime sense of life's transiency. Whoever she was, she was now in her fifties and her nightclub appearances were long forgotten. It put my own obscurity into perspective, for everything is eventually blown hither and yon by the winds of time. The feeling, though, wasn't heavy or depressing, but sublime and liberating. Buber, then, is right--there are signs that are Heaven-sent and the wind had blown one to me, in the form of an old newspaper. And, in an act of grace, the wind then blew away my sadness and regret.

Part Two, of the Case of the Blown Newspaper

I shall preface my remarks by stating that a reverie, or daydream, can sometimes be more powerful and insight-laden than even a dream. Reveries are very brief, and so we are most apt to forget them, which is unfortunate. In any case, I had completely forgotten about discovering the old newspaper, on the bridge, for over twenty years had elapsed. But something occurred that evoked that memory.

I was slated to offer a few non-credit seminars, at a local community college. Along with courses on yoga, PowerPoint, and Chinese cooking, were my popular philosophy seminars. The dean of the college was sure that they would be a big hit and so, on the page where my seminars were listed, she included a large photo of me. A lot of people in town received the course catalogue and saw the philosophy seminars, and my photo. I received a goodly number of compliments about the photo, along with promises that they would surely be attending the fascinating seminars. Yes, I had achieved minor celebrity status, very minor as it turned out.

Two days before the seminars were to run, I received a telephone call from the dean's secretary. All three courses were being canceled, due to inadequate enrollment. Ah, another disappointment! Tired, I lay down on my couch. As I was drifting off, I had a reverie, which lasted perhaps a second, but was intense enough to make me jump up from the couch. I saw myself on the very bridge that I had crossed some twenty years back, on my way home from the auto-repair shop. In the reverie, I was halfway across the bridge, when I picked up a very old community college course catalogue, with yellowed, crumbling pages. On it, I saw my photo, along with the blurbs of the philosophy seminars that I had been slated to teach! The sublime feeling returned, only it was more powerful this time, for I was not viewing the photo of the Latin singer, but a photo of myself. I remembered, then, that no matter what degree of success I achieve as a teacher and counselor, whatever I accomplish is still subject to mutability and decay, and will end up like papers scattered to oblivion by the winds of time.

That insight has not diminished my efforts, for no one can foresee from whence and to where the wind may scatter the seeds of spiritual renewal. Thus did the wind blow through my soul, rekindling my inner fire.

"Scatter, as from an unextinguished hearth
Ashes and sparks, my words among mankind!
Be through my lips to unawakened earth

The trumpet of a prophesy! O, wind,
If Winter comes, can Spring be far behind?

--Percy Bysshe Shelley

"The answer, my friend, is blowin' in the wind,
The answer is blowin' in the wind."

--Bob Dylan

The Case of the Bottlenecked Bicyclist

In my essay about the blown newspaper, I offered an example of what the philosopher Martin Buber calls a sign. We must remember that a sign is not an objective occurrence that holds the same meaning for everyone. When the Thou of the universe speaks, according to Buber, it is for your ears only. May you become attuned to the signs that are desperately seeking to speak to you!

I shall now offer another example. I'll preface my remarks by saying that some years ago I had been very concerned with the question of how to be more effective with my philosophical counseling. I found that my clients would often reach a certain point in their self-development and then become stuck. I pondered why this was so, and what could I do to help them to become unstuck. The answer, if it was a sign from above, took the form of a rather odd incident. Once again, it involved an encounter with the feminine, only this time not in the form of an old newspaper photograph, but of an actual woman on a bicycle. I suspect that Sophia, the goddess of wisdom, can transfigure herself into just the right incarnation, as a teaching device. I certainly wouldn't put it past her. And so here is what happened...

Some summers ago, on a Saturday afternoon in Binghamton, I was taking a walk to a neighborhood cafe that was hosting a music festival. I was almost there, when I heard a woman bicyclist, in her early thirties, with bleach-blond hair, calling to me for help, from the across the street. I went over to her, whereupon she showed me that she couldn't ride her bicycle home because a plastic Pepsi bottle had gotten wedged between the front wheel and the frame of the bicycle. I asked her how it had gotten there. She explained that she had been riding with a small plastic bag of groceries, which included the bottle, hanging over the bicycle's handle bar. When the bag hit the wheel, the bottle miraculously got lodged there, bringing the wheel and the bicycle to a standstill. I then tried to dislodge the soda bottle. I pulled and tugged for a few minutes, but it was absolutely stuck. The problem was that I couldn't get a good grip on it, for only the tapered side with the cap protruded, and only a few of inches.

Then eureka! The solution dawned on me. I asked her permission to turn the knob of the bottle, emptying the contents. She agreed. I opened it and the soda quickly sprayed out like a fire hydrant. It was then easy to dislodge the deflated bottle. She was relieved and thanked me. Then she took out of her shopping bag another bottle of Pepsi. For a moment it seemed like she was going to offer me some, but instead she took a swig before placing the bottle back into her shopping bag. She then lit herself a cigarette.

She expressed to me a combination of perplexity and astonishment that she hadn't arrived at the solution to the bottle problem herself, for she certainly seemed intelligent enough. As we talked, I too became perplexed over why the solution hadn't occurred to her. At that moment, I knew that I was entering into a mystery. Here, again, was what Buber called a "sign," this time taking the form of a rather odd incident. What, though, was the Thou saying to me?

I previously stated that I had been concerned with the problem of counseling. How could I help people who were stuck? Here, then, was the answer to my question. I can only express what I saw as an extended metaphor: What retards us on our journey through life is our attachment to the mother. I do not mean "mother" in the literal sense, i.e., one's personal mother. I mean it in the way that the psychologist C.G. Jung meant it, as a symbol, or an archetype, for a certain reality that we seek. The mother symbolizes life as sweet, easy, no work, a free ride. The sweet soft drink that the bicyclist was carrying home with her, symbolized her attachment to the mother archetype.

The cosmic irony of the situation was that the very thing that she hoped would make her journey through life an easy one (symbolized by the bottle of soda), was what prevented her from getting anywhere in life, quite literally. The reason why the solution did not occur to her was that giving up mother (symbolized by letting the soda pour on to the concrete) was the very thing she was unwilling to do.

This brings us to the question of why people are stuck. Not everyone is stuck for the reason I suggested, but a great many are.

Quite often, the mother wears the aspect of comfort and security. A man or a woman cannot leave a job they hate because their employer promises to take care of them. A company like IBM then becomes "Big Mama." On a more universal level, the mother symbolizes those habits, routines, and ways of seeing life that we know are long outmoded. They're very confining, but we cannot abandon them, for they feel comfortable and secure, as is the realm of the mother.

I realized that to help my clients get anywhere in life, I would need to encourage them to throw away their bottles, whether they be baby bottles, soda bottles, or liquor bottles. It would mean for them to kiss mom goodbye and leave home. Again, I am speaking symbolically, not about one's real mother, but about the mother archetype. As to how I have finally been able to help my clients to leave home is another story.

Questions for the Reader to Ponder

1. Evoke God or the universe or nature or whatever to communicate with you, by means of a sign. Then open your eyes, ears and heart. (You might have to wait for weeks or months.) Then, when you least expect it, a sign might appear. If it does, then look out! It may hit you like a tornado. Were you able to discern its message?

2. Pasteur said, "Fortune favors the prepared mind." Do signs favor the prepared heart? Buber ironically wrote that we're unable to hear God's voice because of wax in our ears. What can you do to remove the wax of quotidian worries and concerns, hopes and fears, from your ears so that you might hear the universe speaking to you?

How Not to Bring Yourself with You, When You Move

"But we breathe, we change! We lose our hair, our teeth! Our bloom! Our ideas!"

--Samuel Beckett

Way up there, on the list of life's most stressful events, is moving, especially if it involves relocating to another city. I recently moved from Binghamton New York, where I'd lived for a real long time, to Louisville Kentucky. I've experienced many of the regrets and anxieties endemic to this major life transition.

It took Hercules a single day to clean the Augean stables. I'd been cleaning for many months sorting through the plethora of items that I've accumulated over the years, deciding what to keep and what to discard. Each object--from an old tennis racket to a pile of love letters, from a ukulele that I never learned to play to the syllabus from a course that I taught long ago--becomes like Proust's madeleine, evoking a flood of memories, some pleasant and some rather painful.

Sorting through one's accumulated possessions, in preparation to move, reawakens all sorts of slumbering ghosts. The most powerful is the specter of regret. After tormenting us for what we did, it then attacks us for the many more things that we should have done. What, then, can be done? Ideally, this journey backwards in time can effectuate a kind of catharsis, leading to a healing epiphany: one could not be the person one is today had one not been the person that one had been, in all one's ignorance and foolishness. Thus regrets are burned away through insight into the necessity of error.

Insight doesn't justify anything, but it allows us to transcend the tragic dimension of our lives--offering peace to our tormented soul--through an enlarged understanding of life. Without exorcising the ghosts of the past, though insight and acceptance, there is a danger that these regrets will follow the moving van to our new abode, taking up residence there. And then we shall be haunted.

The Two Fears

There would appear to be two fears involved with moving. There is the fear of leaving home, severing contact with all that is familiar, indeed of losing one's world--in the ontological sense--and, therefore, no longer being able to be oneself. This fear of losing one's moorings, by virtue of the fact that home no longer exists, is a fundamental anxiety. Freud relates the sense of the uncanny to the disorientation of having what was home transform into something strange and other.

The other fear is of not being able to let go of oneself, of a self that one increasingly suspects is outmoded. This is the fear that we shall bring our old self with us when we move. We would drag along the albatross of memories we would rather forget, along with the habits, routines and outlooks that limit our horizons. If we long for novelty and adventure, if not indeed for self-renewal, then the thought of bringing ourselves with us, when we move, is a source of both depression and dread.

Of course, this dread, that we may bring ourselves with us to the new place, requires a certain degree of insight into ourselves. We might observe, from experience, that we change jobs but, due to retaining our old attitudes, soon transform our new job into our old job. Thus we find ourselves experiencing the same kind of difficulties with our bosses and coworkers that we had previously experienced. Or we find ourselves in a new relationship, but still have the same sort of conflicts we had in the previous one. To become suspicious of oneself, in this way, requires the ability to identify certain attitudes that make our life what it is, no matter what the circumstance.

Apropos is an episode of *The Twilight Zone* that sent a chill down my spine. It is about three astronauts who have one heck of a time getting their rocket to take off from an alien planet. Finally, they are able to do, to their great relief. Well, their joys soon turn to horror when they realize that they have been deceived; they are still on the alien planet. Here was an image of imagining that one has finally become free of an old place, only to realize that one hasn't. To extend the metaphor, it is difficult to escape the atmosphere, or the force field, of the world one has created for oneself.

We might also recall the film *Cast Away* (2000). The protagonist, Chuck Noland (played by Tom Hanks), has his toughest time escaping the pull of the tide surrounding the island, on which he is stranded. That tide is symbolic of our attitudes, beliefs, and worldviews that we must escape, if we are to leave the island of our old self, which has become our prison.

Breaking Free of the Past

If we are to be blessed with a new life, we must discern our way of seeing, or outlook on life. Relocating can help us to discern it, for we begin to wonder how it is that our new situation bears an eerie resemblance to our old situation. Similarly, were we in a number of relationships, we might better grasp the set of attitudes that we bring to bear, which leads each new relationship to be but a variation on an old theme. What has happened, of course, is that our way of seeing, or outlook on life, is still the same. Consequently, we have unconsciously transformed our new living situation into a variation of our former situation. That is why inner freedom and self-renewal requires grasping our inner attitudes and moving can help, in that regard.

A second good reason to move is that we have already inwardly changed, but our present environment is causing us to retain old habits. By analogy, if we learn to walk properly, our old pair of shoes could be forcing us to walk in the old incorrect way, due to the imprint on the shoes of our former stride. Thus, if we are to escape the force of old habits, we need a new pair of shoes. Similarly, we need a new place to live.

Of course, there are other reasons to move, from new financial opportunities to sunnier skies to an enhancement of one's social relations. I've only explored those that relate to self-renewal. In conclusion, the art of moving consists of this: it means, to the greatest extent possible, leaving oneself behind when one moves to a new place.

Questions for the Reader to Ponder

1. Soren Kierkegaard defined despair as the inability to die. Eric Bentley, the theater critic, ads this,

   > "...dying is something we have to do in order to live... one can think of this in relation to one's personal neurotic problems. They are all one problem: the refusal to let go of certain habits, the refusal to die."
   > --(The Life of the Drama, 1964)

   Indeed, most people finally let go of something that they no longer like or believe in--such as a job, a house, a set of beliefs or a lifestyle--ten or more years too late, when it's already thoroughly sickened them and weakened their spirit. Can you offer examples either from the people you know or from your own life?

2. There are many people today, who remain at a job they hate, because they fear losing their health insurance, but staying at their job is making them very sick. Might that constitute theological proof for the existence of the devil?

3. Make a list of ten films that concludes with one of the characters having experienced a self-renewal. (The film *Cast Away*, which we just discussed, would be an example.) Explore the new versus old life of the protagonist and the factors that contributed to his or her life change. Was it merely a change or rather a transformation of some sort?

The Mystery of Being Home & Yet Not Being There

"Though I'm in Kyoto, when the cuckoo sings, I long for Kyoto."

--Basho

Some years ago, I stumbled upon that strange haiku by Basho. It puzzled me how Basho could be in Kyoto and yet, when the cuckoo sings, long to be there. Apparently, the plaintive sound of the cuckoo moved the poet to conclude that although he was physically in Kyoto, he was not there in some other sense. But, what is that other sense?

As a way of deciphering this mystery, I substituted Binghamton, NY, where I was living, for Kyoto. And then a doorway into the poem appeared before me, which I entered. I think that Basho's haiku is about the longing for home. For one can be home in the physical sense, but not fully home in a deeper sense. It can take a moment of intense beauty--the song of a bird, a shaft of sunlight, falling leaves, a haunting melody played on a violin, or some other such moment of splendor--to awaken in us a certain metaphysical nostalgia.

To be home, in this deeper sense, is to achieve that fullness, wholeness, and oneness with the universe that we intuit is our birthright, but which we know we have lost, when we became conscious beings and fallen beings. To regain that lost sense of unity is what it would really mean to return home.

In lieu of that metaphysical return, there is the usual nostalgia. It explains, for example, the popularity of retro-style clothing, antiques, the migration of urbanites to small towns, the popularity of "The Prairie

Home Companion," and old movies. In difficult times--and times are always difficult--we idealize what seems to be a more innocent age. Other people more desperately seek to return home by more desperate means, such as drinking and drugs. But, of course, the gates of Eden are now closed, and guarded by two angels with flaming swords.

There is, though, a real way to return home. Paradoxically, we cannot journey home until we have fully left home. It's what Homer's *Odyssey* is all about; indeed, it took Odysseus twenty years to return. Symbolically, that it what baseball is all about--leaving home, completing the journey through life, and then returning home. More universally, it's the fundamental theme of all such heroic journeys.

If it is true that we cannot return home till we have fully left home, then the practical question is: how to leave home? If you ask deep questions about life, with all the force and power of your being, you will soon find that you are not in Kansas anymore. You may, in an obvious sense, still reside in Kansas or Kyoto, in Binghamton or Brooklyn, in London or Louisville, but you will have entered into the unknown, the unfamiliar. You will find yourself alone. And, then, you must rely on your inner light to guide you homeward.

Questions for the Reader to Ponder

1. Have you left home, in the psychological sense? If not what inner force is stopping you? I.E., to what are you clinging?

2. Have you been able to return home, in the psychological sense? If not, what inner force is blocking your path, on your journey home? (Read Homer's, "The Odyssey" and interpret it symbolically for clues. Also, see the film, "After Hours.")

3. Read Castaneda's "Journey to Ixtlan." Here, too, we find the longing to return home. Relate its theme to the haiku.

Part III
Concluding Thoughts
and
Suggestions to the Reader

Epicurus inquired, "Why does there always seems to be something missing?" The dialogues, essays and commentary, contained here, have essentially sought to answer that question. Of course, what Samantha believes to be missing is very different from what Frank believes to be missing. What we perceive the lack to be determines the route we travel through life and the type of experiences that we are likely to have. We might, for example, believe that we need fame, a new relationship, a world with social justice, a closer connection with nature, financial security, a sense of community, creative expression, or greater autonomy. How very different our life will be in each case! And yet, what's *really* missing is essentially the same for each of us. Only by grasping the obscure object of human desire is there any hope of finding it and overcoming our ever-present sense of lack.

Few people examine their efforts to achieve happiness and fulfillment. But were we to get to the very heart of the matter, we would discern that the requirements for selfhood happen to also be the requirements for true reality. Thus we would realize that we are, more essentially, seeking to achieve reality as a person and to inhabit a world that is real. These requirements hold the key that could unlock Epicurus' riddle and solve the mystery of human suffering.

Are You for Real?

What, then, does it mean to be real?" Our discussion with Dorothy, about her dread of pubic speaking, led to the ironic question, "Who do you think you are?" That question ultimately concerns our reality or lack of it. We've uncovered five criteria that people unconsciously use to determine whether or not something is real:

1. **Physical existence:** Here is the most obvious criterion of what it means to be real. To be real we must physically exist in space and time. Ah, but that is far from sufficient, for there are many people who physically exist and yet who have a sense that their life lacks true reality. Partly, it's because what we take ourselves to be is invariably more than our physical body. We often identify with our expressions and objectifications, such as our clothing, our house, our car and all else, which are our body in the extended sense. Few people are so otherworldly such that they can walk through life like Diogenes, with only a loincloth and a tin cup.

    At the other extreme from an ascetic renunciation of this world is the effort to transform the object (the world) into a single subject. In some totalitarian countries, for example, we see a photo of the supreme leader--be it Stalin, Mao or Saddam Hussein--just about everywhere. This is not surprising, for totalitarianism derives from the word "total."

    In a democracy, on the other hand, any one person's objectification is rarely so totalistic, for there are other subjects who also wish to objectify themselves as well, on that canvas we call the world. Apropos is my discussion with Samantha about owning the health club. The subject (Samantha) seeks to find expression in the world, as do other subjects. That's where competition enters in.

2. **Infinitude, Eternality, Absoluteness:** When we examine what people are really up to, we see that everyone is seeking to connect his or her finite, temporal lives to that which is

absolute, eternal, unconditioned, and infinite. If we fail to make this connection, we then feel that our transient earthly existence--which is destined to vanish into nothingness--is not quite real. Even atheists, like Christopher Hitchens, have sought to create something eternal, something that could outlast their mortal coil, be it a book, the values that they impart to their children, or simply their DNA.

That which a person regards as absolute, infinite, ultimate or eternal might not be God and his commandments. It might be some humanistic vision of a secular utopia made possible through science and human progress. Such people often speak of wishing to "make a difference," as if their efforts were bringing Planet Earth closer to the millennium. How very different is Lao Tzu notion that "A perfect traveler leaves no trace."

Egotism consists in regarding oneself as the center of the universe, and therefore as ultimate, or absolute. Still other people seek infinite power, through money. And some people seek to escape the limits imposed by ego consciousness by means of drink and drugs, for as self-awareness is abolished, so is the sense of limits. Alas, angels, with flaming swords, guard the Gates of Eden. They won't permit us to return to a state of un-self-awareness, or immediacy. No doubt, Slobberchops is often a nuisance, but Tim keeps him because Slobberchops seems to embody the immediacy that Tim lacks and which Tim enjoys vicariously.

We might note that there has been a recent trend of people wishing to adopt mentally challenged children and adults. This derives from a valorization of the immediacy, innocence or un-self-awareness that the mentally challenged seem to embody. It's not really true that such individuals are without self-awareness, but their limited self-awareness seems very appealing to certain other individuals who view themselves as fallen, temporal, finite, limited beings, beleaguered by all of the problems and conflicts that accompanies increased self-awareness.

There are numerous other ways in which people seek to satisfy the requirement for reality that says that they must either be absolute or relate themselves to that which they take to be absolute. It would benefit the reader to uncover how he or she has been seeking to satisfy this criterion of reality. More than likely, it may be in a variety of ways. Furthermore, is the means to achieving true reality really viable? Apropos is a comment by Woody Allen, "I don't want to achieve immortality through my work... I want to achieve it through not dying." Apparently for Mr. Allen, symbolic immortality is not sufficient.

3. **Self-identity:** That which is regarded as real is intelligible, which means graspable by the mind. The mind can only apprehend that which has an identity. As Ricky comes to realize, if he doesn't give his life shape, form and identity, he will feel like a formless blob, or like a soup that has so many ingredients that its identity is indeterminate. To feel like a blob is to feel like one is nothing at all, and therefore unreal.

The problematic of self-identity is also evident in Haley's effort to find existential grounding by tattooing a picture of her hometown on her arm, and by her anxiety--as symbolized in her dream--that her turbulent emotions were threatening to drown out her identity.

Similarly, that which has an identity must be unchanging through time. If we feel that we are completely different from day to day, lacking in focus or direction, we feel unreal. Direction, meaning and purpose are dimensions of the self-identity criterion. It's what links our days together into a unity. If we have a goal, but it no longer appears to be meaningful, it feels like the string holding together the beads of a necklace has been severed. All of our days then lose their connection to each other and we suffer meaninglessness.

There are those who believe that the meaning that they give their lives is the only true meaning. Often, they are intolerant of those who subscribe to other beliefs systems, which offer different meanings. This leads to a war of ideas and sometimes an actual war, as each person, group, culture or civilization seeks to transform the world to conform to its sense of identity. This conflict is inevitable since each person regards his identity as not merely any identity, but as absolute, as the only true identity. After all, who would want an identity that was merely relative?

4. **Self-sufficiency:** Some philosophers, such as Plato, consider self-sufficiency to be a criterion of reality, and all of us do, whether we realize it or not. People pursue self-sufficiency, independence, or autonomy in quite a variety of ways--from seeking to acquire wealth, so as to be freer of conditions, to moving to the woods, where they will be less dependent on society.

There are problems, though, with the quest for self-sufficiency. Plato initially thought that his Ideas, or Forms, were thinkable through themselves alone, and therefore self-sufficient, but he latter realized that that is not the case. We cannot, for example, think of the notion of courage, without thinking of justice, without thinking of other notions as well. A Twentieth Century philosopher, Herbert Bradley, contended that all identities are internally related to other identities.

Could it be, then, that our very identity, as a person, is contingent upon other people's identities? As Rabbi Menachem Mendel of Kotzk wrote, "If I am I because you are you and you are you because I am I, then I am not I and you are not you." If we picture our identity as a circle, that which defines us, the outer edge of the circle, is that which we aren't. For example, one cannot be a Democrat if there do not exist Republicans, and vice versa.

The problem, then, is that we seek to be self-sufficient, but no identity can be self-sufficient. Only the absolute can truly be self-sufficient, which is why it's the true object of our desire, as well as "the final terminus for thought," as

Arthur O. Lovejoy rightly observed. But that which is truly self-sufficient, the absolute, is ungraspable by the mind and, therefore, unintelligible. Furthermore, any attempts to define the absolute, so as to make it intelligible--even by assigning it good qualities--will limit it such that it's no longer absolute. That seems to be the central contradiction.

In any case, if self-sufficiency is a requirement for true reality and therefore, for selfhood, then Houston we have a problem.

5. **Recognition:** Finally, to be real is, as the Eighteenth Century philosopher George Berkeley noted, is to be seen, or recognized. Tim, for example, feels invisible because his customers do not see the deeper significance of the landscape gardens that he is creating for them.

The craving to be seen, or recognized, knows no bounds in contemporary culture or society. It may involve being famous in some way, perhaps breaking some record, such as eating the most hotdogs or singing "Macarthur Park," while standing on one's head, for the longest period of time.

Fashion involves a curious adjudication of opposite interests--conformity and nonconformity. Tattoos would be a contemporary example, and is akin to the long hair that men wore in the 1960s. On the one hand, a person wishes to be regarded by other people as a nonconforming rebel, by virtue of having a tattoo. But they are simultaneously fearful of really nonconforming, which is why they chose a means of rebellion that other people have chosen. Furthermore, when a person is seen in this superficial way, they can have a sense that their true self is invisible. As such they can feel alone and unreal.

If being seen, known or recognized is a requirement for reality and, therefore, for selfhood, then to be recognized we must be recognizable. Ah, but to be recognizable, who we are must be intelligible, which means that we must have an identity. But, as we have seen, no identity is thinkable through itself alone. Therefore, nothing can truly be known, seen or recognized.

What emerged, from our discussions, is that it's impossible to satisfy the criteria of reality and, therefore, of selfhood. It's impossible because they conflict with each other such that contradictions emerge. If, for example, we were to satisfy the criterion of infinitude, we would not be able to satisfy the criterion of self-identity.

People often speak of needing to "get it together." When they run into difficulties, in that regard, they might seek the services of a psychotherapist, who promises to help them to get it together. The assumption, of course, is that it could be gotten together, that life's conflicting and opposing criteria can be organized into a unity, or a balance, as Samantha likes to way. But what if the criteria that we use to determine what is real are contradictory? In that case it's impossible to get it together! That would be a shocking realization. The good news, though, is that it's possible to let go of the puzzle, at the moment when we realize that it cannot be completed. That moment, paradoxically, is the moment when the Self comes to see itself, the moment of our self-realization.

In any case, suffering is really the psychophysical concomitant of the perception of our unreality. It points to the failure of our answer to the question of how to be. Let us, then, return to Epicurus' question. The reason why there always seems to be something missing is because we always fail to satisfy one or more of the criteria for selfhood, which are, as we have seen, also the criteria for reality.

Theoretical Background

I've referred to the type of work that I do as philosophical counseling, but that term is very imprecise. After all, those who bill themselves as such each have their own notion of philosophical counseling. That's not surprising, for if you were to ask twenty college philosophy professors to offer an extended definition of philosophy, you would likely come away with twenty very different definitions.

Philosophical counseling has a certain kinship with existential psychotherapy, which has its theorists, academic journals and practitioners, but it's really been out of vogue since the 1940s. Even back then, it never went mainstream. There have been a number of theoretical formulations of it, including Rudolph Allers' *Ontoanalysis*, Martin Heidegger's *Dasein Analysis*, and Jean-Paul Sartre's *Existential Psychoanalysis*. Theoretical differences aside, these existential thinkers offer a profound analysis of human existence. If existential philosophy and psychotherapy is not more popular today, it's mostly because ours is an age of shallowness.

As is the case with revived and then revised intellectual movements, they are often barely recognizable by their original progenitors. In any case, Rudolph Allers term "Ontoanalysis" expresses what I've been seeking to accomplish throughout these pages. Ontoanalysis tries to uncover a person's hidden ontology. Ontology derives from the root, "onto," meaning "to be," or "to be real." Ontoanalysis, therefore, seeks to uncover how you've been seeking to be real, in all that you do--in your job, your relationships, your food preferences, etc.

Perhaps it would help to contrast Ontoanalysis to psychotherapy. Each form of psychotherapy harbors certain metaphysical assumptions, along with a theory of personality, a theory of health and much more. Psychoanalysis, for example, believes that the driving force in human beings is sexual satisfaction. For Adler, the quest for power is key and for Jung it is individuation coupled with psycho-synthesis of the various components of the psyche. For Rank it was all about the birth trauma. Other theorists have emphasized the importance of social relationships. There have, of course, been many other schools of analysis, apart from those of the depth psychologists. There are, for example, Marxist analyses of everyday life, postmodern analyses, deconstructionist, feminist and probably hundreds more.

The existential modes of analysis recognize, for example, that Freud's insights into sexuality are valid to a certain extent, as are Adler's insights into power, as are the insights of the other theorists. But they perceive, at the root of these various human longings, something more fundamental, something of which they are all but an expression. This more fundamental longing is ontological; it's the longing to be, i.e., to be real, real as a self, inhabiting a world that is real.

In other words, sexuality, power, spiritual yearnings, social relationships, economic factors and all the rest are species of the longing to be real as a self and to inhabit a real world. This idea is foreshadowed in Plato's *Symposium*, where we find Aristophanes contending that erotic love is a search for the completeness we lost when we were born either male or female. The yearning for completeness is a longing to be real.

We've already discussed how psychotherapy mistakenly assumes that we can "get it together." The Ontoanalysts, by contrast, seek to awaken us from the impossible project. Consequently, their goal is not merely for us to attain mental health, but to attain an awakened and illuminated state of consciousness. Furthermore, psychotherapy is theory-laden. My interest in the existential types of analysis lies in the possibility of understanding people and their problems free of the distorting theoretical assumptions that belong to each school of therapy, whether it be Freudian psychoanalysis, Rogerian therapy, cognitive behaviorism or any other school of psychotherapy. Ontoanalysis, for example, simply seeks to uncover and to illuminate the hidden ontology, or worldview, that each of us has and to show how our difficulties in life stem from having unconsciously subscribed to that worldview.

Furthermore, unlike psychotherapy, these existential modes of analysis regard human suffering neither as a disease to be cured, nor as a mistake to be rectified, nor as a problem to be solved. On the contrary, suffering is intrinsic to human existence. Whatever form it may take, suffering--when illuminated--is the road to liberating self-knowledge and wisdom. Ontoanalysis and these other modes of analysis are, in that respect, actually a western route to eastern wisdom.

A Philosophical Puzzle

Before we leave these theoretical concerns, there is a question that some readers may have. We had suggested that insights into our interests, desires, activities, conflicts, and anxieties reveal offer not merely self-knowledge and emotional freedom, but ontological truths, i.e., knowledge of ultimate reality. How is this possible?

We can understand this through a kind of Kantian Copernican Revolution. If we study the history of modern philosophy--from Descartes though to the twentieth century--we see something amazing happening: To an ever-increasing degree, the object is becoming absorbed into the subject. Indeed, the very notion of "out there" becomes "in here." I.E., so-called external reality, the objective world, is understood to be nothing more than a form of cognition, a form of knowing of the subject. (Of course, most scientists still contend that there exists objective reality. Unfortunately, they never took a philosophy course or else never took it seriously.)

All this would seem rather solipsistic, for it implies that all we can't know anything outside our individual consciousness. Ah, but the principle of individuation, whereupon there appears to be a multiplicity of individual subjects--you and I and everyone else--becomes a function of what Kant called "the transcendental illusion," at least that is the reasoning of Schopenhauer.

Thousands of years before Kant, the Hindus had it right: There is only one Self, with billions of faces. Therefore, our interests, desires and all else--as well as those of the billions of individual egos inhabiting the planet, as well as the generations that proceeded us-- are all expressions of Brahman, or the Self, which the Hegelians call "Spirit."

Thus a particular person's struggles to achieve happiness and fulfillment are really the struggles and difficulties of the Self to know itself. Haley's tattoo and Frank's interest in golf, for example, are but two of the many expressions of the Self to know itself. And so, our interests, desires, activities, conflicts and anxieties not only reveal psychological truths about each us, as individuals, but --as expressions of the Self --offer clues to the great mystery. That's why it is correct to say that they reveal not merely psychological truths, but ontological truths.

Suggestions for Expediting the Process of Self-Transformation

It may have been Abraham Maslow who said that we are not really human beings, but "human becomings." It's because we are always undergoing transformation. The process of transformation normally occurs at a slow pace, which is just as well, for the continual process of dying and rebirth is trying on us, both emotionally and physically. Self-knowledge is the catalyst that changes us. Here, then, is another difference between psychotherapy and the various existential forms of counseling. Psychotherapeutic healing is restorative. It restores us to who we had been prior to a crisis. Existential healing, on the other hand, is transformative. It can elevate us to a new level, one in which we gain in insight, judgment and wisdom.

During those times when a person experiences a crisis in his life, the pace of change is accelerated, sometimes even to a dangerous degree. Such crises are often times of significantly intensified suffering. Our psychological stability is threatened and we can experience a kind of metaphysical vertigo. Few would wish to pay the price required to expedite the process of self-transformation, which is why periods of openness to the big questions are relatively rare, and why closure and a renewed stability soon return.

There exist those people whose lust for life, for a real life, is so intense that they are willing to suffer all that the dread spirit casts upon them. They are willing to suffer it all, in the hope that they might eventually discover life's deepest secrets and then live in accord with the truth they uncover. The characters in our trilogy possess this lust and I suspect that the reader--who has made it almost to the end of this tome--does too.

We had suggested that self-knowledge is the catalyst that expedites the pace of change. That is because who we are, our mode of being in the world, is actually a function of what we don't know about ourselves! The light reveals the contradictions internal to who we are. As Soren Kierkegaard's writings illustrate, the awareness of contradiction and therefore of the impossible is the doorway to new stages on life's way. All the same, it's why self-knowledge is a dangerous affair.

Here, then, are some suggestions on making faster progress:

1. **Discerning One's Mode of Being:** It's necessary to get clearer on one's mode of being, i.e., the particular way in which one attempts to achieve selfhood, or reality as a person. Such knowledge isn't easy to acquire. We might begin by asking, what get's us through the day? Is it a hope for a new world order? Is it a romance? A new type of chocolate chip cookie? A hug from our dog? The little things in life often carry powerful symbolic meanings for us.

    Clues to one's mode of being can be found in one's possessions, interests and activities. Examples include: one's car, the clothing that one wears, the music one listens to, one's friends, one's occupation, the problems that one encounters at the workplace, general concerns, one's house, favorite joke, favorite actor, favorite films, how one walks, how one sits, family problems, investments, favorite foods, hobbies and games, etc. Discerning one's mode of being is not an easy thing to do. It is an art that can take years of practice, but one well worth mastering.

    It can sometimes be valuable to assemble a group of people interested in discerning their mode of being. This is because we can sometimes grasp our outlook on life by contrasting it to how other people see the world. The group can then, over time, develop the perspicacity to discern each of the member's mode of being, as it manifests itself in everything about him or her.

    Once we are able to grasp our mode of being, we see it everywhere. This is a disturbing, but potentially liberating perception. It is disturbing because a person then feels trapped by none other than himself. But the perception of our imprisonment is the requirement for our liberation.

2. **Illuminating the Negative:** The negative aspect life, which we experience as suffering, is the best clue to one's mode of being. As we have seen, suffering is the psychophysical

concomitant of the perception of our unreality. Suffering therefore reveals the inadequacy of our answer. It can also point us back to the question.

It's very useful to fully grasp the question, for then we can determine whether any answer could, under any circumstances, be adequate. It may be, in other words, that we have been involved in a contradictory effort. In one of the dialogues, I used the example of Rubik's Cube. Metaphorically speaking, at birth we are given a puzzle to solve. We assume that it can be solved; we very rarely consider that maybe it can't be done. In any case, it is important to get clear on the particular way in which the negative shows up in our life, for it points to the contradictions within our mode of being. It can be devastating to realize that that particular form of suffering that we experience is not accidental, but rather is intrinsic to who we are. We would much rather think that we can continue to be live as we do, but without the necessary negative concomitant.

3. **Memento Mori:** The right sort of psychological stability is necessary, if we are to endure the onslaughts of self-knowledge. That stability, or balance, must come from acknowledging the truth of one's existential predicament, the human condition. Simply stated, it means acknowledging that one is a finite, temporal being, and as such one will one day die.

Carlos Castaneda's teacher, Don Juan Matus, spoke of making death one's advisor as a requirement for living impeccably. As Samuel Johnson had earlier expressed it, "Depend upon it, sir, when a man knows he is to be hanged in a fortnight, it concentrates his mind wonderfully." Indeed, the realization that today could be one's last day on this earth is sobering. That sobriety of spirit often gives one the courage needed to venture into the unknown, for as a wise man once sang, "When you got nothing, you got nothing to lose."

4. **Mastering the Art of Deciphering Clues:** Our interests, desires, conflicts, and all else are written in the language of symbolism. If we are to make sense of our experience, we must be able to decipher the symbolic, mythic and archetypal component of our experience.

    There are times, though, when we might wonder if our interpretation is valid or not. This is the same problem that people have in regard to dream interpretation. The proof, though, is in the pudding. If our interpretation is truly illuminating, bells and whistles will go off. Indeed, you may even hear the archangel Gabriel playing his trumpet. We shall, in other words, intuitively know that it's the correct interpretation. If not, we shall be left cold.

    It takes a lot of effort to master the art of interpreting the symbolic and mythic dimension of human experience. It's certainly an art worth learning. The various dialogues and essays contained in the previous chapters offer lessons in that art.

5. **Patience:** As my student, Ricky, has come to understand, patience is necessary in the quest for self-knowledge and an awakened life. Patience means putting up with finitude and limits, pain and suffering, and not losing one's balance in the quest for knowledge and self-realization. As Goethe told Eckermann, "Any growth in consciousness, without a corresponding growth in self-control, is pernicious." Patience is allied with self-control.

    Forbearance is a species of patience, which requires that one bear a great deal of the world's folly, and not become too aggravated by it, nor attempt to flee from it in frustration. Balthasar Gracian writes, *"Put up with fools... The first great rule of life, according to Epictetus, is to put up with things--he valued this as half of all wisdom. To put up with all the varieties of all folly would need much patience... Out of patience comes forth peace, the priceless boon that is the happiness of the world."* (*The Art of Worldly Wisdom*. Shambhala. Translated by Joseph Jacobs. p. 138.)

6. **A Journal:** It would be a good idea to keep a journal, in which you seek to observe how you have been seeking to satisfy the criteria of reality and of selfhood. For example, do you seek to satisfy the need to be unconditioned by setting off into the woods? By starting our own company? By some other means? Also, what form has the negative taken in one's life? Why has it taken that form? Can we trace the negative back to one's fundamental mode of being? Pursuing these, as well as the questions that I assigned to you, after each of the three dialogues and after each essay, will bear fruit. Write the questions and your answers to them, in your journal. Sometimes, if you feel stuck, the mere act of writing can cause connections to appear, as you write, and open the door to amazing insights. So write, even if you feel stuck. Also, outlining can often prove helpful in causing distinctions to appear.

   Recording one's observations in a journal often helps one to observe various patterns. For example, you might observe that you're having a series of dreams involving transportation, first in a plane, subsequently, in a train, a car, on a bicycle and finally on foot. A journal will help us to detect these significant patterns. In addition to the journal, it might help to have a smaller notebook to carry with you, in your pocket, for on the spot observations and insights.

7. **Practices:** In the third dialogue, I introduced the notion of practices, which are activities designed to undo the fixity of our mode of being. Having Ricky refrain from buffets, but rather have him choose only one menu item is a practice, as it helps him come to terms with choice and limits. Over time, I gave Ricky further practices, to help him, in that respect.

   Elsewhere, Samantha expresses shock, when I suggest giving up donuts or a certain familiar TV show, upon her realizing that those are the things that get her through the day. The purpose of this asceticism--to use a boating metaphor from Castaneda's teacher, Don Juan Matus--is to patch our sails. Then, when the winds of the spirit blow, it can really take us somewhere. The little things that get us through the day would be, to follow along with this metaphor, holes in our sails.

Sometimes what is required is simply to break away with habit, with the familiar, for the wind to catch the sails. Apropos is one of the essays, contained in this volume, has to do with the notion of doing the opposite, which the character, George, from the situation comedy Seinfeld, had success with. The notion of doing the opposite is more powerful, if a person has some grasp of his mode of being. In any case, it is worth experimenting with this practice, as it might produce some valuable insights.

Once we acquire a clearer sense of our mode of being, there becomes a lot more possibilities in regard to practices. Seeing ourselves in everything that we do, we can then do other than we are wont to do. Even a small gesture, like reaching for an item on the shelf of a supermarket, expresses one's way of being in the world. In that particular instance, then, we would reach for the item in a way that was uncharacteristic and therefore free of our mode of being.

8. **Balancing Anxiety with Wonderment:** Here again, we bow to the wisdom of Don Juan Matus, who recommended balancing the terror of life with the wonder of it all. That is excellent advice for those seeking to survive the arduous journey to self-realization. In addition to wonder, there exist other forms of transcendence, such as amazement, awe, and the comic perception.

I might add that many people today suffer from an oppressive *ennui,* as encapsulated in the phrase "been there, done that." This is the "ho-humness" about which Frank complained. Insight into the symbolic meanings that comprise everyday life replaces *ennui* with amazement.

In another discussion with Ricky, the discussion

having to do with dealing with life's sometimes anguishing contradictions, I recommended viewing life's contradictions at a distance. Doing so will sometimes result in wonder, amazement, or laughter. One must, though, not become too distant, or else the delicate balance--of being in the contradiction (and therefore suffering it) and witnessing it from a distance--will be lost. Samantha, for example, has a proclivity to become too distant, at times. When her distance collapses, she's prone to feelings of frustration and anger. She has, though, become much more self-aware, in regard to these shifts of consciousness. Ricky, too, has made progress. In any case, this balancing act improves with practice.

I suspect that the various forms of transcendence--wonder, amazement and awe--are healing to body, mind and spirit. In that respect, they are akin to the comic perception that erupts in laughter. The dialogues and essays contained in these pages have been lessons in the art of wonderment.

9. **Letting Go of Excessive Seriousness:** There is a danger of becoming too emotionally heavy from life's deeper questions. After all, the road to wisdom is not a walk in the park, nor is life itself for that matter. This practice, then, consists in letting go of excess seriousness.

We might utilize comic media--such as humorous TV show, films, and standup comics--to help rid us of excess seriousness. Alas, these media can become a crutch. It is far better to simply not take oneself and the world too seriously. What is required is an attitudinal shift, from seriousness to light-heartedness. This shift takes practice. If such efforts are rarely undertaken, it is because the notion that we must work to become lighthearted does not sit well with people. That's why they prefer to get their laughs by simply turning on the TV.

The ability to laugh amidst one's difficulties indicates that one is not a slave to the world and its meanings, but a free being. Although Nicolai Berdyaev didn't write very much on humor, I suspect that he would have agreed with me that the ability to laugh, especially in trying circumstances, indicates the victory of a free subject over the object. It requires a certain fighting spirit not to allow the world, and its terrible seriousness, to intimidate us into losing our smile. In any case, the cultivation of the comic spirit can provide a necessary inner balance. But our laughter must derive from genuine insight into life's depths, for without that it is as hollow as those who offer seminars to various organizations on laugh therapy or, even worse, those who use laughter as a kind of yoga.

Some people, such as Frank, have a penchant for making jokes. Others, such as Ricky, due to their eccentric personality, become the occasion for laughter. It is valuable to have such people in a group, for it lightens the atmosphere for everybody.

While we cannot prevent our bodies from aging, the pursuit of philosophical wisdom leads to insights that transform our very being, freeing us from all sorts of darks emotions, and which causes our body to shake from cosmic belly laughter and a Buddha smile to break forth on our countenance, which is turn causes our spirits to become younger and lighter. As Mr. Bob Dylan expressed it, "Ah, but I was so much older then. I'm younger than that now."

10. **Keep the Faith:** The journey to self-realization is an arduous undertaking. The ancient *Upanishads* compare it to walking along a razor's edge. Consequently, unremitting effort is required. But here is the good news: the *Bible* rightly tells us, "Knock and ye shall enter." That is true for any genuine philosophical and spiritual endeavor, including the type of analysis in which we've been engaged, which we have suggested can be a western route to eastern wisdom. If diligent efforts are made, one will make signal progress; that is for certain.

In the realm of spirit, there's often a lag between

investment and return on investment. That's why one day we may be surprised--in the midst of a familiar situation--that we react differently than we are accustomed to do. Indeed, we might discover that what we had always taken with dreadful seriousness now seems a mere trifle. Such pleasant surprises are the deferred dividends paid by assiduous efforts. So it is that Samantha may one day be astonished to find that rude drivers no longer get under her skin. We may be similarly rewarded for our earnest efforts.

All of us have our ups and downs. Alas, there are times when we might feel discouraged, concluding that we aren't getting anywhere, with our efforts. Rather than selling short the enterprise, we should heed the words of Winston Churchill, "When going through hell, keep on going."

We might also be discouraged that the moments of insight and inspiration that we had once known have long since faded away. We shouldn't be discouraged for it's been rightly said that any true spiritual advance is never lost. And besides, as I've often explained to Dorothy and sometimes to the other members of the group, as well, it's best not to worry too much about whether or not we are making progress. It's best to just labor away at the task.

About Mark Dillof

Mark Dillof has been offering philosophical counseling for over twenty years. Originally from New York City, he lived in Binghamton, New York for many years, which is the locale of the mystery trilogy, contained in these pages.

He's currently director of **The Dillof Institute for Transformative Knowing** deeperquestions.com and **Plato's Attaché: Life & Business Advisory** platosattache.com, both of which are located in Louisville, Kentucky. Many of the essays that appeared in *Mysteries in Broad Daylight* originally appeared in his popular blog: http://blog.deeperquestions.com/blog/

Dr. Dillof is also author of *Awakening with the Enemy: The Origin & End of Male/Female Conflict* (which is available on Amazon) as well as *The Paranoid Vision: The Worldview at the Root of Evil,* which will soon be available. In addition to counseling and writing, Dr. Dillof offers seminars and workshops throughout the world. Information relating to this book, as well as author appearances can be found at: deepestmysteries.com.

www.ingramcontent.com/pod-product-compliance
Lightning Source LLC
Chambersburg PA
CBHW020742100426
42735CB00037B/167